James P. Mackey, Professor of Systematic Theology in Edinburgh, contributes the introduction. The book reflects the interests of the Very Rev. Professor John McIntyre, and marks his retirement from the Edinburgh Chair of Divinity.

RELIGIOUS IMAGINATION

for John McIntyre

RELIGIOUS IMAGINATION
EDITED BY JAMES P. MACKEY
FOR EDINBURGH
UNIVERSITY
PRESS

© Edinburgh University Press 1986
22 George Square, Edinburgh

Set in Linoterm Plantin by
Speedspools, Edinburgh, and
printed in Great Britain by
Redwood Burn Limited, Trowbridge

British Library Cataloguing
in Publication Data

Religious imagination
1. God—Knowableness
I. Mackey, James P.
211'.01'9   BT102

ISBN 0 85224 512 2

CONTENTS

JAMES P. MACKEY : INTRODUCTION ... 1

The Historical Part

1. GERARD WATSON : IMAGINATION AND RELIGION IN CLASSICAL THOUGHT ... 29
2. JOHN DILLON : PLOTINUS AND THE TRANSCENDENTAL IMAGINATION ... 55
3. THOMAS FINAN : DANTE AND THE RELIGIOUS IMAGINATION ... 65
4. PATRICK GRANT : IMAGINATION IN THE RENAISSANCE ... 86
5. JOHN MCINTYRE : NEW HELP FROM KANT; THEOLOGY AND HUMAN IMAGINATION ... 102

The Philosophical Part

6. A. D. NUTTALL : ADAM'S DREAM AND MADELINE'S ... 125
7. MARY WARNOCK : RELIGIOUS IMAGINATION ... 142

The Exemplary Part

8. J. DAVIS MCCAUGHEY : IMAGINATION IN THE UNDERSTANDING OF THE PROPHETS ... 161
9. D. M. MACKINNON : THE EVANGELICAL IMAGINATION ... 175
10. N. D. O'DONOGHUE : THE MYSTICAL IMAGINATION ... 186

Contributors ... 207
Author Index ... 208
Subject Index ... 214

JAMES P. MACKEY: INTRODUCTION

The theme is an inquiry into the possibility of a *cognitive* role for *imagination* in the specific area of the God-question. This theme is clearly fundamental to much of the use and theory of religious language and it is properly philosophical. On the one hand, the question as to whether God can be known, known to exist, or even known not to exist, has been canvassed in all periods of our philosophical tradition, but this has been done normally without reference to the role of *imagination* in *knowing* the world around us. On the other hand, in several areas of religious and cognate disciplines in recent times, imagination or one or other of its assumed specialities has been invoked, but normally without any reference to a properly philosophical and fundamental analysis of the nature and function of imagination.

To give some examples: Works on religion and literature frequently bring theological presuppositions to literature which hide from view the religious possibilities innate in the best of creative writing. It was once common for literary critics to complain that Graham Greene's novels failed to reach the summit of his art because divine grace was one of his *dramatis personae*, as artificially intrusive as the proverbial *deus ex machina*. Criticism of this kind clearly conceals the assumption that divine presence is not empirical; it takes over quite uncritically those dichotomous distinctions between nature and grace, reason and revelation, science and religion, which by collusion of philosophers and theologians alike have but recently achieved dominance in Western culture, and which threaten to bedevil the theme of this book as badly as they have bedevilled so many others. Literary folk who perpetuate the conflict between the priest and the artist and who cannot see beyond it hold out the same kind of hope, and as much of it, as popular politicians who try to restrict our already miserable prospects to a simple choice between communism and freedom, thereby misrepresenting everything.

There is another quite contrary kind of example. Theologians have recently taken to symbol and metaphor, poetry and story, with an enthusiasm which contrasts very strikingly with their all-but-recent avoidance of such matters. This enthusiasm spills over quite easily into claims that only symbol is adequate to religion, or that symbol by its very nature goes deeper (or higher) than concept. Prodigal imagination with all its offspring is back in the fold before any credentials have been examined, and the shouts of welcome drown out the more sceptical suggestions that symbol and suchlike belong to religion and religion to imagination precisely because neither makes any truly cognitive claim. Your solid empiricist who stands on his claim of the little that can truly be known now consigns both the priest and the artist to the sense of wonder and allows in each case that it is a wonderful way of sweetening the time.

There clearly is a need for a basic epistemological study of the religious imagination. And just as clearly the study must address the twin questions: (1) does imagination have a place for, or in, religion, and (2) does it (still) have a truly cognitive function, a claim to truth?

I

In Wallace Stevens' poem *Angel Surrounded by Paysans*, the angel speaks as follows:

> I am the angel of reality,
> Seen for a moment standing at the door.
>
> I have neither ashen wing nor wear of ore
> And live without a tepid aureole,
>
> Or stars that follow me, not to attend,
> But, of my being and its knowing, part.
>
> I am one of you and being one of you
> Is being and knowing what I am and know.
>
> Yet I am the necessary angel of earth,
> Since in my sight, you see the earth again,
>
> Cleared of its stiff and stubborn, man-locked set,
> And, in my hearing, you hear its tragic drone
>
> Rise liquidly in liquid lingerings,
> Like watery words awash; like meanings said
>
> By repetitions of half-meanings. Am I not,
> Myself, only half of a figure of a sort,
>
> A figure half seen, or seen for a moment, a man
> Of the mind, an apparition apparelled in
>
> Apparels of such lightest look that a turn
> Of my shoulder and quickly, too quickly, I am gone?

Stevens himself commented on the poem in one of his letters (*Collected Letters* No.831):

> in *Angel Surrounded by Paysans* the angel is the angel of reality. This is clear only if the reader is of the idea that we live in the world of the imagination, in which reality and contact with it are the great blessings. For nine readers out of ten, the necessary angel will appear to be the angel of the imagination and for nine

days out of ten that is true, although it is the tenth day that counts.

I quote the poem and the comment because there are few better ways of introducing the cognitive claims of imagination, its possible purchase upon truth, the relationship between imagination and reality; but even more so because of the eschatological note so gently sounded in the last phrase. What promise is held out to us here? What will happen on the tenth day?

II

One of the principal values of Mary Warnock's book on *Imagination* was that in it she demonstrated with the aid of established philosophers the essential role played by imagination in all ordinary knowing. In the common perception—and this is quite arguably common to more than the common people—imagination is seen as the source of creativity, itself ornamental and peripheral to the main business of life which in its cognitive form is carried on by the sciences and in its practical form by technology, by the creation of wealth and the raising of material standards of living; unless, of course, imagination is even further looked down upon as the faculty of the childish and the fanciful. This may explain in part at least why so much theology has been at such pains to prove on behalf of the christian religion it sought to serve, that it too was truly scientific; why it was at times iconoclastic, positively frightened by the word 'myth', nervous of symbolism, and visibly uneasy with metaphor.

For it does seem reasonable to suppose that it was theology's envy of science in the modern period which to a large degree explained theology's reluctance to come to grips with the imagery, the metaphor, the symbol and myth so prevalent in its own sources. After all, in the mind of Descartes, the father of modern philosophy, it was the success of science which dictated the prospects for a newly restructured philosophy, and theology in the western world at least has never ignored philosophical fashion. Few christian theologians followed D.F. Strauss, but fewer still dissented from his view that myth was no more than an infantile substitute for science, and as such unworthy of a scientific age.[1] Instead they set themselves to disprove Strauss's view that myth was everywhere in the Bible. And from myth suspicion easily spreads to the symbols of which it is composed and to the images and metaphors and stories which are its stock-in-trade.

Of course there were many well-advertised clashes between science and religion, beginning with Galileo, and these in time tempered the enthusiasm of theologians to be thought of as just another species of scientists. The most obvious strategy employed to neutralise the worst effects of these clashes was the effort to delimit the disciplines, to insist that theology and science asked different questions, to invite each to stay within the bounds of its own discipline, and by avoiding contact avoid also all hostile encounters.[2] But this strategy never quite worked[3] —possibly by reason of imagination's most natural trajectory with which we must shortly deal. Theology still wished to be as much like science as possible, and on both sides of this somewhat schizophrenic attitude the casualty continued to be imagination and its native tongue, the symbol. As late as 1959 M. D. Chenu's book *Is Theology a Science?* wanted to have it both ways, the clearest distinction of the disciplines but with the closest analogies to bind them.[4] But what is most significant from our point of view is that it is in a section entitled 'Non-Rational Functions' that Chenu deals with what he calls 'certain byways of thought, originating in the imagination, which nourish and sometimes profoundly instruct our faith'; and this section finally yields the statement: 'The symbols and the types are unquestionably part of the revealed truth, but theology, when it is exercising its scientific function, must exclude them from its field.'[5] There are fewer clearer statements in recent theology of the alignment of the scientific with the rational and of the imaginative with the non-rational, and this despite the acknowledgment of the fact that symbols are part of divine revelation![6]

Things have changed, mercifully. The faults and the potentially tragic consequences of such ways of looking at both science and religion have been noticed, as one might expect, by the poet. Wallace Stevens did not confer upon imagination, as did Blake, the status of divine *persona*;[7] Ted Hughes came close to doing so. The achievements of modern science Hughes attributes to 'the precious tool of objective imagination'. But this deals only with the 'outer world', which is only one of the worlds we live in. There is also the inner world, at the depths of which our real selves lie. Religion is roundly castigated for betraying in its quest for scientific status the inner world to which it was once guide and guardian.

> When it came the turn of the christian church to embody the laws of the inner world, it made the mistake of claiming that they were objective laws. That might have passed, if Science had not come along, whose laws were so demonstrably objective that it was able to impose them on the whole world. As the mistaken claims of christianity became scientifically meaningless, the inner world which it had clothed became incomprehensible, absurd and finally invisible. Objective imagination, in the light of science, rejected religions as charlatanism, and the inner world as a bundle of fairy tales, a relic of primeval superstition. People rushed towards the idea of living without any religion or any inner life whatsoever as if towards some great new freedom. A great final awakening. The most energetic intellectual and political movements of this century wrote the manifestos of the new liberation. The great artistic statements have recorded the true emptiness of the new prison.

The inner world, separated from the outer world, is a place of demons. The outer world, separated from the inner world, is a place of meaningless objects and machines. The faculty that makes the human being out of these two worlds is called divine. That is only a way of saying that it is the faculty without which humanity cannot really exist. It can be called religious or visionary. More essentially, it is imagination which embraces both outer and inner worlds in a creative spirit.[8]

Within this vigorous protest lies an agenda, and indeed an agenda which, by simply looking to more recent discussions of science and religion, would produce an alternative collection to the one I here introduce. The key thematic questions could conceivably find an answer in successive attention to the rôle of imagination in science, and hence in the investigation of the most concrete reality; the corresponding rôle of imagination in the realm of religious myth and symbol, with at least the suspicion that, since it is after all the self-same 'faculty', it might be no less capable of truth in one realm than in the other; the reconciling function of imagination in healing broken worlds and allowing human life to blossom again in true creative freedom.

In fact, on this agenda, essays could simply follow unmistakeable signposts in recent philosophy of science.

First, Michael Polanyi introduced his 'personal co-efficient' in all knowing, even the most allegedly scientific, and he did so with such philosophical thoroughness that Patrick Grant[9] could plausibly argue the Augustinian connection through the motif of the faith that always seems to precede and to seek understanding.

Theologians were already rejoicing that something akin to personal faith seemed to be emerging as a prerequisite for scientific research when Thomas Kuhn's *The Structure of Scientific Revolution* appeared (1962)[10] and caused a minor revolution of its own. Kuhn is best known for his insistence on the rôle of paradigms in the course of scientific progress and in the second edition of his book (1970) he explained in more detail that a paradigm comprised a settled tradition, some key 'exemplars' which embodied that tradition, and a set of assumptions about the nature of reality which were connected with this tradition and which could only be considered metaphysical. These paradigms were 'carried' by whole scientific communities, he argued, to the extent that all particular scientific theories were paradigm-dependent, and the new paradigm which heralded scientific advance came about, not simply by the accumulation of objectively observed data as the empiricists would have it, but by a kind of quantum leap (of the imagination?) and the 'conversion' of others to the new way of looking into the empirical world.

After Kuhn came Ian Barbour's *Myths, Models, and Paradigms*.[11] 'It is the thesis of this volume' he wrote, 'that recent work in the philosophy of science has important implications for the philosophy of religion and for theology' (p.3). And in the course of arguing for his thesis he investigates the analogies between the models and paradigms of science and the myths of religion and models of theology. He highlights incidentally the role of imagination in science. Theoretical models in science—as distinct from experimental, logical or mathematical models—are used to help us understand the world, he argues. They are not simply 'useful fictions', useful, that is to say, in the particular pursuit of particular scientific projects, part of the pullulating throw-away facilities of the technological age. But neither are they 'literal pictures of reality'. They originate, rather, he says, 'in a combination of analogy to the familiar and creative imagination in inventing the new' (p.47); 'they are partial and inadequate ways of imagining what is not observable' (p.48); they 'seem to require a special kind of creative imagination' (p.30).

Max Black carries further than Barbour, as Barbour himself acknowledges, the analysis of the role of imagination in the sciences; he maintains that scientific models are systematically developed metaphors. And it does seem as if Barbour himself could go a little further in the analogies he draws between science and religion. 'Other functions of religious models have no parallel in science', he wrote (p.8) and he gave as instances the expression of commitment, of ethical dedication and policies of action. Yet he himself had written shortly before that 'The function of scientific language is the prediction *and control* of nature' (p.5, my italics), and shortly after that 'all symbol systems are selective, ordering those aspects of experience which men consider significant' (p.8). Now of course there can be working models created by the imagination for purposes of a particular problem-solving exercise and then discarded, but can those models which he calls the theoretical models of science be so easily separated from the further reaches of human interest and evaluation where hope and moral choice and commitment are part of the very fibres of the experience? What else does control involve except commitment and action? And what does selection of the significant imply if not ethical policies? And how far away then is the metaphysical?

The milestones are clear and they are topped by even clearer signposts to this new direction of contemporary thought. Nevertheless it is necessary to have the humility to recognise that the proper pursuit of this new direction in converging paths of science and religion would require another collection, a separate volume. Partly because, as a Latin poet once put it, *non omnia possumus omnes*. Partly because the scientific community still has severe problems with Kuhn in particular, and with the nature and function of imagination in general, and these are still far from satisfactory resolution. The role of imagination in

INTRODUCTION 7

science and the influence of science upon the modern imagination must inevitably appear at times in the story of philosophers and creative writers which now unfolds. But the agenda for this present collection must confine itself to the history and present status of the epistemology of imagination, with particular reference to its religious uses, and to literary folk who have no problems at all about the place of imagination in their work. It is sufficient to have pointed to the perhaps unwitting influence of modern science on the odd attitudes of religious writers to imagination and its varied offspring, but the tentative changes in the philosophy of science are not the only, and perhaps they are not the major, forces for demolition of such odd attitudes. Philosophers have rediscovered the cognitive claims of imagination which had already grown in stature, particularly in philosophical theology, in the classical period; creative writers have never lost interest in religion; and in addition to all such influences, modern theologians have not proved altogether incapable of discovering the central place of parable and plot, of symbol and even of myth, in their own Biblical sources.[12] The brief look at modern science has also highlighted, I hope, the need for a more adequate epistemology of imagination which the theme of this volume proposes: to this the work of philosophers and creative writers must contribute, and of this the products of the religious imagination may well prove to be the test case.

III

A good start has been made by Mary Warnock in providing, at last, an adequate epistemology of imagination. I shall not attempt to summarise her work, but since I have suggested to all the contributors to this volume that it should act as a common point of reference, I wish to draw attention to those elements in *Imagination* which bear most directly on questions raised by the theme to which this collection is devoted. Mary Warnock first investigates the imagination topic in Hume and Kant, and I will begin with some of the results of that investigation. She then looks at Schelling whose thought on the subject anticipates Hegel in many ways; and I shall have a little to say about Hegel on my own account, if only because Hegel points up very sharply indeed some of the issues which *Imagination* did not, except in the most incidental manner, discuss: the traditional place of imagination in Western philosophy, an inferior to intellect, and the rôle of imagination in religious faith. In this way I can best introduce the chapters of this collection which carry the themes of *Imagination* back to the formative period of Western philosophy and on to the furthest religious reaches of Western thought.

Mary Warnock successfully argues that 'we use imagination in our ordinary perception of the world. This perception cannot be separated from interpretation. Interpretation can be common to everyone, and in this sense ordinary, or it can be inventive, personal and revolutionary. So imagination is necessary, I have suggested, to enable us to recognise things in the world as familiar, to take for granted features of the world which we need to take for granted and rely on, if we are to go about our ordinary business; but it is also necessary if we are to see the world as significant of something unfamiliar, if we are ever to treat the objects of perception as symbolising or suggesting things other than themselves' (p.10).

First, then, the essential role of imagination in all ordinary perception of the world is secured. Far from being a faculty which only conjures up the non-existent or represents things in their absence, imagination is necessary in order that we should at all be able to perceive the world about us. For impressions of the world of which we are the recipients are not serial and atomic, as Hume at times suggests, so that it is the customary 'clusterings' of these which enable us to 'name' cats and dogs and such things; nor are series of atomic impressions organised without intermediary by the analytic mind. Rather is the world about us perceived by us already organised into continuously existing objects to which we can then apply the abstract concept of substance, quality, and so on, categorise into species and genera, and investigate their inter-relationships; or, to put the same matter another way, to perceive the world about us at all is already to construe it as a world in which we can live and move and have our being. Images, restricted or comprehensive, *are* our ways of perceiving things present as they were and will be, and they are extensions of the immediately perceptible which go beyond the limits of immediate perception or attention. They are therefore themselves the very genesis of ideas and of thought. As Kant put it in his own peculiar terminology, 'Intuitions are always required to verify the reality of our concepts. If the concepts are empirical the intuitions are called examples; if they are pure concepts of the understanding, the intuitions go by the name of schemata.'[13]

What, then, in Mary Warnock's words, of the 'inventive, personal and revolutionary'; what, in other words, of the creative, the artistic rôle of the same imagination? Two elements of the answer to this question are worth pursuing, one of which we may attach to Hume's phrase 'impressions of reflexion', and the other to a similar-sounding phrase of Kant's, 'reflective judgment'. As Mary Warnock reminds us, the connection between desire and imagination goes back at least as far as Aristotle. And Hume attributed to imagination the power, in recreating immediate impressions, to evoke desire and aversion, love and hate. This power to suffuse the recreated perception of reality with the most powerful of the subject's emotions will prove to be a key element in the fuller understanding of imagination which is now sought.

Kant, with his similar sounding phrase, 'reflective judgment', meant

INTRODUCTION

to indicate the fact that over and above its routine work of exemplifying concepts or instantiating categories, the imagination is also capable of envisaging what in the case of science must be called a 'finality of nature', and in the case of art, what is simply referred to as 'an internal finality'. That is to say, whereas in the ordinary course the 'chaos' of sense impressions is put in order by 'intuiting' the received concepts and schematising the categories of the understanding, reflective judgment comprises the act of imagination whereby the scientist envisages further order or pattern, and the artist in his creative work brings to light form and inscape never before seen. And in the ensuing 'harmonious interplay of understanding and imagination' the peculiar pleasure of art is to be found. It is a clear implication of this philosophy that imagination is at once the means of knowing our world as conventional science knows it, and of advancing that knowledge; and there are further implications for analogies between art and science which, to the best of my knowledge, still wait to be drawn.

But Kant goes further than this, and much further than Hume, as he approaches the third subject, theology. It is well known that Kant wrote of ideas of reason which were however quite beyond the limits of conceptual thought—the principal examples of these are freedom, immortality and God. Now partly as a result of his difficulty of finding many instances of the creation of pure artistic form—i.e. a painting of a horse into the appreciation of which would go no consideration of how it exemplified horses we know—Kant describes how artistic genius is capable by the forms it creates of carrying us beyond the limits of conceptuality altogether. Hence 'aesthetic ideas' are analogous to 'ideas of reason'. An aesthetic idea he defines as 'a representation of the imagination which induces much thought, yet without the possibility of any thought whatever, i.e. *concept*, being adequate to it'.[14] This is the realm of the symbol properly so-called, the gift to us of the artistic genius. 'Symbols are analogous to schemata', writes Mary Warnock, 'they are intended to present ideas, as schemata present concepts.' And she adds: 'What we perceive as sublime in nature, or what we appreciate or create in the highest art, is a symbol of something which is forever beyond it' (p.63). And the ideas of reason, we know from Kant, include the unknown object of religious faith. Hence imagination carries us from the most mundane knowledge of the meanest thing we may know, beyond the frontiers of conventional science, beyond the categories of the understanding and the limits of all conceptuality. Add to this the power of the deepest human emotions which seem inseparable from the more creative exercises of imagination, and the whole elan of the human spirit comes into view, echoes of the Platonic eros, the passion which can carry men to God, perhaps because it was first the passion of a God who created in his own image.

There is here, I think, a tolerable sketch of a comprehensive philosophy of imagination, but if it is to be philosophically respectable it will need a very great deal of testing and tightening. So how can one proceed?

Well, it is seldom wise to omit Hegel altogether if one has been seeking light on a subject of deep spiritual significance and one has already visited the words of Kant. And isn't the impression we have just been given by Kant, the impression of imagination luring us forever beyond anything that we can analyse or conceive, is not this the very impression that Hegel consistently throughout his philosophical life criticised as the most misleading and the most enervating of Romantic wishful thinking, 'perennierendes Jenseits, perennierendes Sollen', though he had Fichte in mind more than Kant, or for that matter Schelling?

Certainly Hegel's vision was one of universal reconciliation, so that one should feel *bei sich selbst*, or as Marx later put it, *zu Hause* in this universe that we so little know and so imperfectly appreciate. Yet for this vision he constantly used traditional christian symbolism. He declared: 'To embrace the whole energy of the suffering and discord that has controlled the world and all forms of its culture, and also to rise above it—this can be done by philosophy alone.' Yet Hegel sought in his philosophy 'a new religion in which the infinite grief and the whole gravity of its discord is acknowledged, but is at the same time serenely and purely dissolved'.[15] Can one then conclude, without hesitation, that Hegel's persistent antipathy to whatever would carry us forever beyond what can be conceptualised is in fact a straightforward antipathy at one and the same time to imagination and to traditional christian convictions about a God who, in addition to being immanent, is also 'beyond' this world?

The way to reconciliation, for Hegel as for Kant, was through the universal, universal significance, universal relevance, universal efficacy; in phrases from another place, it meant 'belonging to the universe', 'being grandly related'; and this was because there is something of universal relevance, significance and efficacy about the apperceptive ego itself, equi-present in all states of passion and action to all its objects of mind and will. It is not, however, in the abstract concept or category, or law or formula, that the apperceptive ego encountered the universality which corresponded to its own inner drives (*Triebe*) to know and to mould according to its own nature and thus to be fully reconciled and unconditionally happy. For such abstractions of which the ego is capable still stand abstracted from the real which is so impenitently concrete, Kant's unknown 'noumenon' is still unknown, and spirit is still alienated in its own world.

Reality itself, rather, is dialectical and the rhythm of its very being in all its regions is the dialectic of affirmation, negation and negation of the negation. That is to say, into every settled state of things in the world and of the myriad relationships that make them what they are, a negative element inevitably enters by reason of the very dynamism of the states and the relationships themselves; as the disturbing element of reflection and consequent recognition of the rights of others inevitably enters the at first unreflective uroboric unity of the child's world. This 'negation' always causes suffering, and it can always be fatal, unless it is in turn 'negated', unless it is assimilated and becomes a stair of transcendence to higher perfection and more nuanced bliss. This rhythm holds together all the levels of nature and its whole majestic structure, and it is the true logic, the true law of mind.

Now when mind comes to recognise this universal rhythm, or the whole dialectical system of such rhythms at all levels of nature and in every region of reality, it recognises its own innermost law, it recognises itself in what had seemed Other. Then full reconciliation and limitless joy is found at last.

This is the Absolute Idea that concludes Hegel's *Logic*, and though it finds itself described there in the necessarily abstract expressions of philosophy, it is not itself an abstract idea. It is, rather, in Hegel's own phrase 'Pure Personality'. As mind by engendering its own logical categories recognises itself more and more in the world of *Dasein*, it approaches more and more the status of Pure Personality or Absolute Idea. As the grand rhythm of the cosmos, working simultaneously in Mind and Nature, reaches its full reflective synthesis, we find ourselves in the presence of Absolute Spirit: Spirit all in all and fully conscious of its own objectivity in all. This absolute state can be described in terms of consciousness, knowledge, recognition—and so it most frequently is described—but since spirit is voluntary and active as well as receptive and knowledgeable, the absolute state can just as well be described in terms of love. Recognising oneself in the Other in order to be reconciled is just as easily and just as accurately described as actively losing oneself in the Other in order in this way alone to truly find oneself.

But does this Absolute Idea, this Pure Personality, this Absolute Spirit of Hegel's bear any real resemblance to the christian God or, for that matter to the God of any known religion? Or has the implacable enemy of all Romantic yearning for the Forever Beyond, of those whose highest satisfaction lay in perpetual dissatisfaction, has Hegel confined our ambitions for happiness to the conceivable progress of this universe, and in the process with one stone put an end to the fanciful flight of both Kant's Ideas of Reason and his Aesthetic Ideas? One need not enter here into the details of historical Hegelian exegesis, or consider again the paternity suits brought by Feuerbachian or Marxist atheists or more recent death-of-God theologians. But one is bound to be impressed by the fact that a careful philosopher like Franz Grégoire could finally give as his considered opinion that God for

Hegel meant 'l'ensemble des esprits finis, ou mieux leur système, c'est-à-dire, les esprits finis groupés en différentes religions et différentes philosophies enchâinées entre elles dialectiquement'; in other words, Hegelian spirit is most likely entirely immanent in our universe and works out its destiny entirely through the human spirit in this universe.[16] Thus the christian symbolism in Hegel could be no more than decorative, a kind of allegory in reverse, a use of familiar motifs in order to establish in our dull heads a complicated and unfamiliar logic.

Hegel, however, like many another genius, like Plato in particular, is not so simply and clearly systematised. His pages too are pregnant with thoughts which go far beyond such straightforward answers to such obvious questions as: is God just a name for totally immanent (human) spirit, or does God (also) transcend this universe? One is reminded of Mary Warnock's comment on those who would demand clear categorising of a poet's belief as pantheistic or not pantheistic: 'The beliefs themselves, because of... their inevitable non-literalness, defy such treatment' (*Imagination*, p. 109). Or of the poet Yeats who, when naming the faith into which he was born, had lived, and hoped to die, said: 'My Christ, a legitimate deduction from the Creed of St Patrick as I think, is that Unity of Being Dante compared to a perfectly proportioned human body, Blake's "imagination", what the Upanishads have named "Self"; nor is this unity distant and therefore intellectually understandable, but immanent, differing from man to man and age to age, taking upon itself pain and ugliness, "eye of newt, and toe of frog".'[17]

A unity that takes up into itself all pain and all particularity, is all too reminiscent of Hegel's vision. And notice the marvellous phrase 'distant and therefore intellectually understandable'. So it is the poet who really poses the question to Hegelian exegetes: is the traditional religious symbolism really reducible to a visual aid for the lesson in logic? Or is the 'either–or' form of the immanent or transcendent question about God a crude imposition by a pedantic discursive reason destined, because such matters are beyond its unaided comprehension, to leave us with all the forms of reductionism which Hegel's own century so eagerly produced in Feuerbach and Marx, and later in Freud and Durkheim, and sometimes in Hegel's name? 'Les esprits finis groupés en différentes religions et différentes philosophies enchâinées entre elles dialectiquement'—that would not be beyond the power of any reductionist to describe, and the more reductionist the view the more facile the description of all that has been and now is and, worse still, of all that is to be.

It is more than a little significant, then, that one cannot pursue the question of Hegel's God without looking to Hegel's views on art and religion. For in art and religion, as well as in philosophy, Hegel's Absolute Idea comes to 'an adequate existence'. And it is of more than

INTRODUCTION

incidental importance to remark that the pursuit of Hegel on this point shows how closely our two thematic questions are linked together—does imagination have a place for religion? and does it have a claim to truth? For it must be either purely ornamental or also substantive in what it has to say. That either–or at least seems unavoidable.

Art, religion and philosophy are the three 'forms' of Absolute Spirit, the three ways in which Spirit, conscious of itself and reconciled in the other, intentionally and lovingly losing itself to find itself in the Other, manifests or expresses itself as such. Spirit is always present as Spirit in art, religion and philosophy, but in different ways and at different levels. For art uses the images or symbols of sense, religion uses intellectual symbols or inadequate concepts, and philosophy uses adequate concepts (or, better *Begriffe*, since for philosophy as much as for art or religion, it is not a matter of inspecting reality at a distance through abstract concepts, but of living intellectually also within the very rhythms of being).

Art, of course, can be used merely to entertain, to illustrate or to adorn. But then thought can also be restricted to what Hegel calls 'useful science'. But when, like thought, art rises freely to its own expression of truth, the concrete truth of Absolute Spirit, then 'It enters into the same circle with Religion and Philosophy, and is only a special mode and form of bringing the Divine, with the deepest interest of man and the most comprehensive truths of the spiritual life, to consciousness and expression'.[18] In fact, 'Art stands higher than Nature. For the beauty of art is beauty that is born again and again of the Spirit';[19] 'The hard rind of nature and the common world makes it more difficult for the spirit of man to penetrate through them to the eternal and absolute Idea than through works of art.'[20] Art in fact is a kind of 'reconciling medium' between the world of sensible reality and finitude with which presumably the 'useful sciences' have to do and the 'supersensible world that thought strives to penetrate'.[21] The world of art is thus a mediator between finite nature and infinite freedom. A noble role for art indeed vis-à-vis what we should nowadays call science and technology, and one which it exercises by virtue of its power to represent the true reconciled nature of the human spirit. But what is art's relationship to religion?

Can we say of art and religion what Hegel himself said about philosophy and religion, namely, 'what they have in common is, that they are religion; what distinguishes them from each other is merely the kind and manner of religion which we find in each'?[22] I think so. He has already been quoted to say that art is a mode of bringing the divine to consciousness and expression, and he has also said that art may be our only access to the religions of some peoples.[23] He is most explicit in the *Logic*. There he writes of the Absolute Idea: 'Nature and Spirit are different manners in which it comprehends itself and gives itself an adequate existence. Philosophy has the same content and end as art and religion; but it is the highest manner of comprehending the Absolute Idea, because its manner is the highest—the Notion.'[24]

But two things must be noted: first, religion properly so-called uses inadequate concepts rather than sensible symbols, and second, philosophy is a 'kind and manner' of religion which is intrinsically superior to both the other 'kinds and manners', namely, art and religion itself. Now religion properly so-called uses inadequate concepts and this inadequacy of its concepts, compared, that is to say, to the adequacy of the *Begriffe* of philosophy, normally consists in the fact that these concepts are either still too immersed in sense imagery though they may be dialectically inter-related (as in the story of a Father-God giving birth to a Son and sending him to die so that he can then return as Risen Lord or Spirit), or they are concepts all right (such as First Cause, Necessary Being) and clear of such immersion, but dialectically undeveloped.[25] Now the dialectic, grand rhythm of all individual rhythms, enters to regulate this triad also of art, religion, philosophy. For just as religion introduces the negative, reflective, critical element of thought into art, so philosophy by highlighting in the concepts of religion the dialectic already present in its religious imagery gives the highest expression to the truth which is contained in both art and religion. Negating the negation in religion allows transcendence to take place from the immediate intuitions of art to the mediated and now highest affirmation of Truth. Spirit is supremely 'chez soi' as artistic and religious life, but it is so most of all in philosophical life for only in philosophy is Spirit fully conscious of the achievements of art and religion.[26]

The dialectic sometimes works chronologically or historically as well as logically, and this is true also in the case of the triad of art, religion and philosophy. 'Art', Hegel wrote, 'no longer yields that satisfaction to our spiritual wants which earlier ages and peoples sought and found in it.' And he attributes this fact to 'the reflective character of our contemporary life'. 'Even the producing artist himself', he continues, 'is too often infected and misled by the reflection growing everywhere more articulate around him, and by the unusual habit of criticising and judging about Art. It is thus that he is led to aim at introducing more reflective thought into his works. The whole spiritual culture of the time is so embracing that he stands himself within this reflecting world and its relations, and cannot by any act of will or resolution withdraw himself from it. Nor could any special training or removal of himself from these relations of life, restore to the artist in solitude what has thus been lost, or artificially bring back the former simplicity again.'[27] This does not, of course, mean that we are now historically beyond art, or beyond religion properly so called, that Hegel thought of art and religion as Strauss, by distorting his influence, thought of myth. What Grégoire said of religion in Hegel's view of things is true equally of art: 'The philosopher himself nourishes his soul with these (religious) symbols, which feed at one and the same time the spirit of the non-philosopher and non-philosophical parts of the philosopher's spirit.' And he adds: 'Philosophical thought and admiration for the Rational in things, religious thought and adoration, and in addition the great artistic intuitions of reality: such is the supreme goal and the primary *raison d'être* of the universe.'[28] But it is nevertheless very clear that to the question as to whether the primacy should go to imagination or reflective thought, then, in so far as imagination is the faculty of art, Hegel quite clearly accords the primacy, the lead and the more comprehensive role to the pure concepts of philosophy. Otherwise we might return to hypocritical yearning,[29] to *perennierendes Sollen, perennierendes Jenseits*. The control of reason is crucial.

A number of questions push through the fertile soil of the subconscious mind at this point, and attract attention as they begin to multiply.

Even those who do not question this second-rating to the claims of 'pure' reason of the imaginative and the symbolic, might still wonder how in the history of Western epistemology such second-class status first came to be established—for Hegel like every truly original genius is very traditional in his approach to things. In order to answer this most elementary question Gerard Watson goes back beyond the philosophers with whom Mary Warnock began her book, back in fact to the dawn of Western philosophy which, even as it dawned, was already philosophy of religion. But the story that he unfolds does not quite turn out to be confirmatory in any straightforward sense of the prejudice against imagination. Like many a good story it has its detective element as he tries to discover who forged the very creative links between the very different epistemologies of imagination which came successively from Plato, from Artistotle, and from the Stoa. And the story itself reveals how imagination, partly as a result of these creative links, and despite the fact that it was considered 'a lowly faculty at the beginning of Greek philosophy',[30] grew steadily in epistemological stature as the classical period of Western philosophy progressed until, at the Middle Ages, 'imagination had become the pathway to divine life.'

John Dillon takes the exemplary and most influential case of Plotinus and illustrates even more graphically the tension between a traditionally supercilious attitude to imagination and an ungrudging awareness of how powerful an access to the highest truth 'dynamic images' can be. Thomas Finan unfolds another story, which illustrates how very far imagination had come from its lowly origins, at least in the mind of one Medieval author. It is a story that Dante himself tells about his

Beatrician vision, how he decided in the wake of that vision that he would study very hard indeed before writing. When he did write, of course, it was poetry that he wrote: so that the exercise of reason seems now to be contained between vision and poetry much as Blake was much later to reverse Hegel's priorities between art and philosophy. On any reading of it, the history of Western philosophy up to the high Middle Ages is less a sustained confirmation of an original lowly estimate of imagination, and more an increasing and simultaneous awareness of the role of imagination both in 'ordinary' knowledge and in religious faith. The original prejudice, far from finding more rational support as time goes on, finds more and more need for qualification. And yet it persisted, as the most straightforward reading of Hegel proves, and it persists to this day.

So the question of fact raises a question of law. If *de facto* imagination was held subservient to reason, should it be so *de jure*? Is it *right* that imagination should be required to be led by reason, and whenever necessary corrected by it, a court jester to the king, or to the teacher the little man from the audio-visual department who comes with slide-projector and slides? As Patrick Grant continues the history of imagination's image into the period of the Renaissance he comes upon some of those humanists who have produced the most enthusiastic endorsement of the free creativity of imagination, the one 'faculty' it would seem equal to the stature of a human being who can by God's already given graces make himself, if he so wishes, a partaker in God's own divine nature. To this there corresponds a castigation of pedantic logicians and, on one occasion, the warning from Erasmus to such people that 'word-mongering, power-mongering, and war-mongering are closely allied'. But the very exaggeration of claims for images liberated from close logical scrutiny only serves to feed the old suspicions of imagination's wildness, its destructive, or in religious terms, its demonic potential. So Grant takes us at last to Hamlet and to an exegesis of his speech to Rosencrantz and Guildenstern, where Hamlet 'deconstructs', as it were the very scale of nature itself, and is left with nothing, and worse still, with no one even to talk to. What restraint can there be on such wildness except common sense, patiently argued positions and, in religious terms, the Nicene Creed, or while it lasts, some common christian consensus? Must not Luther always reprimand Erasmus when the latter's humanism leads him to its pathless ways?

And yet . . . and yet . . . has not pure reason and cold logic also been guilty of its own destructive excesses? The Dionysian can undoubtedly destroy by dint of sheer uncontrollable exuberance, but the Apollonian has long mastered the more systematically destructive techniques of the bureaucratic machine in churches as well as states, ideologies and creeds have become weapons of oppression, and Erasmus' words on the alliance of word-mongering to power-mongering are all too true. Nor is the point relevant to religion merely because churches sometimes learn too much from dictatorships, nor relevant to states because institutions inevitably compromise visions. The most comprehensive philosophy of life to arise in recent history under the banner of 'scientific' thinking, I mean Marxism, is a proper alternative to religion, for although it claimed the kind of scientific underpinning which nineteenth-century rationalism required, it presented a moral imperative demanding the most unselfish service to an ideal, and indeed a redemptive faith which looks to human salvation in this world. And with the best of both worlds, a substitute religion in the clean white garment of science, it became one of the best examples of the worst authoritarian abuses of reason.[31]

There does seem to be a case, then, for suggesting that imagination, although it can be wild, can also be less domineering, can enhance rather than restrict human freedom. This may be because of its native connections with the deepest and finest of human emotions, because it lures and haunts rather than orders people about or hounds them. Or, to put the matter in more cognitive terms, it may be that imagination in all its works and pomps always manages to elicit just that tentative yet gently tenacious quality of assent which alone truly corresponds to the measure of truth and certainty which alone is available over the whole range of human questing and questioning in this world.

In the first essay of the Philosophical Part, A.D. Nuttall takes up Keats' philosophical credo: 'I am certain of nothing but of the holiness of the heart's affections and the truth of imagination'. He places this beside the contrasting philosophical credo of the empiricists and notes carefully the paradox that while the flag of empiricism still flies over the fortress of science more and more of what we should normally call experience is excluded in favour of the less and less that is strictly measurable and quantifiable by the very abstract criteria of the mathematician. But the more instructive contrast in this essay is between the philosophical credo just quoted ('I am certain of nothing but . . .') and a poem, between a work of discursive reason and a work of imagination, and both of them by Keats. Nuttall concluded that Keats' philosophical credo 'does not survive when tested in the fire of a real poem'. In short, the philosophical conviction that imagination gives us reality does not survive imagination's own attention to this matter. I suggested to him that this was too brash a conclusion to the arguments from Keats, philosopher (amateur) and poet, as he had presented these. I pointed to his own assertion that the 'thought' of the poem was more alive—and of life and living more later—more exquisitely tormented and divided; and I argued for a conclusion which would allow that although the apodictic certainties which philosophers might seek were not available, the delicate quality of uncertain assent which imagination elicits in all that it works upon, including the reality of its own dream, corresponds in fact quite clearly to our pilgrim state. Nuttall replied that 'the poem cannot forget the commonsense truism that dreams are dreams and imagination the natural antithesis of cognition (and from these humdrum contrasts wins great poignancy).' 'This means, in effect,' he continued, 'that the imagination is not, after all, certainly true. Thus the credo is broken in its central assertion, even as its power to haunt, to enchant is lovingly presented.' But he did offer a compromise conclusion to the essay.

I decided in the end not to substitute the compromise conclusion; partly because I was not sure after the correspondence that we were all that far apart, partly because it is really up to the reader to decide on this important issue of the quality of conviction and the kind of assent that is possible in the case of things we claim to know, and what kind of literary form best preserves such kind and quality; and because Mary Warnock in the second essay of the Philosophical Part revisits the poets of *Imagination,* Wordsworth and Coleridge, and argues with less hesitation, though with no less awareness of pitfalls all around, about the truth-claims of even the religious imagination. In all of this there is more than enough food for thought on the acceptable quality of human assent, over all the vast range of such assent, from earth-bound science to soaring religious vision.

Perhaps, however, when we ask the question which of the two, imagination or reason, must by *right* be led and guided by, or contained within the more comprehensive purview of the other, we are still to some extent victims of a simplistic faculty psychology, of lower and higher souls, or lower and higher parts of the soul, where demons and gods may dwell, but never cohabit. John McIntyre's chapter closes the Historical Part but its argument spills over into the Philosophical Part, for he takes the story forward from Kant. Kant has come down to us as the definitive critic of all possibility of *knowledge* of God; quite frequently, in the time between, religion has been confined to the imaginative, understood as the fanciful, the fantastic. McIntyre brings Kant forward once more as the proponent of imagination as 'a fundamental human activity', fundamental to every part of the cognitive enterprise. Now, because imagination in aesthetic judgment can reach as high as 'aesthetic ideas' and thus into the realm of religion, the question of the cognitive nature of religious faith is reopened whether or not one wished it closed forever. That, however concerns our next and last question. What is important to note here is McIntyre's conclusion that as it is by no means unusual in philosophy 'to employ the same term to cover a wide range of mental activities, such as, for example, understanding, reason, experience or will', so 'imagination' may be thought to cover at least as wide a range as any of these.

Indeed, if the Philosophical Part had been carried beyond Kant, as in a small way I have in this introduction carried it forward to Hegel, one would find a closer look at Hegel quite instructive on this present question. Hegel at first sight seemed clearest and most consistent in his determination to segregate art, religion, and philosophy, and to keep the former two quite distinctly inferior to the last. But as Noel O'Donoghue remarks in the final chapter of this book, on 'The Mystical Imagination', however much we may analyse and measure a great philosopher, however lucidly we may expound him, we have not really encountered him until 'we are lifted and carried along by the sweep and power of the vision' that inspires and sustains him. One is reminded that it was art and religion *tout court*, not imagination, which Hegel held subservient to philosophy, that philosophy was in fact religion in essence and in its highest mode, that art had become irreversibly reflective.

As a matter of fact, the seed which contains the whole genetic code of Hegel's most complicated system is a kind of proleptic vision of 'reality perfected and reconciled' which appears at the end of the *Logic* as the concluding description of Absolute Idea. Or, to change the imagery, at the very opening of Étude I of his *Études Hégéliennes*, Franz Grégoire states that he intends to expound the mature thought of Hegel by beginning with the 'fundamental experience' which, he believes, sustains it throughout. He continues: 'The schematic description of that experience, of that attitude to existence, occupies in fact in the *Encyclopedia*, under the name of Absolute Idea, the centre from which echoes proceed, progressively weakened or progressively strengthened and enriched, to the very outer limits of the system.' One need only think of the characteristic descriptions of Hegel's Absolute: pure personality, total reconciliation, fruition, limitless joy, love (and it is of more than incidental interest to note, with Grégoire, that Hegel's most impressive philosophy of love occurs precisely in his commentary on mainly christian art).[32] No doubt Hegel, a man of his age, preferred to point to the most *logical, rational* account of that vision, that proleptic experience. Yet who could deny that if imagination had been given then the extended range since claimed for it, the whole System might not have been comprehended in alternative terms by means of it? Key terms for the understanding of Hegel, such as his fundamental experience, his attitude to existence, his vision, suggest as much.

We should then find it possible to argue that terms such as imagination and reason are by reason of their very range and their similar varieties of application, largely co-terminous or co-extensive as regards subject-matter: that relationships between them are perhaps better described in terms of reason's ability to control imagination's 'wildness' by analysing the structures and implications of imagery, measuring past effects on human praxis and passion and, on the basis of this, estimating present and future prospects, while imaginative vision inspires and sustains the otherwise lifeless round of analysis and synthesis. This would seem a more promising approach to reason and imagination than that which would continue to argue the issue of which should lead or contain the other.

But all this simply brings us to the final question, a question that has been developing like a new shoot out of the previous one: what are the truth-claims of imagination? or, to put the question even more stringently: what truth-claims are left to us at all if imagination is such a fundamental human activity without which no effort to know could even begin, much less proceed? I do not pretend to know how philosophers of science or scientists with philosophical leanings would answer that question. One gathers that in the course of this century they have become increasingly aware of it, and one might suspect that it is the anticipated difficulty of giving it a satisfactory answer which dissuades many of them from talking about the rôle of imagination in science in the first place. In the case of the more 'human' sciences it is instructive to note that those psychologists, for example, who allowed value to symbol and myth, at the very least as psychic regulators, still suggest that it is the scientific demythologising of their content that reveals whatever truth they may carry, so that truth-claims really belong to science and to ratiocination, not to imagery which would presumably be incapable of distinguishing the veridical from the fantastic, history from myth.

But however the matter may rest with the scientists and their in-house philosophers, no one who reads the three chapters of the Exemplary Part of this volume could for a moment be unaware of how crucial this final question of imagination's truth-claims must be for religion. For if the three chapters of the Exemplary Part show nothing else, they certainly show how centrally and essentially imaginative is the source-experience of christian faith—for it is christian faith that the writers in this volume have mostly in mind. By source-experience here I mean a number of things. First, following Noel O'Donoghue, I mean the source to whom religious experience is attributed and the fundamental experience of that source upon which all forms of religious expression follow. Noel O'Donoghue's chapter on the mystical imagination illustrates quite amply the imaginative nature of that experience and raises again from his point of view the question of continuity with the deepest or highest of poetic experience. But I also mean by source-experience the Biblical source which in all the christian traditions is thought to be supremely normative for the shape and content of the christian faith, and the vexed question of the manner in which we are best to approach and experience that source. A bewildering variety of scholarly approaches and critical methods have recently coincided or replaced each other in scholarly esteem: plain textual criticism, history of religions school, form and redaction criticism, and so on. Davis McCaughey in a sense returns to the case for literary theory and criticism, never altogether neglected, to the need to understand the force of inspiration, the power of a dream ('I have a dream'), the creative nature of words, their overspill into drama and action, the hopes they arouse ('Words are for those with promises to keep')—if the experience of the prophets is ever to be ours, albeit in our own form.

D. M. MacKinnon takes up the theme with the Gospel writers, the evangelists. The role of imagination in the construction and in the reading of the Gospels is most frequently challenged these days by the apparently contrary claims of history. But if there is any reason to think that the 'coldly factual' which historians seek refers in this case to 'the unique, unrepeatable presence of the transcendent in and to the world around us', and if we are ever 'to capture even the outskirts of that drawing near', then MacKinnon must insist on our imaginative entry to a literary tradition that has been imaginative from its inception. 'We cannot, if we are literate, ignore the imprint in our imagination of Milton's rendering and he was responding to what Luke had done with a tradition before him. We do well to heed the fact that we are dealing with great literature, where the imagination of a creative artist has transcended the limitation of bare factual record' if only to touch the hem of mystery's barely tangible garment.

Such centrality of imagination to the source-experience of christianity—and presumably of other religions also—does serve to render even more acute the question of the truth-claims of imagination, of 'the world of imagination', as Stevens put it, 'in which reality and contact with it are the great blessings'. Now the kind of answer to that question which this volume provides must be a function of the combined arguments of its varied chapters rather than a summary formula which could already be written down in the introduction. But there is one particular approach to an answer which I might finally summarise here; partly because it involves a theme which peeps through momentarily in many different chapters but never stays long enough for fuller inspection, partly because it raises broader issues in epistemology which professional theory of knowledge still leaves largely unsettled. It is the theme of truth-claims that can only be settled by action, not by logic alone, and the corresponding suggestion that all of the really important truth-claims, from science to religion, are such. It is a theme which finds its own form of expression in the works of Wallace Stevens, and as I began with Stevens I might as well end with him.

'It is belief and not the god that counts.'[33] That sentence, I think, was unworthy of Stevens. It suggests simplistic assumptions about a distinction between imagination's beliefs and its 'objects' in the real world which Stevens' own tenacious analysis would do least to support. It was Stevens after all who wrote the equally pithy sentence on imagination, 'It has the strength of reality or none at all'.[34] That is not to say, of course, that imagination cannot and does not produce 'purely imaginary' objects that have no further reality. Nor is it to say that the poet must not resist the pressures of a too mundane reality when that threatens to rob human existence of all possible nobility. But it always remains true, as he put it, that 'The imagination loses vitality as it ceases to adhere to what is real'.[35] And in that word 'vitality' lies the clue to our final theme, for Stevens is convinced that it is the poet's vocation to help us all to live our lives.

The quite specific links that bind imagination to emotion and to moral action are already occasionally visible in Watson's survey. Indeed, at one point, it is to imagination as part of the quasi-corporeal 'spiritual' vehicle of the soul, that Augustine attributes the power to continue and to receive our dominant joys and sorrows in an after-life and another world. During the Renaissance the power of *bonae litterae* in the divine transformation of human nature was, if anything, overstressed. But the more sober Hume still pointed to that unique quality of imagination by which it could evoke the most significant and effective of human passions. The clarificatory pursuit of this essential connection between imagination and emotion brings us to Wordsworth, to the fateful struggle between fear and love, respectively the most destructive and the most enhancing of human passions, and it goes a long way towards explaining Mary Warnock's interest in the formative educational prospects of renewed attention to the imagination. In the end, only those who remain unaware or unconvinced of all of this could possibly be surprised to find precisely in the chapter on mysticism the strongest critical stress upon the quality of moral responsibility and the strength of active commitment.

For it is certainly noticeable in the source-documents of christianity—whatever may be said of other religions—that the God-question is never really a question of the existence of God; it is rather a question of the discernment of spirits or powers, so many of which appear to be malevolent. Much, if not all, that has more recently passed for philosophy of religion of course takes the God-question to be a question about the existence of God, almost as the existence of yet another entity. It is this philosophy which really deserves Sartre's retort: 'Even if God did exist, that would *change* nothing' (my italics). Jesus, however, was not concerned with the existence of God, and this was not because it was for him some sort of theoretical assumption making sense, for example, of origins. He sought instead to introduce the reign of God, to release in this world—this and no other—a power which would change it utterly and for the best. And it is no accident that he adopted for this purpose the aid of imagination. It was through the poetry of parable, of prayer and of dramatic action, that he elicited recognition of and encounter with what he called the reign of God; and in this way he made new perception possible, marshalled emotion and moved people to action—though much of the emotion turned out to be hatred bred from fear of the enormity of the demands made and much of the action was finally aimed at his own destruction. More people, then as now, preferred lesser, more manageable, even if also death-dealing Gods, like Mammon. But it is as true now as it was then that the perception and partaking of this benevolent reign requires what can only be called an act of historical imagination, and that the truth of this act of imagination is in the transformation of life, of perception, emotion and action.

It may be then that, still victims of an old faculty psychology however much we explicitly denigrate it, when we think of the truth-claims of imagination we compare it unfavourably to intellect and reason, and to the more theoretical of rational processes. It may be that, instead, we should be in pursuit of a more comprehensive epistemology, and that closer attention to the power of imagination—to forge the unity of vision, passion and pattern of attitude and action—could prove to be the most promising directive for such pursuit. Marx and his followers have restricted the question of truth-claim to praxis but Marxist philosophy is not widely respected outside of Marxist societies; American pragmatism has been slighted, unfairly no doubt, as the philosophy of American entrepreneurs; so the larger task of epistemology still waits to be completed, and the final claims of imagination may still wait to be settled.

The most generous settlement would possibly allow that it is the peculiar strength of imagination to be able to see simultaneously what is and what might yet be for the best, to engage at the same time the most creative of human passions, and consequently to lure into action and to sustain commitment. Heaven and earth both cleared of their 'stiff and stubborn, man-locked set', both truly heard and seen for the first time, their incoherent promise given tongue by dreamers who awake to find that visions can materialise and dreams can be 'true'? If that is what happens on the tenth day, then it is indeed the tenth day that counts.

NOTES

1. On the history and career of the word 'myth' see Maurice Wiles 'Myth in Theology', chapter 8 of *The Myth of God Incarnate*, London: SCM Press 1977.
2. See Langdon Gilkey's *Maker of Heaven and Earth*, New York: Doubleday 1965.
3. The fact that men as far apart in time and philosophical temperament as Engels and Bertrand Russell saw in modern science the basis of post-christian atheism, can hardly be attributed either to their ignorance of a simple reasonable strategy or to simple human perversity. See Bertrand Russell's essay 'A Free Man's Worship' in

his *Mysticism and Logic*, London: Pelican Books 1953. See Marx–Engels, *On Religion*, Moscow: Foreign Languages Publishing House 1955, pp.154, 164, 297.
4. London: Burns & Oates 1959. See pp.10, 88ff.
5. *Is Theology a Science?* pp.81, 88.
6. For some testimony to the fact that philosophers of religion as well as theologians of this country took this view, and that non-rational is truly the equivalent in this view of non-cognitive, see for example Richard Kroner, *How Do We Know God?* New York: Harper 1943, p.99 where faith, to which imaginative reception of revelation is central, is said to be 'something different in principle from all knowledge'. See also his *The Religious Function of Imagination*, New Haven: Yale 1941.
7. We must shortly take note of Stevens' religious indecision. For the moment it must suffice to quote from Holly Stevens (ed.), *Letters of Wallace Stevens*, New York: Knopf 1966, p.370: 'If one no longer believes in God (as truth), it is not possible merely to disbelieve; it becomes necessary to believe in something else. Logically, I ought to believe in essential imagination, but that has its difficulties.'
8. Ted Hughes, *Writers, Critics, and Children*, London: Heinemann 1983. Chapter on 'Myth and Education'.
9. Patrick Grant, 'Michael Polanyi: The Augustinian Component', *The New Scholasticism* 48 (1974), pp.438-63.
10. Chicago University Press.
11. New York: Harper & Row 1974.
12. See Norman Perrin, *What is Redaction Criticism?*, Philadelphia: Fortress Press 1969, p.21. Also see James T. Burtchaell, *Catholic Theories of Biblical Interpretation since 1810*, Cambridge University Press 1969. John Dominic Crossan, for example, went from *In Parables*, New York: Harper & Row 1973, to *Dark Interval: Towards a Theology of Story*, Niles: Argus 1975.
13. I. Kant, *Critique of Judgment*, Oxford University Press 1952, p.59.
14. I. Kant, *Critique of Judgment*, p.314.
15. Fragments quoted by Richard Kroner in his introduction to G. W. F. Hegel, *Early Theological Writings*, University of Chicago Press 1948, p.38.
16. Franz Grégoire, *Aux Sources de la Pensée de Marx, Hegel, Feuerbach*, Publications Universitaires de Louvain 1947, p.111. For other possible options and a fuller discussion, see his *Études Hégéliennes*, Publications Universitaires de Louvain 1958, Étude III.
17. James Scully (ed.), *Modern Poets on Modern Poetry*, London: Collins 1966, pp.21-2.
18. Hegel, *The Philosophy of Art*, Edinburgh: Oliver & Boyd 1886, p.12.
19. Op. cit., p.4.
20. Op. cit., p.15.
21. Op. cit., p.13.
22. Hegel, *Lectures on the Philosophy of Religion*, London: Routledge & Kegan Paul 1895, vol.I, p.20.
23. Hegel, *Philosophy of Art*, p.12.
24. Hegel, *Science of Logic*, London: Allen & Unwin 1929, vol.II, p.466.
25. Grégoire, *Études Hégélinnes*, p.153.
26. Grégoire, *Études Hégéliennes*, p.29.
27. Hegel, *The Philosophy of Art*, pp.17-18.

28. Grégoire, *Études Hégéliennes*, pp.260-1.
29. Hegel, *Philosophy of Religion*, vol.1, p.50.
30. As Watson points out, and other contributors also intimate, imagination is not the only word used for what this volume sets out to examine, and it certainly does not tie us down to one member of an out-dated 'faculty psychology'. It might be interesting to note in this connection that when Newman was writing his *Grammar of Assent* he considered using the phrase 'imaginative consent' for that which he finally decided to call 'real assent'. See John Coulson, *Religion and Imagination*, Oxford University Press 1981, p.82.
31. See L. Kolakowski, *Marxism and Beyond*, London: Paladin 1971, pp.191ff.
32. Grégoire, *Études Hégéliennes*, p.35.
33. Scully (ed.), *Modern Poets on Modern Poetry*, p.154.
34. Op. cit., p.131.
35. Op. cit., p.130.

THE HISTORICAL PART

« 1 »

GERARD WATSON : IMAGINATION AND RELIGION IN CLASSICAL THOUGHT

Imagination is a lowly faculty at the beginning of Greek philosophy. At the end it was to be praised as the faculty which could give us a vision of reality which we would not normally expect, a vision indeed of a divine reality. That end for us will be St Augustine who, though he wrote in Latin, thought in Greek. Imagination was lowly because it was connected with the senses and what appeared to them; and they are constantly associated with *phantasia*. Phantasia is not the only Greek word for the English 'imagination', but it is the most obvious and important one, and tracing its history will help to provide a guiding thread through what might prove a maze. The word phantasia (not in italics henceforth) occurs comparatively late in Greek thought, and we must begin with a brief look at a context which is important for imagination and its theological uses, in Xenophanes, c.570–475 BC. He emphasised the limitations of human knowledge, but the first clear warning of the unreliability of the senses occurs in a philosopher of the next generation, Heraclitus. Both he and Parmenides made a deep impression on Plato, the most influential of all the Greek philosophers, and a preliminary glance at their thought will help to explain why we might expect from philosophy a negative attitude to any sense-derived knowledge, including imagination. We shall then turn back to Xenophanes.[1]

Heraclitus says that most men do not recognise the *Logos*, the plan or principle which governs all things; they are taken in by appearances and fail to see the hidden harmony in things. They do not reflect sufficiently on what they see and hear. Consequently, he says, 'Eyes and ears are bad witnesses for men, if they have souls which are barbarians' (fragment 107), souls which do not understand what the senses can tell them. Intelligence is needed to reach the deeper reality, for the sensible world is in a state of perpetual flux, everything is always changing.

Parmenides adopted what appeared to be a directly antithetical position: he maintained that Being is, there is no such thing as change. 'Being is ungenerated and imperishable, whole, unique, immovable and complete . . . Unmoved . . ., it is without beginning and it never ends, since coming into being and perishing have been driven far away, driven out by true conviction. Remaining the same in the same place it rests by itself . . . There is not, nor shall be, anything else besides Being, since Fate fettered it to be entire and immovable. Therefore all things are mere names which mortals have agreed upon believing them to be true: coming into being and perishing, being and not being, change of place and alteration of bright colour' (fragment 8). No comment is needed on relevance to the question of God.

What united Heraclitus and Parmenides, in spite of their differences, was the conviction that if one were to reach ultimate reality, one must reject *doxa* (appearance, mere opinion, ordinary judgement), a term which later was to be much linked with phantasia. And as was mentioned just above, something else which they had in common was the fact that they were both greatly admired by Plato. The notion of two 'worlds', two contrasting 'realities', is central to his philosophy. On the one hand, there is the 'world' which is always in a state of becoming and never really existing, which falls within the scope of a combination of sensation and belief, and on the other there is that which always is, to be grasped by intellection and reasoning (*Timaeus* 27d–28a, 52a). Most of us take the first as the real world. But, according to Plato, we might as well make the pig or the baboon or the tadpole the measure of all things, if there is nothing more to man than sense-perception (*aisthēsis*) (see *Theaetetus* 161).[2] Plato takes it for granted that the human being has criteria for deciding right and wrong. They are based ultimately on the distinction in the human being between *epistēmē*, real knowledge, which only man has (leaving the gods aside for a moment), and *aisthēsis*, which the animals share. For Plato, education consists essentially in turning our attention from sensation to intellection.

But we must leave a fuller discussion of Plato until later. It is clear where the feelings of Heraclitus and Parmenides lay, even if it would be forcing the evidence to say that they rejected the help of the imagination in the search for God. But if we return now to Xenophanes we can see in him clearer warnings about the dangers of what we would call the imagination. In one application of that word for us nowadays it is concerned with creating or enabling us to see an ideal world. Xenophanes, however, warns us that we tend to create gods in our own image and likeness. He censures the uncritical use of the imagination at some length. 'Mortals consider that the gods are born, and that they have clothes and speech like their own'. 'The Ethiopians say that their gods are snub-nosed and black, the Thracians that they have light blue eyes and red hair'. 'But if cattle and horses or lions had hands, or were able to draw with their hands and do the works that men can do, horses would draw the forms of the gods like horses, and cattle like cattle, and they would make their bodies such as they each had themselves'. Against this, Xenophanes asserts what is the true position concerning the divinity: 'There is one god, greatest among gods and men, in no way similar to mortals either in body or in thought . . . Always he remains in the same place, moving not at all; nor is it fitting for him to go to different places at different times, but without toil he shakes all things by the thought of his mind'. He warns, however: 'No man knows, or ever will know, the truth about the gods and about everything I speak of: for even if one chanced to say the complete truth, yet oneself knows it not; but fancy is involved in all things'. (Translations of fragments 170–4, and 189, except last sentence, Kirk-Raven 1957.)[3]

Plato draws on all these traditions. For him, men live in the world of appearance, *doxa* (what Xenophanes calls *dokos*), and most of us, seduced by the body and deluded by the senses, believe that this is the only reality. A powerful restatement of the warning of Xenophanes is to be found in the *Republic*. In Book 2 Plato is discussing the formation of the ideal state, and the first and most important topic there is education, and above all religious education. He says they must begin by rejecting most of the stories current in contemporary education from Homer and Hesiod and the poets, because they misrepresent gods and heroes (377d–e). The truth is that 'God is good and he must be so described' (379b). 'The state of God and the Divine is perfect; and therefore God is the least liable of all things to be changed into other forms' (381b). 'God is without deceit or falsehood in action or word, he does not change himself, nor deceive others awake or dreaming, either *kata phantasias* or by words or by signs' (382e). This is the first occurrence of phantasia in Greek literature, and there is some ambiguity in its use (which is why I have transliterated and italicised the phrase). It may mean that God does not deceive us by visions, phantasia being given a passive sense, or on the other hand it may mean that we are not to blame God for our wrong interpretations of sense experience, an active sense of phantasia.

This active sense is to be found in the *Sophist* where the most explicit description of phantasia is given. It is given in the course of a long hunt for the definition of the sophist. He is a very troublesome sort of creature to hunt down, and deception is his native element. Once we grant the possibility of the existence of deception, it is said, 'of necessity everything will be full of images and likenesses and phantasia' (260c). The sophist, to defend himself, wants to deny the existence of falsity and, consequently, of deception. Therefore, Plato says, 'we must examine discourse (*logos*) and opinion (*doxa*) and phantasia so that we may see their combination with not-being, and so prove that falsity exists' (260e). The result of this examination, for our purposes, is the declaration that when judgement (*doxa*) occurs, not independently, but by means of sensation (*di' aisthēseōs*), this is called phantasia (264a).

The *Sophist*, as I have just said, contains the most explicit discussion of phantasia by Plato. But it also plays an important part in the immediately preceding dialogue, the *Theaetetus*. It is introduced subtly into the discussion of the suggestion that knowledge, *epistēmē*, is best described as *aisthēsis* (see 152a ff). He uses his concept of phantasia, in fact, to demonstrate how misleading the appealing dictum of Protagoras, that 'Man is the measure of all things', could be, in ethics as well as in epistemology, and ultimately, therefore, in ontology and theology. Plato wants to show how easy it is to take human sense-perception for granted, and how far astray a mistake even at this apparently primary level can lead us. He wants to make it clear that human sense-perception involves judgement, and judgement involves the use of meaningful language and thought.

The *Theaetetus*, dealing as it did with a central problem in philosophy, the nature of knowledge, had a great influence, notably on Aristotle and the Stoics.[4] Two further dialogues should be noticed for important discussions of Plato's concept of phantasia. In the *Philebus* it is said that we can think of a man's soul as like a book: the memory, in meeting with *aisthēseis*, and the judgements, which result from this meeting, write, as it were, 'discourses' in the soul, and the man keeps these judgements, true or false, within him. Moreover, there is a second artist within (39b), a painter who comes after the writer and paints, in the soul, pictures of the judgements we make. These images help to determine our conduct (40a). Here we can see the beginning of the extension of Plato's concept of phantasia into the area of the preservation and utilisation of images. The knowledge which can be described as phantasia is evidently useful, in spite of the initial hesitation. And that is clear from the *Timaeus* where the formula for phantasia is again used (27d ff). This is the two 'worlds' passage referred to above: the eternal unchanging world, to be grasped by intellection with reasoning, and the changing world, which is the object of opinion accompanied by *aisthēsis*. Even though the accounts to be given of the second world will not reach absolute exactitude, we shall do the best that human nature can and therefore give a 'likely' account, which will be as accurate as possible (29b–d). Phantasia then, which is opinion following on sense knowledge, has a very extensive scope, even if its status is secondary.

Aristotle, as we shall see, will disagree with Plato's description of phantasia. But before turning to him reference should be made to another passage in the *Timaeus*, particularly because of the influence it had in Neoplatonism, and therefore Augustine. Here (70e ff) Plato says that the gods placed the inferior part of the soul between the navel and the midriff. God composed for it the structure of the liver and placed it there as its home, making it solid and smooth and bright and sweet and yet containing bitterness. The idea was that the force of thoughts proceeding from the mind should be received there as in a mirror which gathers impressions and makes images appear. The helping gods who shaped us had been commanded by their father to make the mortal kind as good as possible, and so they improved even the inferior part of the soul in that they placed in it the power of divination so that it might have some contact with truth. The proof of this is that people do not practise inspired and truthful divination when they are in full possession of their senses, but rather when their power of reflection is hindered through sleep or illness or when their character has been changed through enthusiasm. It is the part of the man in full possession of his senses to make careful discriminations through the use of reasoning when what has been communicated in sleep or in a waking state through the power of divination or divine possession has been recalled, and the visions which have been seen brought up, and as a result of this examination he is to try to say how these experiences are significant and for whom they indicate good or evil, future, past or present. That is why a distinction is made between spokesmen or interpreters (*prophētai*) and seers (*manteis*). It is the work of the prophetai to interpret the riddles given in words or visions (*phantasis*, a rare alternative form for phantasia).[5]

It is clear then that though phantasia in Plato refers to knowledge that is tentative (*Philebus*), sometimes false (*Republic*) and in any case second rate, inferior (*Timaeus*), it is by no means simply to be dismissed. First-rate knowledge is after all, according to Plato, confined to the gods and a minuscule portion of humanity. Phantasia would in fact cover the vast bulk of our knowledge. And the *phantasis* of the *Timaeus* introduces the possibility of transcending ordinary knowledge through inspiration. But, most important of all for the future positive evaluation of imagination and for its interest to theology, there is inherent in Platonism the urge towards transcendence, which is in effect a version of the ontological argument. For it is in that direction that Plato's theory of Forms leads us. With the imagination we stretch beyond the sensually verifiable, and reach or create a world which we feel should exist, and which satisfies a longing which seems to us reasonable. It ought to exist and we would like to say that therefore it does exist. Plato said that the world of Forms exists because it must exist. There must be something beyond the buzz of sensation which gives it meaning and direction. Mind, too, gives a superior vision, particularly of beauty which, because of its degrees, points beyond itself and so creates a desire which cannot be satisfied by the seen. The God of the unseen has laid everyone under his spell (*Cratylus* 403c). Or, as 'Longinus' put it, referring specifically to Plato, in chapter 35 of *On the Sublime*: 'Nature has brought us into life, into the whole vast universe, there to be spectators of all that she has created . . .; thus from the first she has implanted in our souls an unconquerable passion for all that is great and for all that is more divine than ourselves. For this reason the entire universe does not satisfy the contemplation and thought that lie within the scope of human endeavour; our ideas often go beyond the boundaries by which we are circumscribed, and if we look at life from all sides, observing how in everything that concerns us the extraordinary, the great and the beautiful play the leading part, we shall soon realize the purpose of our creation' (Penguin translation).

Aristotle was a great admirer of Plato personally, but was frequently highly critical of his philosophical positions. And in his treatise on psychology, the *De Anima*, he starts his main discussion of phantasia by rejecting Plato's view of it (III 3, 427b14).[6] Phantasia does not occur without sensation (*aisthēsis*), and even though, like sensation, it is common to man and beast, it must be conceived as something different from sensation. He then shows its difference from the distinctively human faculty of thought (*dianoia*). 'Taking-something-to-be-the-case' (*hypolēpsis*) is characteristic of thought, covering as it does various forms of human knowledge, and being of immediate importance for human action. Plato had confused the issue with his mention of judgement or opinion (*doxa*), which is a form of 'taking-something-to-be-the-case', in his description of phantasia. He had thereby prohibited the beasts from sharing in phantasia, and at the same time he had skipped a stage in the description of human knowledge. So, according to Aristotle, phantasia is neither of the two things, or combination of two things, which Plato said it was, sensation and judgement. Phantasia is not perception, nor knowledge, nor intuitive apprehension, nor belief, nor any form of combination such as Plato proposed. But it is something *like* perception, a movement caused by perception, veridical or misleading depending on whether the perception was true or false, and a cause of action in men and animals. It is understandable that phantasia should be confused with perception, for the two are closely connected, and it is understandable also that as a consequence it has been confused with judgement. But phantasia is simply involved in the process of supplying the materials on which the mind builds judgements: it is not itself a judgement.

We are, then, to envisage the development of human knowledge as follows. Movements arise from sensations. The movement which remains in the soul similar to the sensation which caused it is phantasia. This is then involved (Aristotle does not say exactly how) in the mutation of sensations into images (*phantasmata*), which are then, in the case of man, available for the activity of the intellective soul. In the case of animals the process ends with such images. In the case of human beings the mind or *nous* can act on the images and educe thoughts (*noēmata*); how exactly again Aristotle does not say. But the soul never thinks without such an image (431a8–17, and cf. *De Memoria* 450a12, where he says that memory, even of intelligibles, does not take place without a *phantasma*). We can calculate on the basis of

IMAGINATION AND RELIGION

images as such or on the basis of thoughts in the soul, as if we were actually watching something going on, and we estimate the course of future events in the light of what is in this form present to us. It is in this way, i.e. on the basis of retained images in the soul, that the avoidance or pursuit of things is generalised.

Valuable though Aristotle's sober account of the functioning of the imagination is, there is little in it to suggest that imagination would one day be regarded as a quasi-divine faculty, the symbol of all that is best in man. In fact, the enemies of the imagination could cite Aristotle as their witness. He says, for instance, that because the phantasiai persist and are like the perceptions, animals do many things in accordance with them—some, like the beasts, because they lack reason, and others (men) because their reason is sometimes obscured by passion, disease or sleep (*De An.* 429a4–8). Or again he says, though admittedly in an eristic context, that phantasiai are for the most part misleading (428 a11–12). But Aristotle's patient building of a bridge from sense to intellect by way of imagination was ultimately to prove very important for theology. When integrated into Christian medieval philosophy, it made impossible the dismissal such as we find in Eusebius (*Prep. Ev.* VII 2,1) of pagan philosophers as people who were prisoners of sensation and the lowly reality which it revealed.

Aristotle's theory, then, is to be understood as a correction of Plato's, a correction which many later Platonists tacitly accepted, while some managed to profess both this theory and that of Plato, contradictorily, at the same time.[7] It could appear to them that Plato and Aristotle shared basically the same knowledge frame, with *epistēmē* at the top and *aisthēsis* at the bottom, and *doxa* and phantasia in descending order in between. There would be all the more temptation to make this assimilation if one were joining ranks against the materialists, the Epicureans and the Stoics. The Stoics maintained that what was real was body; on the other hand, at first sight paradoxically, they were also regarded as 'most religious' philosophers, because of their great emphasis on God as the artist designing and governing the world. Their effort to avoid the postulation of an immaterial mind brought phantasia to the centre of their theory of knowledge. The knowledge obtained from phantasiai which depended directly on sensation (*aisthētikai*) was extended through the phantasiai not directly dependent.

Sextus Empiricus reports concerning them: 'The Dogmatists (i.e. the Stoics) maintain that man does not differ from the irrational animals by speech taken simply as uttered (*prophorikos logos*) (for crows and parrots and jays produce articulated sounds), but by the reasoned speech which is internal (*endiathetos logos*); nor does man differ by the simple phantasia only (for the animals too have phantasia), but through the phantasia of transition and composition (*metabatikē kai sunthetikē*)' (*Adv. Math.* viii 275–6). This is illustrated elsewhere. Through various processes, from something that is actually present to us, concepts are also formed of what is not directly perceived. We form a concept of Socrates by resemblance, for instance, from a likeness of Socrates that is present to us. Others are formed by analogy: Tityos or the Cyclops, for example, by enlarging the normal man, the Pygmy by decreasing him, and the centre of the earth through our experience of smaller spheres. Through transformation we get the notion of eyes on the chest, through composition that of the Centaur, and through contrariety that of death. Some notions come through transition, like the *lekta* (what can be expressed), and place. The notion of something just and good arises naturally, *physikōs*. Finally, a notion might be conceived through privation, like that of being handless (Diogenes Laertius, *Lives of the Philosophers* vii 53).

The possibilities here for the emergence of the creative imagination are obvious, and the potentiality is clearly realised at the beginning of the third century AD in the *Life of Apollonius* by Philostratus.[8] But before seeing what he has to say it should be emphasised that the preparatory work for his statement goes back most probably to the first century BC, and that it came about most likely through the syncretism of Stoicism and Platonism which is well attested for that period. The form of Philostratus' work allows him to raise any topic that comes into his head, and one of these is the question of the value of painting. The discussion develops into a consideration of *mimēsis* (II 22). We are told that human beings have the power of imitation, but artists have it in a more developed way. It is because we share in the power of imitation that we can appreciate the skill of artists, either in reproducing what we have all seen, or in conjuring up what perhaps has never happened but can be imagined, as for instance the expression of Ajax emerging from his delusion.

In this whole section there is no mention of phantasia. Later in the *Life*, however, phantasia is contrasted specifically with *mimēsis*, in VI 19. Here, in a conversation with Thespesion, an Egyptian Gymnosophist, Apollonius ridicules the manner in which the gods are represented in local temples. Thespesion, somewhat annoyed, asks sarcastically were Greeks like Phidias and Praxiteles so privileged that they could go to Heaven and look around and use the gods there as models for the statues they make on earth. Oh no, Apollonius replies, they relied on something else. But what could that be other than *mimēsis*, asks Thespesion. It is something other, however, is the reply—phantasia. Phantasia is a more skilled craftsman than *mimēsis*. 'For *mimēsis* will produce only what she has seen, but phantasia even what she has not seen as well; and she will produce it by referring to the standard of perfect reality'. When someone wishes to produce Zeus he must do it as Phidias did, and when Athene, he must conjure up armies and intelligence and the arts and how she sprang from the head of Zeus.

Apollonius suggests finally to his hosts that it would be better to honour the gods by making no representations of them at all: they should leave the picturing of the shape of the gods to the worshippers because the *gnōmē*, imagination or mind, makes better pictures and plastic representations than art.

We see then in Philostratus how 'phantasia' was extended in its meaning from a term practically confined to epistemology to something more like the creative imagination. It is to be noted also that this occurs in a theological context, though the theology cannot be called rigorous. This happened, as I said above, about the beginning of the third century AD. It seems, however, as I also said, that the term must have been used in this sense much earlier, and phantasia was described as creating, or enabling us to see, an ideal world. Mention of 'ideal world' suggests Platonism. It might, however, appear unlikely, as we saw earlier, that a Platonist would praise imagination as a faculty which would help us to create art, which is, according to Plato, an imitation of an imitation, or that he would use phantasia as a term of approbation for a higher kind of knowledge. On the other hand, by the first century BC, philosophical syncretism, or the mingling and combination of philosophical traditions, had become quite common, and in Rome Platonism and Stoicism were frequently blended. I think it probable that it was a Platonising Stoic who made the transformation. As a Platonist he would say that there are two basic kinds of knowledge, corresponding to two different levels of being. Following the *Timaeus*, the best-known and most admired Platonic dialogue during these centuries, he would distinguish the eternal unchanging world and the changing world. The first is to be grasped by intellection with reasoning, the second is the object of opinion accompanied by sensation/perception. The first kind of knowledge, the direct vision of the truth, is possessed only by the gods and a few exceptional human beings. The majority of people, including the artists, have to rely on the second, the combination of sensation and opinion which Plato called phantasia. Even when an artist wants to create a vision of the gods (and this was a much discussed topic in the period), it is this form of knowledge, phantasia, he must rely on.

My reasons for thinking such a thing probable are as follows. More than two hundred years before the time of Philostratus, views remarkably similar to those we have seen in him are put forward in a passage in Cicero's *Orator*. The context (7 ff) is the discussion of ideal orator. The supreme orator he is painting has never perhaps existed, says Cicero, and the eloquence we are seeking is at the very most suggested, now and again, in speeches, copies as it were of the perfect. We see various beautiful things, but none of them is so beautiful as that of which it is a copy. 'This cannot be perceived by the eyes or ears or any sense: we grasp it only through thinking (*cogitatione tantum et mente complecti-*

mur)'. He refers to parallels from painting and sculpture—Phidias and the statue of Zeus. 'Accordingly, as there is something perfect and surpassing in the case of sculpture and painting, with the vision of which in the mind there are associated those things which are never actually seen in the process of imitation, so with our minds we conceive the ideal of perfect eloquence, but with our ears we catch only the copy. These patterns of things are called *ideai* by Plato . . .'.[9]

Here, as distinct from Philostratus, the reference to Plato is explicit, and the obviously Platonic 'something perfect and surpassing', 'things which are never actually seen' corresponds to what Philostratus says in VI 19 about phantasia and what has not been seen. But that by which we grasp what has not been seen is referred to as *cogitatio*, *mens* and *animus* in Latin. Are they translations of phantasia in a Greek original? And would this original, if influenced by Stoicism, have referred to phantasia as 'producing even what it has not seen'? Passages in 'Longinus', Quintilian and Dio Chrysostom suggest that it might.

The 'Longinus' who wrote *On the Sublime* was perhaps a Hellenised Jew of the first century AD.[10] He has a number of references to the term phantasia in his work, but the central passage is chapter 15. There he seems, for a number of reasons, to be using Stoic sources. He says that the term is 'generally used for anything which in any way suggests a thought productive of speech', from which we may conclude that he was aware of the Stoic technical definition of *logikē* phantasia as one 'in which what is presented can be conveyed in speech' (Sextus Empiricus, *Adv. Math.* viii 70), and the associated definition of the *lekton*. 'Longinus' wants to discuss phantasia not in philosophy, but in poetry where its primary aim is to move your audience. You have something vividly before your mind, and through your words you try to bring it before your hearers. As an example of the use of phantasia in poetry he gives the old instance of the Furies in the mad scene in the *Orestes*. This is so familiar because of the constant recurrence of the Furies as an example of delusion in the criticism of the Stoic phantasia *kataleptikē* (see Sextus, *Adv. Math.* vii 170, 244 and 249; viii 63 and 67). He praises all three of the great classical tragedians for their use of phantasia. What he says about Euripides and the Furies is particularly interesting as a parallel to what Philostratus has to say on picturing the despair of Ajax and on phantasia producing even what it has not seen. 'Longinus' says: 'In these scenes the poet himself saw the Furies, and the picture in his mind he almost compelled his audience to behold'. If 'Longinus' is using Stoic sources, was the notion of phantasia 'producing even what it has not seen' to be found in those same sources, mingled perhaps with the Platonism which was also present?

That ideas like those of 'Longinus' were current is indicated by a passage in Quintilian, who may have been a younger contemporary, but cannot be shown to have read him. Quintilian (c. 35 AD–post 95) is explaining that we must have the capacity of feeling something ourselves before we try to move others. He says (*Inst. Or.* 6.2.29) that the orator who will be most effective in moving feelings is the one who has acquired properly a stock of what the Greeks call phantasias and we might call 'visiones': i.e. 'those things through which the images of things not present are so brought before the mind that we seem to see them with our very eyes and have them before us'. If we use them properly (ibid. 8.3.61 ff) the speech will not merely reach the ears: its content will stand clearly before the eyes of the mind. Here once again Cicero is the master. For who is so weak in imaginative power that, when he reads a certain passage from the Verrine orations, he not only seems to be looking at the people involved, the place and the rest, but even adds further details which are not mentioned?

Not long after, in 105 AD, Dio Chrysostom[11] delivered his Twelfth Oration at Olympia where Phidias' statue of Zeus was to be found. In the oration Dio concerns himself with the question of what shapes men's vision of the divine. There we have a large extension of the brief passage in Philostratus, but it obviously shares a large number of ideas with him, even though Dio does not use the actual term phantasia. Both are concerned with representations of the gods, and that raises the question whether it might not be better to have no representations at all. It would certainly be better to have none if the gods are to be represented in animal form. If they are to be represented, the less 'realistic', naively imitative the representations are, the better. Poetry is better than sculpture in suggesting the nature of the gods, as can be seen through the comparison of two leading representatives of these arts, Homer and Phidias. It is so because it is less encumbered with the physical world and with what is obvious to the eye. The higher reaches of art are concerned with the unseen, and the less earth-bound the medium of expression is, the less controlled by the eye, so much the better. As Philostratus puts it, the inspiration of the better craftsman comes from what the eye has not seen.

What Philostratus has to say, then, has been anticipated in one form or another by writers in the three centuries before him. From what context may he have taken his views on phantasia? I suggest from a context like that which we find at such great length in Dio, a context where the question of our knowledge of the gods and what shapes our vision of the divine was discussed. The philosophers of the Roman period were extremely interested in theology,[12] and both Philostratus and Dio had an extensive literature to draw on. We need only glance through Cicero's *De Natura Deorum* to realise how far back the tradition went. But how did phantasia come into the context? Texts in Maximus of Tyre (b. c.125 AD) and Philo of Alexandria (1st cent. AD) which are relevant suggest that it happened in a discussion of or commentary on the *Timaeus* of Plato (see Maximus' second speech on the question of setting up images to the gods, and Philo's *De Opificio Mundi* 16 ff). The *Timaeus*, as remarked above, was one of the best known and most popular of Plato's dialogues. Commentaries were multiplied, and one of the questions raised by it, whether or not the world was created in time (*Tim.* 27d–29d), had been discussed interminably since the time of Plato's immediate successors.[13] The passage which was of interest for creation also contained the exposition (27d–28a) referred to already of the doctrine of the two 'worlds', one of which, the changing, is the object of opinion accompanied by unreasoned sensation. This exposition was obviously useful as a concise summary of the core of Platonism and as such known, like the picture of the demiourgos, wherever Platonism had penetrated.

Whatever their other differences, Platonists and Stoics could agree on the notion of God as an artist shaping the world. If God is like the artist, that the artist is like God seems a natural conclusion. It follows that in the discussion of human artistic creation in the Roman period the same authorities, especially the *Timaeus*, were used as in the discussion of divine creation. What is perhaps most remarkable in a series of authors in the period is the insistence on the vision which the great artist, literary or plastic, must possess. We have mentioned Cicero in the *Orator*, 'Longinus' and Quintilian, Dio and of course Philostratus. To these we can add the elder Seneca, who contrasts what the eyes see and the vision in the mind, again with the example of Phidias (*Contr.* X 34). The younger Seneca, in a discussion of the 'causes' (Epistle 65, 4 ff), mentions the views of the Stoics and Aristotle and then says: 'To these Plato added a fifth, the exemplar, which he calls "idea"; it is to this that the artist looks and brings about what he was planning. It is irrelevant whether the exemplar to which he turns his eyes is outside or something inside, which he himself has conceived and placed there. God has the exemplars of all things within himself . . .'.

Cicero, Philo and Seneca the Younger obviously belong to a Platonist context: if Philostratus' views on phantasia belong to the same context, a context where we do not expect the word 'phantasia' as a term of commendation for reasons already given, how do we explain the introduction of the term? A passage from Maximus of Tyre, who wished to be known as a 'Platonic philosopher', may again be relevant.[14] He raises the question of the importance of vision in the eleventh discourse where he discusses the question of Plato's God. He says (Hobein XI 3) that even Homer's famous description of Zeus in *Iliad* I 528 (the description which is constantly quoted in the comparison of Homer and Phidias) is ridiculously inadequate. All such pictures are due to weakness of vision, dullness of mind: the painters, sculptors, poets and philosophers merely present their vision of God after what seems to be the most beautiful, as best they can, borne up by phantasia (*exairomenoi tēi phantasiai*). This usage is obviously very close to that of Philostratus. It occurs in a Platonic context, and, as might be expected there, phantasia as a form of knowledge is presented as inferior to the perfect vision of perfect beauty. Nevertheless, the artists are borne upwards by phantasia: the term does, therefore, suggest in the context also that phantasia has been assigned a rôle in the extension of knowledge which resembles that of the Stoic phantasia *metabatikē*, that which permits a transition. How could this fusion have taken place?

The passage which, in my opinion, throws most light on how a Stoic phantasia might be introduced in a Platonic background is to be found in Calcidius' commentary on the *Timaeus* (Calcidius lived some time after Philostratus, in the fourth century, but we may use him as an indication of sources which he and Philostratus possibly had in common). Calcidius comments on *Timaeus* 52a where Plato is talking of the two 'worlds': the second is that perceptible by the senses, which comes into being and is always in movement, comes about in a specific place and is to be grasped by belief accompanied by sensation (*doxēi met' aisthēseōs*). Calcidius comments (chapter 343: p.335 Waszink) that here Plato wants to give us an idea of 'the second *species* which comes into being when the artist conceives in his mind the outlines of the work that is to come, and, with the likeness of this fixed within him, on its model shapes what he has started on; it is therefore said to be in some place . . . He says that this *species* is to be known through the senses, because the shape which is impressed on the work is seen by the eyes of the people who look at it; and to be known by belief, because the mind of the artist does not make this appearance come into being from a firmly existing model but he takes it as best he can from his own mind'.

The artist, then, according to Calcidius, has a vision like that of God looking at the Forms, but in the case of the artist the vision is conditioned by the limitations of human capacity. He draws from his own mind, as best he can, that is, he relies not on perfect knowledge but on 'belief'. The result of his artistic activity is perceived by the senses, of course. Therefore, says Calcidius, when Plato talks of the kind of knowledge which is the combination of perception and belief he is thinking of the type of vision which is to be found in the activity of the artist. What Calcidius does not point out here is that the combination or mixture of belief and perception is how Plato explains the word 'phantasia' in the *Sophist* and *Theaetetus* (and cf., as earlier, the *Philebus* and *Timaeus*).

Calcidius' commentary, here as elsewhere, leaves something to be desired. What Plato in fact is referring to is our knowledge of the sensible world. On a topic so fundamental as this it is easy to imagine a commentator much earlier than Calcidius pointing out that Plato's *doxa met' aisthēseōs* is called by him elsewhere phantasia. If he were a strict Platonist he would hesitate to expand the term beyond its Platonic meaning of tentative knowledge. But by the first century BC, and certainly by the third century AD, few Platonists were as strict as that (Plotinus, for instance, is known as the Neoplatonist, but, as his disciple Porphyry said in the *Life of Plotinus* 14.4 f, 'His writings contain an admixture of Stoic doctrines which are not noticed and Peripatetic teachings'). If he were a Stoicising commentator following the line which Calcidius does here, it is easy to imagine him pointing out that there was no serious divergence of opinion between Plato and the Stoics on the question of the artist's vision. He would explain that the Stoics too say that our sense knowledge comes through the phantasia *aisthētikē*, and that the knowledge derived from sense experience is extended through other phantasiai which are not *aisthētikai*. The latter are to be thought of as making a transition, and are indeed, with the *logos endiathetos*, the abilities which distinguish human nature. The commentator would add that, in the Stoic system also, it is phantasia which is responsible for human works of art. For it is phantasia which enables us to transform what we have seen and to create even what has never existed, like the Cyclops or the Centaur. The philosophers also say that it is through phantasia that we can see God, and, also, the best pictures of God are in words or thoughts, *logoi*.

Such a commentator seems to have been the ultimate source of Philostratus, whether Philostratus knew it or not. But whoever he was, and however far back he goes,[15] it is certain that, by the beginning of the third century AD at the latest, something approximating to our notion of the creative imagination had been introduced. What is particularly important for the future is that at least from this time the word phantasia can be used by some Platonists to refer to a kind of knowledge which is indeed a second-best, but which can nevertheless help us to a vision which goes beyond the human. When this kind of knowledge is called no longer 'phantasia' but 'imaginatio' by Augustine, the word and concept is set on the road to the great career it was to have in European thought. The most important link in this was Porphyry, the second great Neoplatonist.

To say that is not to underestimate the importance of the contribution by Plotinus, the first great Neoplatonist, to the theory of the imagination: John Dillon brings out the value of that contribution. Nevertheless, for the continuity of the story of the transition from phantasia to imagination, it seems to have been Porphyry who was of particular importance to Augustine. He in turn managed to make imagination respectable for Christians, precisely because of its connection with the body: he used Neoplatonist theorising on phantasia and the *pneuma* or *spiritus* to buttress Christian doctrine, and in doing so gave Christianity a vested interest in the imagination. Here too

IMAGINATION AND RELIGION

Porphyry forms a bridge between Augustine and Plato.

We have seen the passage in the *Timaeus* on the lower part of the soul as a mirror. This was taken up eagerly by the Neoplatonists, and helped to anchor the imagination more firmly in their system. According to the *Timaeus* (70e ff), as we saw, the lower part of the soul gathers thoughts proceeding from the mind and receives them as in a mirror. In this lower part of the soul the power of divination has been placed so that it might have some contact with the truth, and through it we receive warnings or consolations in visions. The visions come when we are asleep or ill or exalted: in short, when the power of reflection is hindered; and consequently the visions have to be interpreted.

Whatever Plato meant by all this, there can be no doubt about the enormous significance it had for later thought. For here we have a physical medium of contact, of daily occurrence (sleep), with the divine world. Closely connected with this is another physical medium which is ubiquitous in later Neoplatonism. This is the notion of 'pneuma', which we may translate 'spirit', as long as we remain aware of the ambiguity, an ambiguity which, as we shall see, Augustine thoroughly exploited. According to Porphyry phantasia is responsible for many of the affections of the body (*In Tim*. 38, 15 ff Sodano), and through these it affects the soul. When the soul begins its descent into body it is accompanied by the spirit (*pneuma*) which it had gathered in the spheres (*Sent.* 18, 7 Lamberz). (This will be called elsewhere the 'vehicle', *ochēma*, of the soul).[16] Varieties are to be observed in the spirit. The more inclined the soul is to the body, the more it fattens or thickens the spirit, making it like a thick, wet cloud, and the spirit takes on the colouring which is imposed on it through the operation of phantasia (*Antr. Nymph.* 64, 15 ff N; *Sent.* chapter 29). When the soul leaves the body and goes to Hades, it is accompanied by the spirit which it had gathered in the spheres. Because of its attachment to the body the mark of phantasia is impressed on the spirit, and hence the soul draws with it the image which is as it were stamped on it (*Sent.* 29, 18, 1–13 L). The close association of *pneuma* and phantasia, spirit and imagination, is obvious.

Like many of his contemporaries Porphyry had a live interest in *daimones*, intermediaries between God and man, both good and bad. All of them are invisible to human perception, but they can take all sorts of shapes, and the forms which characterise their spirit can sometimes be visible. The good *daimones* are upborne by spirit which they control in accordance with reason. They are concerned to do us good in every way, and among them are those who carry our prayers to the gods and convey through divination the advice and instructions of the gods to us. They defend us against their evil colleagues, warning and helping us through dreams, through a divinely inspired soul and in other ways. Not everyone, however, is capable of interpreting their messages correctly. Evil enchantment, on the other hand, comes through the bad demons, who are full of phantasia and deceit, and whose spirit is fattened by sacrifices (*De Abstinentia* II 38–42).

These chapters seem to form the background to the connection of spirit, imagination and inspiration which Porphyry may have made in other works. 'May', because much of Porphyry is lost to us. We are frequently forced back on fragments, or on writings by other people which seem to depend on him. One of these is Synesius, who wrote a work *On Dreams*, taken to date from 404 AD.[17] In that, we are told (see 134 ff Terzaghi), it is through phantasia that we frequently come into contact with the gods, who warn us, prophesy to us, and otherwise inform us about the future. No wonder, Synesius says, that sleep can be regarded as a gift: even the uncultured meets the Muses in his dreams and becomes a proper poet. Sleep can allow you to look at perfect being and unite yourself with the *noēton*, the higher world. If to see God with our own eyes is a blessing, to grasp him with the help of phantasia is an even greater privilege. Phantasia is the sense of senses, because the *pneuma phantastikon* is the most all-embracing sense organ, and the first embodiment of soul. The *pneuma* dwells inside and rules over the living being as if from an acropolis. The *pneuma* is very sensitive to the condition of the soul, and as the soul's first and proper vehicle, *ochēma*, is fine and ethereal when the soul is in good condition, and coarse and earthy when it is in bad. All in all, *pneuma* is on the border between the irrational and reason, the incorporeal and body, and is common territory for both, and through it the divine comes into contact with matter. To go beyond phantasia is difficult, and blessed; what is dear to a man in his old age, says Plato, is intellect and wisdom, meaning by that the cessation of phantasia. But that is something else: life as we know it is one of phantasia or a life of *nous* using phantasia. This psychic pneuma, or pneumatic psyche can become a god, a multi-faceted *daimōn* and a phantasmal being, and in it the soul undergoes its penalties (137D).

This is merely a partial summary, but it is clear, as Lang has shown in *Das Traumbuch des Synesius von Cyrene* (1926), that much of what appears here in Synesius was already to be found in Porphyry. Of particular interest to us is the use of the term *psychē pneumatikē* by Synesius. This appears in St Augustine's report of Porphyry's *De regressu animae* as *anima spiritalis*, where it is explained as that 'per quam capiuntur rerum imagines', that in which the images of things are held (*Civ. Dei* X 9). This is to be distinguished from the first soul: the distinction in Porphyry, again according to Augustine, is between *anima intellectualis* and *anima spiritalis*. It seems clear that Augustine, like Synesius, drew on lost material, and that even for *De Genesi ad litteram* XII he and Synesius' *On Dreams* may have used a common source.

Augustine is in any case fascinated by the imagination, and by capacities related to it like dreaming and memory (one needs only to think of Book Ten of the *Confessions*). Some of the earliest and clearest evidence of Augustine's attitude to the imagination appears in his correspondence. Nebridius was one of his closest friends and shared his interest in matters philosophical. In one of the earliest letters, Ep. 6 (Nebridius died in 390), Nebridius asks a series of questions about phantasia, the *animus phantasticus* and *intellectualis*, which even as questions reveal such a knowledge of the tradition we have been reviewing that one is almost inclined to suspect that this is the bright student showing off, or the friend playing the dumb straight man to give the master a platform. Augustine replies in Ep. 7 at some length. Among other things he tells him that *imaginatio* is nothing other than a blow inflicted through the senses—the reminiscence of Plotinus seems fairly obvious, even if his name is not mentioned.[18] All these *images*, which Nebridius and a lot of others, he says rather sourly, call phantasia, can be divided into three kinds. Examples of the first kind are a memory of your face, or of Carthage or of our old friend from Milan, Verecundus. They are sense images. Under the second class come all the things which we imagine (*putamus*) to have been or to be so and so, as for instance when we give shape and form to things when we are reading history, or hear or make up or refuse to believe fabulous narrations. So I can imagine (*fingo*) the appearance of Aeneas, or of Medea with her team of winged dragons. Or again, in the course of a discussion we might say 'Imagine (*puta*) that three worlds, like the one in which we live, were placed one on top of the other'. We create pictures for ourselves of all such things. This third class of images contains essentially those which are used to assist scientific theorising of various kinds or, as Augustine says, those concerned with numbers and dimensions. We think out the shape of the whole world and on this there follows an image in the mind of the thinker. We also use these kinds of images in geometry, music and all sorts of numbers. Imagination here is liable to be misleading, however, so reason (*ratio*) must be on its guard.

Augustine has strong words to say on the deceptiveness of the senses (Ep. 7, 5), before going on to consider the question of how it is that we can imagine (*cogitemus*) what we have not seen. The reason is, he says, in words which have a Stoic colouring, that the soul has an inbuilt power of increasing and diminishing what it is thinking of: a particularly clear instance is the case of numbers ('Think of a number. Double it. Subtract five', etc. might be our example). From our image of a crow we can construct a completely different bird we never saw by adding and subtracting. From a little water in a cup we were able, when we were children, to imagine oceans. People who get into the habit of immersing themselves in such imaginings find that after a while the images come flooding in on them of their own accord.

Augustine ends the letter with a ritual warning to Nebridius about the danger of being overcome by the senses, and by the blows and wounds inflicted through the senses, that is the imagination. But in spite of this it is obvious that he is highly interested in the workings of phantasia or what he calls *imaginatio*. It is through him particularly that we have imagination (or the close equivalent) used as the commonest translation for phantasia in many modern European languages. (That does not imply that the word was first used by him: see the elder Pliny, *N.H.* 20, 68, and Tacitus, *Ann.* 15, 36, and Calcidius 190, 16–17 w.)[19] But it was Augustine who gave it currency in the Latin West. We can see in this letter a certain reluctance to use 'phantasia' transliterated: too much, however, should not be made off this, and his linking and interchanging of the two was to be long continued.

The correspondence continued (see Ep. 13 and the mention of the *vehiculum animae*, the *ochēma*), but we must leave it there. Long after this the *De Trinitate* appeared (c.414 AD), and it is consistent with what we have seen in Augustine's letter (see XI 2 ff). But for a fuller consideration of phantasia we turn to a work which was written in roughly the same years as *De Trinitate*, the *De Genesi ad litteram*. As a Christian apologist Augustine seized enthusiastically on Neoplatonic doctrines which could provide support for Christian doctrines on the body, and he is able to use Neoplatonic speculation on *pneuma, spiritus* to suggest an explanation of the resurrection body which even a Neoplatonist could accept. In Book XII of the *De Genesi* he shows how their psychology of the imagination was consistent with, and could be used to support, the Christian doctrine of the after-life. He begins by distinguishing three forms of vision: 1) through the eyes, by which the letters of a word, for instance, are seen, 2) through the *spiritus hominis*, by means of which your neighbour is imagined, and 3) through the vision of the mind, intellectual vision (chapter 6). It is immediately obvious that in spite of the superiority of the third type of vision, it is the second which he is most anxious to consider in this book, and that at considerable length. It is not difficult to suggest what it is, he says: it is that through which we can think up (*cogitamus*) the sky, the earth and all we can see in them, even if we are sitting in darkness and not actually seeing anything with the eyes of the body but nevertheless are looking at bodily likenesses (*imagines*) in the mind. These can be either derived from experience directly, as when we have seen the bodies and retain them in our memory, or made up. For we have a different kind of picture of Carthage which we know personally than we have of Alexandria, which we don't know. It is the *spiritus* in which these images are contained, and this genus of vision we call the *spiritale* (chapter 7). Earlier in the work Augustine had used that adjective in connection with the body: in VI 19 he had distinguished between 'animale corpus', such as we now have, and 'spiritale', that of the resurrection.

Here in Book XII there follows a long discussion of 'spiritus' and 'spiritale', beginning with a host of citations from Scripture illustrating the usage of 'spiritus'. He says that he is going to use the word as it was used in the letter to the Corinthians I 14, 14 where *spiritus* is very clearly distinguished from *mens*. In fact, his interpretation sounds very much like a Neoplatonist reading of the *Timaeus*: *spiritus* and 'tongue' are taken to be referring to images or likenesses of things which need the vision of the mind to be understood (chapter 8). As regards prophecy in Scripture we are told that the prophet is not so much the one who has seen, but the one who has interpreted what another has seen. So prophecy belongs rather to the mind than to what we call *spiritus*, a power of the soul inferior to the mind, where the likenesses of corporeal things are produced. But he says he prefers to leave the consideration of the causes and progress of visions and divinations to some one else. He would prefer to devote his time to the investigation of an everyday occurrence like dreams which no one bothers about, or bothers very little about, than to questions about visions in ecstasy which are very rare experiences for the soul. Are dreams less wonderful because they are a daily occurrence or less worthy of attention because they are a universal experience? 'For my part, I wonder much more at and am more astonished by the speed and facility with which the soul creates within itself images of the objects which it has seen through the eyes than all the visions of dreamers or ecstasists' (chapter 18).

Augustine summarises what he has been saying in chapters 23–4, and concludes: 'Therefore it is not absurd, I think, nor unfitting, that *spiritalis* vision should play a mediating role between intellectual and corporeal vision. It is not unfitting that it should be called a medium between what is really body and that which is neither body nor similar to body, since it (i.e. the *spiritus-pneuma* and its vision) is not a body but it is similar to body' (chapter 24 end). When the soul leaves the body it is carried to 'spiritual' regions, resembling corporeal, for reward or punishment. It is not right to speak of these as false rewards or punishments: they are rather true joy or sorrow experienced in the imagination ('facta de substantia spiritali'), just as the joy and terror we experience in dreams or nightmares are due to the same faculty but are very real. The after-life, then, is a reality, but one that we can understand better by thinking of it in terms of the imagination rather than those of the body (chapter 32). He concludes (chapter 36) by saying that in the state of glory the body will still exist, but now as *spiritale*.

That much of Book XII of *De Genesi* is Neoplatonic and not simply the original creation of Augustine is, I think, obvious, and would be even clearer from a fuller summary than we have had space for here. Augustine's own particular background, training and interests are also apparent, of course, as in the anecdotes and the Scriptural references and quotations. But the whole texture is Neoplatonic. The typical Neoplatonic mixture of traditions is to be observed. Phantasia is stimulated by sense to form its images which are then at the disposal of intellect, and it already possesses within itself the forms through which knowledge is guaranteed. Aristotle's emphasis on the intermediate position of phantasia is accepted in the Neoplatonic way, and the mediating role is then interestingly extended in a Christian way for the next life also. The Neoplatonic grading of the different types of knowledge is preserved. Perhaps there is more of Augustine's own experience in his insistence on how images can flood the mind whether we want them or not, and how this can develop into a habit. I have not mentioned the phantasia *lektikē/sēmantikē*, but it is a feature which appears frequently in the Neoplatonists: Augustine gives us the clearest explanation of how it is to be envisaged.[20] Phantasia in dreams had also been a recurring element in the tradition, though once again Augustine's keen interest in psychology and in introspection gives it a fresh and personal note. 'Are dreams less wonderful because they happen every day?' The similarities to the *On Dreams* of Synesius, Augustine's contemporary, direct us to a common Neoplatonic source, and it is hard to see who else other than Porphyry this might have been. Augustine's concealing of the name of his source, the well-known anti-Christian Porphyry, is understandable; and Porphyry had after all insisted that 'the soul must avoid all union with the body in order to abide forever happy with God' (*Civ. Dei* x 29).

Augustine, with Boethius, passed on Neoplatonic Greek speculation on phantasia to the medieval Latin world. It was clear to anyone who read the two authors (and Courcelle among others has shown how much they were read)[21] that they used *imaginatio* as the Latin translation of the Greek phantasia, particularly when referring to the faculty. In this way they are ultimately responsible for the use of that word in the modern world. Finally, it should be noted that they did not attempt to make any distinction between phantasia and imagination. Those who would later distinguish phantasy or fancy from imagination could not call on the authority of the Latin Neoplatonists.

The medieval world cannot be dealt with here. In order, however, to give an indication of how the tradition we have been discussing was continued, I may refer briefly to the two leading figures, in prose and poetry, without pretending to any full exposition of their thought on imagination. These are Thomas Aquinas and Dante. Aquinas preserves two main streams, those of Aristotelianism and Neoplatonism, and manages fairly successfully to keep them apart, or, if he combines them, to use them both to explain in a positive way the workings of phantasia. His main source for his Aristotelianism in this instance is the *De Anima*, on the translation of which he had written a commentary,[22] and for Neoplatonism, Augustine's *De Genesi ad litteram* XII (although he does not appear to be aware of the Neoplatonic background of that book). Aquinas uses Augustine's threefold partition of vision into corporeal, intellectual and 'spiritualis', which is explained as coming about through the imagination or phantasia ('. . . spiritualem, quae fit per imaginationem sive phantasiam', *ST* 1, 78, 4. It is to be remarked that Aquinas uses *spiritualis* whereas Augustine had used *spiritalis*).

Yet although Augustine's three-fold distinction is authoritative for Aquinas and occupies a very important place in his work, there is a considerable difference of emphasis in the two thinkers. In the *De Genesi ad litteram* XII Augustine is largely, if not exclusively, concerned with the use of the distinction to provide philosophical support for Christian theological doctrine on the after-life, and particularly on the nature of the resurrection body. Aquinas used the distinction of the three visions for a wider purpose. He too saw an essential continuity and unity between philosophy and theology, and like Augustine thought that philosophy's search for the truth would end only in the vision of God. 'Vita aeterna consistit in visione divinae essentiae' (*ST* 1, 12, 4). The problem was, how was this vision to be achieved and what were the stages on the road to it. And here, perhaps for reasons of personal experience,[23] Aquinas, in different parts of his work, put the three-fold vision to work in a more systematic way than Augustine had done, and in so doing made it central to the history of contemplative theology. It is due mainly to him perhaps that MacIntyre can say: 'Contemplative theologians customarily distinguish three classes of vision, the external, the imaginary or the imaginal, and the intellectual'.[24] There can be no question of covering thoroughly this vast and complex topic in this space, but as an introduction to it we may take some of Aquinas' remarks in *ST* 1, 12 on how God is known by us.

There, in 1, 12, 11 he addresses himself to the question of whether anyone in this life can see God in his essence, and one of his reasons for raising the question is because Augustine has said (in *De Gen. ad litt.* XII 24) that by our intellectual vision we see what is in the soul by its essence. Aquinas' reply is that the ordinary human being cannot see God in his essence unless he is taken up out of this mortal life. He puts forward as an indication of this the fact that the more the soul is taken away from corporeal things the more capable it becomes of understanding abstract intelligible things. And thus it is that divine revelations and visions of the future are perceived more frequently in dreams and alienations from the senses. God can, of course, work miracles, and so certain minds can be raised up to see his essence in this life, but not through the use of the senses. We can, indeed, see God in the imagination (*imaginaria visione*), and seeing God speaking (by way of the imagination) is a specially distinguished form of prophecy as he promises to explain later. But he emphasises in 1, 12, 3 *ad* 3 that the essence of God is not seen in the imagination: a representation of God, like the metaphorical descriptions of God in the Scriptures, is all that is formed there. The blessed, however, do see the essence of God (1, 12, 1).

The Neoplatonism of this passage is obvious, as channelled to Aquinas through Augustine. And while the limitations of the senses and the imagination are clearly displayed, so too in 1, 12, 7 are those of the human intellect: 'it is impossible for any created intellect to comprehend God'. The senses and the imagination are not despised: they must keep their place, but they are accepted and must play their rôle. Aquinas is faithful to the Aristotelian tradition as we shall see. But before we take a glance at that we must turn to a closely related field which drew Aquinas' attention, referred to in 1, 12, 11, that of visions, dreams and prophecies. I think it is fair to say that a discussion of the foretelling of the future by means of dreams, etc. is not the sort of thing we would expect to find in a modern theological text-book. But the visions, dreams and prophecies of Scripture, both Old and New Testament, had fascinated the early Church, and much elaborate speculation had gone into their exegesis. We must remind ourselves that Scripture and its interpretation, then and in the later Middle Ages, occupied a central place in Christian intellectual life, and the discussion of problems arising from it had a correspondingly dominant influence in art, literature and philosophy. There is, besides, the very important tradition of mystical theology, and in Aquinas the topics just now mentioned and ecstasy are brought together (IIa, IIae 171–5).

Prophecy is there stated to be a knowledge remote from the knowledge of men (171, 1, backed by a false etymology), a knowledge which is above natural reason (171,2), and comes about through a divine light, because of which all things can be known, divine and human, spiritual and corporeal (171, 3). Aquinas agrees with Augustine (*De Gen. ad litt.* II 17) that sometimes the prophet's mind is instructed even unknowingly (171, 5). That brings us back to an earlier part of the *Secunda Secundae*, quaestio 95, where divination is discussed. Aquinas is not slow to make clear his opposition to divination, 95, 2, and to astrology, 5. In 6 he turns to consider whether divination through dreams is illicit, and here the views of his two favourite authorities, Christian and pagan, must be considered. As he puts it in 172, 1, prophecy apparently can be natural, for Augustine (op. cit. XII 13) says that the human soul can foresee the future in as much as it is abstracted from the senses of the body; and prophecy foresees the future. Similarly, Aristotle says in *On Divination in Sleep* 464a17 that some people while asleep naturally foresee some future events. Aquinas' answer in 95, 6 finally is that using dreams for divination is not illicit when one knows that they come from a divine revelation, being caused spiritually, or from a natural cause 'insofar as the power of such a cause can extend'. In 172, 1 he says that prophecy strictly so called cannot be from nature, but only from divine revelation.

It seems to me that there is an uneasiness here which may go back ultimately to Aquinas' failure to recognise Augustine's sleight of hand with *pneuma-spiritus*. What is quite clear in all this section is how deeply he is impressed by *De Genesi* XII. He goes back to the point he had made in I, 12, 11 about foreknowledge in dreams. 'When a soul is abstracted from bodily realities it is more adapted to coming under the sway of spiritual substances; it is also more sensitive to those subtle impressions which natural causes leave upon the human imagination ... These modes of knowledge (i.e. foreknowledge in dreams) are more active during sleep than when awake, for the soul of one who is awake is taken up with exterior tangible realities, and is accordingly less capable of sensing the delicate impressions made by spiritual beings or even by natural causes' (172, 1). And a final familiar Neoplatonic note: 'God ... reveals things to men in dreams through the ministry of angels ... (But) Sometimes the appearance of certain images to persons in their sleep is the work of demons, and then some of the future may be disclosed to those who have entered into an unlawful compact with them' (95, 6. Blackfriars translation in above quotations). The activity of demons in this field is further discussed in 172, 5 and 6, and there again *De Genesi* XII 19 is the authority.

Prophetic vision does not, then, allow anyone to see God in his essence, to return to the question of I, 12, 11. Rather, the mind of the prophet is enlightened so that it reflects likenesses or images of the truth of the divine foreknowledge, as if in a mirror, another Neoplatonic echo of the imagination (173, 1). But God's enlightening of the prophet's mind is not confined to activity through the senses or the imagination: sometimes intellectual likenesses of realities are impressed on the mind itself, as is clear in the case of those who like Solomon or the Apostles received infused knowledge or wisdom. And sometimes too an intellectual light is infused into the human mind by God to enable it to judge things seen by others (173, 3). The prophecy which allows a supernatural truth to be perceived in accordance with intellectual vision is more valuable than that in which supernatural truth is manifested through imaginative vision. Yet, because prophecy implies a certain obscurity or remoteness from truth, we are inclined to use the term 'prophet' more specifically for those who see in visions of the imagination (174, 2). These can occur during sleep, in dreams, or when awake, in visions in the narrower sense: waking visions are a higher form of prophecy, because a more powerful prophetic light is required to detach someone who is awake from the things of sense and draw him towards supernatural truth than that which is needed in the case of a man already, because of sleep, detached from the objects of sense. For a prophet to see someone speaking to him is a particularly high grade of prophecy, as mentioned before, because the prophet's mind is thereby shown to be nearer to the cause of the revelation (174, 3). Finally, it should be recalled that prophecy is primarily a knowledge and only secondarily speech, when the prophets proclaim what they have learned for the edification of others (171, 1).

After this comprehensive discussion of prophecy Aquinas returns, in question 175, to the experience of ecstasy, in which the three-fold vision was first deployed by Augustine, and particularly to that of the ecstasy of St Paul in 2 *Corinthians* (see also here 180, 5). He says that there are three ways in which the human mind is rapt up to God, firstly by imaginative likenesses, as in Peter's trance in *Acts* 10, 10, secondly by the effect on the intellect, as with David in Psalm 115, 2, and, finally, the divine truth may be contemplated in its essence. The ecstasy of Paul was of the third kind. Now the divine essence cannot be seen by created intellect except through the light of glory, and this in two ways. The first is that of the saints made blessed in heaven, by way of immanent form. The second is by way of a passing affection, and it was in this way that Paul was rapt up. He was not, then, in a permanent state of blessedness, but nevertheless while this rapture lasted he experienced utter joy (175, 3).

There we must leave Aquinas on visions, dreams, prophecy and ecstasy. There can be little doubt that in this sort of speculation Dante saw intellectual support for his own visions in the *Divina Commedia*. The substructure is essentially Platonic, but mixed with it, particularly when purely human knowledge is touched upon, there is thoroughly Aristotelian epistemological theory, and it does not need to be stated that both Dante and Aquinas were great admirers of Aristotle. Aquinas is a faithful follower of 'The Philosopher', and expounds him conscientiously in his commentary on the *De Anima* which he read in William of Moerbeke's version. That commentary leaves no doubt as to Aquinas' grasp of Aristotle. One point which he emphasises particularly is that of the dependence of intellect on sense, with the imagination playing its part as intermediary (see *ST* 1, 84, 6–7). His treatment of phantasia or imagination is marked by a sober appreciation of its necessity for the normal functioning of intellect. Imagination has its defects, of course. 'In the case of ourselves, deception comes about really in accordance with phantasia, through which occasionally we cling to the likenesses of things as if they were the things themselves, as is clear in the case of people sleeping or the mad' (*ST* 1, 54, 5 ad fin.). Sometimes, too, we can deceive ourselves by refusing to rise above the imagination. 'The first of those who began to study the nature of things, not being able to transcend the imagination, maintained that there was nothing beyond bodies. And therefore they said that God was a sort of body, because they thought that He was the principle of other bodies' (*ST* 1, 90, 1). But there is in Aquinas no rhetorical condemnation of phantasia such as we can find in some Neoplatonists.

Dante I leave to Thomas Finan. With Dante the imagination gains a higher place than it had yet been accorded in poetry or philosophy. It is obvious, however, that he had not brought it to this peak by his own efforts alone. His debts are many, even though he could not always have been conscious of them. The justification of the vision which comes through the imagination goes back ultimately to Plato in the *Timaeus*. This justification had been taken up enthusiastically by Porphyry, if we are permitted to use Synesius' *On Dreams* and Augustine on *Genesis* as evidence for his views. Augustine had Christianised the whole process of the vision, and in so doing gave imagination a more central place than would have seemed possible to his pagan contemporaries and Neoplatonic predecessors. The elevation was then completed by Aquinas, following Aristotle with his calm acceptance of the centrality of imagination in the ordinary course of human thinking, and following Platonism and Augustine in establishing the schema of the threefold vision, with the *visio imaginaria* again the intermediary. Imagination had become the pathway to the divine life.

NOTES
1. For English-readers the most comprehensive account of the Presocratics mentioned here is to be found in Guthrie's *A History of Greek Philosophy*, vols I and II (Cambridge 1962, 1965). Highly recommended also is Kirk and Raven, *The Presocratic Philosophers* (Cambridge 1957, 1983, second edn). References to further literature will be found in these volumes.
2. The commentaries on the *Timaeus* by Taylor (1928) and Cornford (1937) are still the most important modern works. Cornford's discussion of the *Theaetetus* is to be found in his *Plato's Theory of Knowledge* (London 1935).
3. Parallels between Xenophanes and Parmenides are to be observed. For a discussion see Guthrie, op. cit., vol.II, pp.37 and 46, and Kirk and Raven, pp.171-2.
4. For the influence on Aristotle, see his *Metaphysics*, Gamma 5. For the Stoics, see my *Phantasia in Classical Thought*, chapter 1.
5. On the passage in the *Timaeus*, and on much else discussed here, see M. W. Bundy, *The Theory of Imagination in Classical and Mediaeval Thought* (Urbana 1927).
6. See my '*Phantasia* in *De Anima*, 3.3', *Classical Quarterly* 32 (1982), 100-13.
7. Simplicius, commentator on Aristotle and Neoplatonist, shows a remarkable ability to combine both theories. See my *Phantasia*, chapter 5.

8. On Philostratus, see O. Schönberger, *Philostratos Die Bilder* (Munich 1968), pp.10-20. F. Solmsen's two essays on Philostratus and the Philostrati are to be found conveniently in *Kleine Schriften* (Hildesheim 1968). The English version of Lesky's *History of Greek Literature* (London 1966) has a useful discussion on pp.836-8, with bibliographical references on p.844. On Apollonius, see also Rose's article in the *Oxford Classical Dictionary* (second edn).
9. In the Latin original of my version I retain the 'non' before 'cadunt'. See H. Sjögren, 'Kleine textkritische Beiträge', *Eranos* 19 (1919-20), 163-6.
10. See D. A. Russell, *'Longinus' On the Sublime* (Oxford 1964). For further bibliography, see D. St Marin, *Bibliography of the 'Essay on the Sublime'* (Privately printed 1967).
11. On Dio, see Lesky, op. cit., pp.834-5.
12. See John Dillon, *The Middle Platonists* (London 1977), p.45.
13. See A. J. Festugière, 'Le "Compendium Timaei" de Galien', *REG* 65 (1952), 101, and M. Baltes, *Die Weltentstehung des Platonischen Timaeus nach den antiken Interpreteten* (Leiden 1976 I and 1978 II).
14. See Hobein in *RE* XIV 2 (1933), 2558.
15. Arguments have been made for Antiochus of Ascalon, the Stoicising Platonist of the first century BC, especially by E. Birmelin in two articles in *Philologus* 88 (1933) entitled 'Die kunsttheoretischen Gedanken in Philostrats Apollonios', invoking W. Theiler's *Die Vorbereitung des Neuplatonismus* (Berlin 1930). Posidonius the Stoic has also been mentioned, but it seems to me impossible to fix on any one author in the present state of our knowledge.
16. On the *ochēma* in Neoplatonism, see Dodds, *Proclus. The Elements of Theology* (Oxford 1963, second edn), pp.313ff.
17. W. Lang, *Das Traumbuch des Synesius von Cyrene* (Tübingen 1926), p.33.
18. See *Enneads* 1.8.15.
19. The elder Pliny spoke of a wonderful power belonging to the seed of lettuce: if crushed taken in wine it prevented libidinous dreams, 'libidinum imaginationes in somno compesci'. Not long after him Tacitus wrote of Nero considering to himself trips to the provinces of the East, especially Egypt—'provincias Orientis, maxime Aegyptum, secretis imaginationibus agitans'. Calcidius uses it as the Latin translation of the Greek phantasia.
20. There are passing references in Porphyry, Iamblichus, Syrianus and Proclus which would remain opaque were it not for Augustine.
21. See his *Les Confessions de S. Augustin dans la tradition littéraire* (Paris 1963) and *La Consolation de Boèce dans la tradition littéraire* (Paris 1967).
22. An English translation of this commentary by K. Foster and S. Humphries was published by Routledge and Kegan Paul, 1951.
23. The restlessness of Augustine made optimism about the mystical vision in this life difficult for him. Aquinas seems to have had some form of mystical experience, at least towards the end of his life: see F. Copleston, *Thomas Aquinas* (London 1955, 1976), p.10. See the excellent remarks in chapter 15 of Peter Brown's *Augustine of Hippo* (London 1967), especially pp.146-8.
24. In 'Visions', chapter XIV of *New Essays in Philosophical Theology*, eds Flew and MacIntyre (London 1955), p.254. This, however, is a twentieth-century perspective, and the classes do not correspond exactly with those of Augustine and Aquinas.

« 2 »

JOHN DILLON : PLOTINUS AND THE TRANSCENDENTAL IMAGINATION

I

The status and role of *phantasia*, or imagination, in Platonism generally is low. The nearest thing to a definition of it by Plato is to be found at *Soph.* 264AB,[1] and Aristotle's discussion in *De Anima* III 3 is essentially a development of the Platonist position.[2] It is a faculty or activity of the 'lower' soul, dependent upon sense-perception, from which the soul must purify itself in the course of its ascent to knowledge of, and unity with, the divine. Only outside the philosophical tradition, in the spheres of rhetoric and of art-criticism is there any sign of a higher valuation of what the imagination can be.[3]

However, that is not quite the whole story, and the exception arises from a quarter from which one should expect it, the fertile mind of Plotinus.[4] Plotinus of course also assigns to *phantasia* its normal Platonic role,[5] and as such recommends that we transcend it, but his profound speculations on the consequences of postulating immortality for the individual soul, and the survival, in some form, of the personality, involves him, especially in *Enneads* IV 3, 23–32 (in the course of his major enquiry, *Problems of the Soul*, divided by Porphyry into three tractates, *Enn.* IV 3–5), in a discussion of memory, and thus of the faculty of imagination, on which he finds memory to be based.

The conclusion that the disembodied, 'purified', soul must retain memory of at least some aspect of its earthly existence necessitates, it seems to him, there being a faculty of imagination dependent on the activities of the higher soul, as well as those of the lower (IV 3, 30–1). At this point, it may be useful to quote from IV 3, 30, where Plotinus raises the question, 'Is imagination involved also in mental acts?' He answers as follows: 'If in fact every mental act is accompanied by an image (*phantasia*), we may well believe that when this image, which woud be as it were a picture of the thought, remains on, this would explain how memory of an object of knowledge would take place. But if this is not the case, another suggestion may be made. Perhaps memory would be the reception into the imagination of the discursive sequel[6] (*logos*) to an act of intuitive thought (*noêma*). The thought itself, being indivisible and never, as it were, rising to the exterior of the consciousness, remains hidden within, but the *logos*, unfolding and proceeding from the thought into the imagination, displays the thought as it were in a mirror,[7] and thus results the apprehension of it, its continued presence, and consequently memory.'

For our present purpose it does not much matter whether the *noêma* itself or its *logos* is 'mirrored' in the imagination. The main thing is that the imagination is clearly recognised as receptive of images from 'above' as well as of sense-data.[8] The imagination is thus situated interestingly at the border, as it were, between the two levels of soul. This Janus-like position for the imagination bothers Plotinus, and he would prefer to postulate *two* imaginative faculties, one serving either level of memory. He then was faced with the problem of how these two would coordinate while the soul is in the body (IV 3, 31).

They cannot, he agrees, simply operate side by side, or we would have some consciousness of this fact—of throwing a mental switch, as it were, to activate one or the other. His solution involves conjuring up one of those vivid images for which he is noted, and about which I will have more to say presently: 'when the two souls are in harmony, and the two imagining faculties do not stand apart, but that of the superior soul is dominant, then a single image only is perceived, the less powerful being like a shadow on the other, like a lesser light merging into a greater.'

The image is that of a stronger and a weaker light focused on a common field, so that the weaker light is not noticed. When the two imaginations are in conflict, he goes on to say, we notice the two lights as separate, though we are still not conscious of the presence of two levels of soul. This image is both striking and apt, as it portrays exactly the sort of double life Plotinus envisages for the imagination. He gives no illustrative examples, but we may propose one. Suppose one is engaged in meditation, conjuring up, perhaps, just such an image of light as he has suggested to us here, and one's bodily organs and senses are totally under control, providing no distractions; the 'lower' imagination is not inoperative; it has simply subordinated its activity completely to that of the higher. On the other hand, if one is an unsuccessful meditator, then conflicting images—perhaps of a friend, or of one's garden, or of a gin-and-tonic—may come crowding in. Here the second 'spotlight' is no longer focused on the same spot as the first; it begins to wander here and there, and distracting images impinge upon the central one.

This image, as I say, is striking, but it may also involve Plotinus in certain problems.[9] Do we really need two imaging faculties? Is it not better to see *phantasia* as a pivotal faculty of the soul, able to serve both the reason and the passions? Possibly, but not for Plotinus, since he is concerned here with preserving *phantasia* in the disembodied soul, without being able to deny its traditional Platonic role as the servant of *aisthēsis* and the passions. We can salute his acuity, I think, without necessarily adopting his particular solution. What his speculations have led to, for the first time, as far as we can see (our knowledge of Middle Platonic speculation is sadly deficient), is the opening of a rôle for *phantasia* as the servant of intellectual (and theological) speculation, such as was not open to it in traditional Platonism.

It may be helpful at this point to confront Plotinus' theory of the imagination with that of Kant. In the *Critique of Pure Reason*, in the course of his 'Deduction of the Pure Concepts of the Understanding' (pp.A115ff),[10] Kant distinguishes between the 'productive' and the merely 'reproductive', the transcendental and the empirical, imagination. The former he describes as follows (A120):[11]

> What is first given to us is appearance. When combined with consciousness it is called perception ... Now, since every appearance contains a manifold, and since different perceptions therefore occur in the mind separately and singly, a combination of them, such as they cannot have in sense itself, is demanded. There must therefore exist in us an active faculty for the synthesis of the manifold. To this faculty I give the title, imagination.

The role of the transcendental imagination is, then, 'the synthesis of the manifold' of experience. To decide whether Plotinus' higher imagination has anything in common with this, we must consider what it does when the soul is in the body (which is the situation Kant is addressing himself to, and the only one in which we are interested at the moment). An interesting text in this connexion is III 6, 4, 19–21 (discussed by Blumenthal, pp.92–3), where Plotinus makes a distinction between 'imagination in the primary sense (*prôtê phantasia*) which we call opinion (*doxa*)', which is the faculty in the soul which synthesises the data of sense-perception (in this case, that there is or is not something to be feared), and delivers an opinion on the basis of them, and a lower imagination, involving no synthesis or judgement (*anepikritos*) which presumably just takes in the data as discrete images.[12]

Although III 6 (26) immediately precedes IV 3–5 (27–9) in Porphyry's chronological list, there is no mention here of two levels of soul, with one imagination each, but this would be explained by the fact that Plotinus is here talking exclusively of the soul in the body, where the distinction between the two levels is not clearly discernible. At any rate, Plotinus' *prôtê phantasia* here seems to have very much the role of Kant's transcendent imagination.

However, there is more to the higher imagination than that. Besides synthesising the reports of the senses, it is also the recipient, the 'mirror', of the operations of the intellect. In *Enn.* I 4, a late treatise (46), in the course of a discussion as to why we are not always conscious of the activity of *nous* within us, Plotinus presents *phantasia* as a mirror for intellectual activity (I 4, 10, 7ff), which only performs properly when the 'surface' of the soul, so to speak, is unruffled by passion, and thus 'smooth'. 'But when this is broken because the harmony of the body is upset, thought and intellect operate without an image, and then intellectual activity takes place without *phantasia*. So one might come to this sort of conclusion, that intellectual activity takes place with the accompaniment of *phantasia*, though it is not identical with *phantasia*.'

Here, as in IV 3, 30 (quoted above), the imagination is the receptacle for *noêseis*, intellectual acts. One might well ask, what are these intellectual acts which the imagination, if the soul is in a harmonious state, can mirror? No doubt Plotinus has various types of intellection in mind—solutions to mathematical or geometrical problems being one possible example, a witty riposte that one failed to make in the Common Room last night being another—but there is one particularly interesting type that I would like to focus on, and that is Plotinus' well-known 'dynamic images',[13] those spiritual exercises which he prescribes for us at various points in the tractates in order to make vivid some knotty point of doctrine. These require the active, creative use of the imagination for the clearer grasping of a truth which transcends all sense-perception, though one must start from physical images in one's ascent to understanding.

One example is to be found at *Enn.* V 8, 9, where Plotinus explains to us how to imagine the intellectual world:

> Let us, then, grasp with our mind (*dianoia*) this cosmos, each member of it remaining what it is, distinct and apart, yet all forming, as far as possible, a complete unity, so that whatever comes into focus, say the outer orb of the heavens, shall bring immediately with it the image (*phantasia*), on the one plane, of the sun and of the other planets, with earth and sea and all living things, as if exhibited upon a transparent globe.
>
> Let there be, then, in your soul the gleaming image (*phantasia*) of a sphere, a picture holding all the things in the universe whether in motion or at rest, or rather, some at rest and others in motion. Keep this sphere before you, and from it imagine another, a sphere stripped of magnitude and of spatial differences; cast out spatial conceptions and the image (*phantasma*) of matter within you; do not simply substitute an image reduced in size, but call on God, the maker of the sphere whose image you now hold, and pray him to enter. (translation by MacKenna, emended)

Here we are being called upon to use our imagination creatively, to attain to a purely intellectual conception. It is worth while, perhaps, to try to perform the exercise as Plotinus prescribes. I have attempted it repeatedly, and the sticking-point is always the instruction, once one has conjured up the universe (as a luminous, diaphanous globe, with all its parts distinct and functioning), then to think away the spatiality ('*aphelōn ton onkon labe*')—and not just by shrinking it! It is in fact an excellent spiritual exercise. Calling upon God here is no empty formality. If done effectively, it has a quasi-theurgic result: 'He may come, bringing his own cosmos, with all the gods that dwell in it—He who is the one God, and all the gods, where each is all, blending into a unity, distinct in powers but all one god, in virtue of that one divine power of many facets.'

In other words, if you perform the exercise correctly, you will achieve a mystical vision of the noetic cosmos. And Plotinus knew what he was talking about.

Let us consider another passage, this time from *Enn.* VI 4, where Plotinus is trying to convey to us how an immaterial force, such as Soul, may be present equally at all points in the universe. In chapter 7, he adduces two images. The first is that of a hand carrying a long plank. The hand supports the whole plank, though its actual contact with it only covers a fraction of its length. 'Now,' says Plotinus, 'think away the corporeal mass of the hand, but retain the same power as it exerted previously. Is not that same power, indivisible, present integrally over every part of the object?'

He follows this up with another image, characteristically involving light, in this case a flame lighting up a translucent globe:

> Or imagine a small luminous mass serving as centre to a transparent sphere, so that the light from within shows upon the entire outer surface, otherwise unlit: we surely agree that the inner core of light, intact and immobile, reaches over the entire outer extension; the simple light of that small centre illuminates the whole field. The diffused light is not due to any bodily magnitude of that central point which illuminates not as body but as body lit, that is by another kind of power than corporeal quality: let us then abstract the corporeal mass, retaining the light as power: we can no longer speak of the light in any particular spot; it is equally diffused within and throughout the entire sphere. We can no longer name the spot it occupied so as to say whence it came or how it is present; we can but seek, and wonder as the search shows us the light simultaneously present at each and every point of the sphere. (translation by MacKenna)

Here again, the imagination is being asked, first to construct a model of a physical object or situation, and then to 'abstract the corporeal mass'. That is a job for a creative imagination, and one in the service of intellect, not of the senses.

II

Having seen the 'transcendental' imagination at work (in one of its rôles, at least), let us return to the problem of the two imaginations. As I have said, the chief reason for postulating this duality in *Enn.* IV 3 is that Plotinus feels that the disembodied rational soul will retain a (selective) memory of its earthly existence, and that the prerequisite of memory is a faculty of imagination. We, however, are discussing the embodied soul, where the imagination behaves, at least, like a unitary faculty. As such, it both reproduces and produces (synthesises) images derived from both sense-data and from purely intellectual operations.

One might ask, though, will the two imaginations ever concern themselves with the same object? Plotinus addresses this question in *Enn.* IV 3, 32, and answers in the affirmative. Once again, he is thinking of the disembodied soul remembering *without passion* (*apathōs*) events or people (a wife, for example) which evoked passionate images in its bodily existence. But we frequently have the experience, surely, of being able now 'calmly and dispassionately' to conjure up the memory of a past event, such as the death of a wife, an old love-affair, an act of injustice that enraged us, and consider it free from the passionate feelings that came with it, or even accompanied earlier memories of it. In such a case, would we not be justified, using Plotinus' formulation, in saying that we are now contemplating the event with our 'higher' imagination?[14] This is certainly, in his view, how we would contemplate it after death.

But the proper rôle of the higher imagination is plainly the representation of mental acts, and of intelligible reality. We hear more of this in the first chapters of *Enn.* IV 4, still in connection with memory. Plotinus, it must be said, does not accord memory or imagination a place of unalloyed honour. Neither the higher beings, even down to the heavenly gods, nor the human soul in its highest state (in contemplation of the intelligible realm), have any use for either memory or imagination. These only arise when the soul descends from its highest state, and then reflects upon it:

> But it leaves that conjunction (sc. with the Intelligible); it cannot suffer that unity; it falls in love with its own powers and possessions, and desires to stand apart; it leans outwards, so to speak; then, it appears to acquire a memory of itself. (*Enn.* IV 4, 3, translation by MacKenna)

And where memory arises, there the imagination necessarily is also. This less-than-perfect status for the imagination explains Plotinus' unwillingness earlier (IV 3, 30, 5–6) to allow intellectual acts themselves to be mirrored in it, but rather their *logoi*, or projections.

Memory, and thus imagination, are only possible for beings whose state changes, and who are thus creatures of time rather than eternity. In the next few chapters of IV 4, Plotinus explains why it is inappropriate to postulate memory of various classes of higher being, even down to the World Soul, which, though the originator of time, is not properly itself *in* time. In chapter 13, in connection with a description of Nature (*Physis*) as the lowest emanation of the World-Soul, and too dim an entity to have memory or imagination, he places imagination interestingly at the mid-point, in some sense, of the Soul's life:

> ✷ For this reason Nature does not possess even imagination. Intellection (*noêsis*) is superior to imagination. Imagination is between the levels of Nature and of Intellection. Nature, after all, does not have apprehension or consciousness of anything, while Imagination has consciousness of what is external to it; for it allows that which has the image to have knowledge of what it has experienced. Intellection, on the other hand, is a generation and activity from the active (intellect) itself.

It is not clear to me whether Plotinus is positing a level of the World-Soul which employs imagination—if so, we should hear more of it—or whether he is really just thinking of the levels of the individual soul, and brings in imagination here just to show how far *physis* is inferior to *noêsis*. I would prefer the latter alternative, but I cannot be sure. In any case, we are not concerned here with the anatomy of the World-Soul, and what he says is true of the individual, that the imagination is a median faculty, on the borderline (*methorion*, IV 4, 3, 11) between the intelligible and the sensible.

III

Finally, a word on the subject of the imagination as an organ of artistic creativity. Plotinus was, of course, not interested in art for art's sake, but he was concerned with both beauty and art in the service of theology. The famous ascent to the Beautiful Itself set out in Diotima's speech in Plato's *Symposium* (210A–212A) is an important exercise of the imaginative faculty, which he celebrates in *Enn*. III 5 and elsewhere. But in one important respect Plotinus goes beyond, and indeed against, Plato, and that is in the value he places on the artistic imagination—or at least in the imagination of *some* divinely-inspired artists, such as Phidias.[15] His doctrine here was a great consolation later to Platonically-minded artists of the Renaissance, such as Michelangelo, to whom Plato would have given short shrift. In an important passage near the beginning of his tractate *On the Intellectual Beauty* (V 8 (31)), he says the following (chapter 1, 36–40):

> Still, the arts are not to be slighted on the ground that they create by imitation of natural objects; for, to begin with, these natural objects are themselves imitations; then we must recognise that they give no bare reproduction of the thing seen, but go back to the Reason-Principles from which Nature itself derives, and, furthermore, that much of their work is all their own; they are holders of beauty and add where nature is lacking. Thus Pheidias wrought the Zeus (in Olympia) upon no model among things of sense, but by apprehending what form Zeus must take if he chose to become manifest to sight. (translation by MacKenna)

In other words, Phidias used his transcendental artistic imagination, to mirror forth a true representation of Zeus himself.

IV

What we see here, I think, in the case of Plotinus, is a significant broadening and upgrading of the concept of the imagination by comparison with the norm of ancient philosophic thought, a development which has considerable significance for later Neoplatonism. By way of appendix to this paper, I will present a few significant passages.

First, a notable statement by Iamblichus, in the *De Mysteriis* III 14 (132), in the course of replying to remarks of Porphyry's about that branch of divination called *phôtagogia* or 'drawing down of light':

> This (activity) illuminates the aetherial and luminous vehicle (*ochêma*) of the soul with divine light, in consequence of which divine images (*phantasiai*) take hold upon our faculty of imagination (*tēn en hēmin phantastikēn dynamin*), stimulated by the will of the gods. For the whole life of the soul and all the faculties in it are subject to the gods and moved by them, in accordance with the wish of its conductors (*hêgemones*).

Porphyry said that in this type of divination, the practitioners remain conscious (*parakolouthountes heautois*), in other respects, while being divinely possessed as to their imaginative faculty (*kata to phantastikon epitheiazousi*). Iamblichus is not basically quarrelling with this statement, merely elucidating it. He goes on to say (133) that the divine light does not fasten on the *dianoia*, or reflective consciousness, but rather on the imaginative faculty, because it allows itself to be stimulated by the gods directly, where the *dianoia* would interpose a degree of self-consciousness.

This is admittedly not to grant a very exalted role to the *phantasia*. It is favoured by the gods precisely because it is subrational. But it is allowed by Iamblichus to have direct access to divine inspiration, which makes it a faculty open to influences from above as well as from below, as it is in Plotinus.

The double nature of *phantasia* is a doctrine preserved also by the Athenian School, though in a less radical form. Plutarch of Athens is reported by Pseudo-Philoponus (Stephanus?) on the *De Anima* (p.515, 12–15 Hayduck, *CAG* xv) as follows:

> Plutarch considers the imagination to be double, and that its upper boundary, which is to say its originative principle (*archē*), is the (lower) boundary of the discursive intellect (*dianoêtikon*), while its other boundary is the upper limit of the senses.

This duality, as Blumenthal points out (*art. cit.* p.134), is one of function rather than of essence. The commentator goes on to report Plutarch's comparison of the imagination to a point where two lines meet, one coming from above, the other from below. What we have here, then, is not two *phantasiai*, but rather a Janus-faced figure, such as Plotinus in fact presents us with, in *Enn.* IV 3, 30 and I 4, 10, but rejects in favour of his double *phantasia*, for special reasons which I have explained.

Proclus' position on *phantasia* is a good deal more complicated, probably simply because we have so much more of him,[16] but in most cases he gives it its traditional low ranking, as something dependent on *aisthesis*, and a function of the lower soul, and associates it closely, and confusingly, with *doxa*. Only in his *Euclid Commentary* do we find a more exalted role being accorded it. At p.141, 4ff Friedlein, Proclus speaks of the soul, 'while acting cognitively, projecting upon the *phantasia*, as upon a mirror, the *logoi* of (geometrical) *schemata*', which the *phantasia* processes, and, as it were, throws up on a screen for the soul to contemplate.[17]

The circumstance that we are concerned with the contemplation of geometrical constructions presumably accounts for this promotion of the *phantasia*, but it is still, here, no more than a 'two-faced', median faculty, not really part of the rational soul, but rather acting as a 'mirror' to it, and there is no trace in Proclus, any more than in Plutarch, of the distinctive Plotinian theory of two imaginations.

V

On the whole, then, Plotinus' successors, as in a number of other areas, tend to back off from his more adventurous innovations, in the direction of a more orthodox Platonic, and indeed Aristotelian, position. Nevertheless, the concept of the imagination as receptive of noetic perceptions as well as of sense perceptions does persist in the tradition, and leave the way open for a higher valuation of it among Renaissance Platonists.

NOTES

1. Other relevant passages are *Tim.* 52A and *Phileb.* 39B.
2. Aristotle also touches on *phantasia* in *De An.* III 7, and in *De Memoria* 1, 449b31ff, in both of which places he makes the troublesome statement that no *noêsis* takes place without *phantasia*, but this does not imply either that *phantasia* is a faculty of a higher part of the soul, or that any *phantasia* derives from *nous*.
3. The fullest pre-Plotinian discussion of *phantasia* in the Platonic-Aristotelian tradition occurs in Alexander of Aphrodisias' *De Anima*, pp.66, 9-73, 13 Bruns (*CAG*), and it is merely an amplification of Aristotle's remarks in *De An.* III 3, embellished with some Stoic terminology. A key passage for the sophistic revaluation of *phantasia* occurs in Philostratus, *Life of Apollonius of Tyana* VI 19 (Philostratus being more or less a contemporary of Alexander).
4. See the useful article of E. W. Warren, 'Imagination in Plotinus', *CQ* n.s. 16 (1966), pp.277-85. (The remarks of H. von Kleist, in *Plotinische Studien*, Heidelberg, 1883, p.87, are still valuable.)

5. Plotinus gives succinct definitions of *phantasia* in its more traditional sense, e.g. *Enn.* I 8, 15, 18-19: 'Imagination is brought about by the irrational part (sc. of the soul) being struck from outside. But (the soul) receives the blow on account of its divisible nature'. *Enn.* VI 8, 3, 10-12: 'But as for ourselves, we call imagination, strictly speaking, what is awakened from the passive impression of the body'.
6. Adopting here the formulation of Henry Blumenthal (*Plotinus' Psychology*, Nijhoff, The Hague, 1971, chapter 7, p.88). No straightforward translation of *logos* will quite do here, as what Plotinus seems to mean is a 'projection' of the original intuition (*noêma*) onto the discursive level of thought, which involves mental images. Bréhier's 'formule verbale' is harmlessly uninformative, as is Harder's 'Begriff', and Armstrong's 'verbal expression'.
7. This 'mirroring' role for the *phantasia* is to some extent anticipated by Plato's interesting presentation of the rôle of the liver, in *Tim.* 71B-D, as receiving 'as in a mirror' images of *dianoemata* from the intellect. But, of course, these images are not themselves rational, nor does the liver indulge in rational activity.
8. This is actually adumbrated as a possibility by Aristotle in *De An.* III 3, but nothing much is made of it.
9. Such as are raised by Blumenthal, op. cit. pp.94ff.
10. Using Norman Kemp Smith's edition (A before the page number refers to Kant's first edition pagination).
11. Quoted by Mary Warnock on p.28 of her *Imagination*.
12. The close connection here between *phantasia* and *doxa* is noteworthy, since the relation of these two faculties is quite tortuous, both in Plotinus himself and in later Platonists, such as Plutarch of Athens and Proclus. See on this Blumenthal, 'Plutarch's *De Anima* and Proclus' in *De Iamblique à Proclus: Entretiens sur l'Antiquité Classique*, XXI, Vandoeuvres-Genève, 1975, pp.123-51.
13. By 'dynamic image' is meant an image which is designed to develop as one contemplates it, thus leading the mind to a deeper comprehension of reality.
14. Plotinus' distinction here is reminiscent of that made by Aristotle between *doxa* and *phantasia* in *De An.* III 3, 427b21ff, where he describes *doxa* as being accompanied by *pathos*, while *phantasia* is free of this, 'as if one were contemplating terrible or encouraging things in a painting'.
15. The use of Phidias as an exemplum goes back at least to Cicero (*Orator* 7ff) but it occurs, significantly, in the discourse of Apollonius of Tyana on *phantasia* composed by Philostratus (see n.3 above).
16. I am indebted here to Blumenthal's discussion of Plutarch's and Proclus' doctrine in the article quoted above n.9.
17. The *phantasia* is described as a mirror for the *dianoia* also earlier, at p.121, 5-6.

« 3 »

THOMAS FINAN: DANTE
AND THE RELIGIOUS IMAGINATION

I

Two preliminary questions are omitted from this essay. They are omitted because I presuppose them as asked and variously answered by other contributors. Both questions have to do with *imagination*: what kind of 'faculty' have we in mind? and how do we understand its cognitive mode and estimate its cognitive value—especially in comparison with logical reason? Another justification for dispensing with these questions is that they can be answered only after a 'phenomenological' study of the actual working and achievements of the imagination. After which we might work inductively towards definition and theory. Or maybe, like à Kempis in *The Imitation*, happier to feel than define, just rest content with the self-validating savour of the apple.

Something like that is the case with Dante himself. Few men's work better embodies the two poles of our problem, reason and imagination. Reason we might expect, *il ben dello intelletto*, from a man whose *corpus* is the distillation and crystallisation of the great Classical and Scholastic achievements of intellect. That he is also a man of the imagination must be obvious even *a priori*, merely from the implications of the rôle played by what we may call the Beatrician experience at the heart of his perceptions and the works that embody them. Yet he seldom or never called this mode of experience and knowledge by the name of imagination in any sense coextensive with our contemporary 'imagination', 'a licentious and vagrant faculty, unsusceptible of limitations, and impatient of restraint'.[1] And, despite the status of *intelletto* in him, no more did he feel obliged to address himself to our problem, the theoretical justification and evaluation of the imaginative vis-à-vis that *intelletto*. One explanation is that he could take for granted—and confirmed in his experience—a great deal of traditional theory about modes and levels of knowing that we are less familiar with, or cannot be so naive about. Theory which puts imagination—though without calling it such—in a locatable position on the map, in a way that the moderns, for all their Romanticism (or because of it?) cannot do.

A first example and very early instance of what Dante could and did take for granted will serve also to introduce us to both radical experience and radical questions about the understanding of it. The example I take is that which occasioned the first sonnet of the *Vita Nuova*[2] (*VN*), a sonnet therefore from among the earliest that Dante wrote, the first written expressly out of the Beatrician experience, or in any case chosen as the starting-point for reflexive analysis of that experience. It represents therefore the starting-point of the imaginative and poetic process which culminated in the penetration to the heart of reality at the summit of the *Paradiso*.

The occasion of this sonnet is narrated in the prose of *VN* 3. In a dream on the night after the famous greeting by Beatrice to Dante in his eighteenth year he has a *maravigliosa visione*—of Love ('a lord of awesome aspect') and of Beatrice sleeping in his arms. Love awakens the sleeping Beatrice and forces her to eat Dante's burning heart. And now the hitherto joyous Love begins to weep, and clasping Beatrice in his arms he is seen to turn away and carry her off up to heaven. Out of this strange experience Dante writes his sonnet (*A ciascun alma presa*), addressing it to his fellow-poets, the *fedeli d'Amore*, and asking them to interpret the experience it describes.

Of course there is much here that, especially out of context, may sound naive, if not fictive. But we have the evidence of surviving replies to the request for interpretation. And there is the fact that once we start to question the historicity of *maravigliose visioni* in Dante we can hardly stop. But in any case I do not think the question of historicity affects our present point—which is the extent to which Dante accepted the imaginative as significant and susceptible of interpretation. This point is reinforced when we remember that the *VN* is a 'confessional' book written out of experience seen in retrospect. A book therefore which singles out what has already been *seen* to have significance.[3] And in fact this vision does turn out to foreshadow essential elements in the course of events to come, as they are unfolded in the *VN*. Nobody fully understood it at the time, he tells us, *ma ora è manifestissimo a li più semplici*.

And Dante's own sense that there is a meaning is reinforced by the replies of his poet friends. Even if nobody fully understood that meaning at the time there was one, Guido Cavalcanti, who, by good luck or good guidance, did divine a lot that events validated (No. 6a in FB). 'He took your heart away, seeing that your lady was sinking towards death . . .' But it is not this temporally *prophetic* significance of the imaginative that shall most concern us in Dante—rather the 'vertical' significance of sign, symbol, image, as disclosing a higher plane of reality. And here Cavalcanti is much to our purposes. 'What you saw, I think, was all nobility (*valore*) and all joy and all the good (*bene*) that man can know . . .'[4] These are among the prime 'values', the sense of which, pursued, will lead Dante to the heart and fount of reality, to 'the Love that moves the sun and the other stars'. The *sense* of these values, I have said, not just the intellectual concepts and theory of them, a sense first 'felt in the blood and felt along the heart', and only then, and from there, passing into the 'purer mind'.

By way of this first example of an imaginative experience with a felt significance we have been able to come to a point where we could speak intelligibly of higher reality translated into image or symbol, and not only of the 'realities' but of a dimension of their reality that we can only designate by that poor, homeless concept of 'value'. We have been able to speak also of a special mode of awareness of those realities and values, a pre-conceptual mode, but not one which we may therefore feel free to devalue. For the pre-conceptual may very well be the condition, and provide the material, of the conceptual. Concepts without percepts, said Kant, are empty, percepts without concepts are blind.[5] Dante, as already indicated, was supremely a man of both modes.

With this minimal *mise-en-scène*, including our insistent *mise-en-valeur(s)* (as we might label it) my hope is that we have insinuated ourselves into an angle of viewing from which the rôle of the imagination in Dante will be intelligible without too much heavy annotation. Intelligible, that is, in its original and originating experience, in its progress, in the cadres of its interpretation, and in its supreme point of arrival.

This essay, of course, cannot hope to trace the *organic* development to that supreme point. Besides, it is a point that is long since far beyond mere imagination—

All' alta fantasia qui mancò possa,

High imagination here broke down.

We are in the domain of *mystical* experience[6]—once again whether Dante's own or at second hand does not really affect the issue of the process he describes. Neither does it matter that we are *beyond* imagination. What matters is the rôle of imagination on the way to its own transcending. For we are beyond not only *fantasia* but *intelletto*—

As the geometer his mind applies
To square the circle, nor for all his wit
Finds the right formula, howe'er he tries.
(*Para.* 33.133–5, trans. Reynolds)

As is well known, it is Beatrice who has been the inspiration first and then the guide of the ascent to this supreme point. And if we are to understand in organic detail the process of the imagination in Dante we must return to the Beatrician experience, and starting from there follow its development through the three great stages of its unfolding. The first of those three stages is the *Vita Nuova*, a retrospective, systematising, 'confessional' work, composed about 1295, five years after the death of Beatrice, ending with visions of Beatrice in glory, and supremely, in a *mirabile visione* in which Dante 'sees things' that determined him to write no more of 'this blessed lady' until by study he was qualified to 'say of her such things as have never been said of any woman' (*VN* 42).

The *Convivio*, composed about ten years later, is unfinished, but it gives us a glimpse of what that projected study was. It represents in fact nothing less than another profound experience, a kind of 'conversion'[7] to philosophy; philosophy, that is, in the old high, sapiential, contemplative and cosmic sense of Greece and the Wisdom literature of the Bible. In this *filosofia-sapienza* drive passion fuses with intellect, the earthly Beatrice with the visionary Lady Philosophy of Boethius, and, still more sublimely, with *la bellissima e onestissima figlia de lo Imperadore de lo universo* (*Conv.* 2.15.12). She is the hypostatised, feminine Sophia of the Creator. *Ego ex ore Altissimi prodivi primogenita ante omnem creaturam* (*Eccli.* 24.5—and cf. *Conv.* 3.12.14).

The *Commedia* . . . how shall it abide our question? It is the fruit of the projected studies and the fulfillment of the idealising promise. But of course no such work could ever come out of study alone. It needed what for shorthand we are calling imagination. It could not even come out of imagination alone. It needed those higher states of spiritual awareness, in which, as we have indicated, imagination is transcended. And this is precisely what it purports to be written out of, a visionary experience in Holy Week of 1300. It is the fruit of another, or other, 'conversion' experiences—sudden light from out the dark wood of crisis,

Nel mezzo del cammin di nostra vita

But what is strange, and more to our purposes, is that it needed Beatrice too—in Dante's case, that is, for of course we do not make a rule out of such an exceptional instance. The strange thing is that this journey to the heart and fount of reality, this succession of revealings of glory within glory, is also a deeper and deeper perception of the reality of Beatrice, a revelation of glory after glory in her fully realised and glorified state. And it is essential to understand that her function as guide in the *Paradiso* is not only through didactic instruction—and even that only because she has a light of higher knowledge that Dante had not. She is in her own self the guide, through being the reflecting image of what she reveals. In the luminous phrase of *Purg.* 6.45, she is the light between Truth and intellect, *lume . . . tra 'l vero e lo intelletto*. She reflects the rays of the eternal (*Para.* 31.72).

> Of all that I have looked upon with these eyes
> Thy goodness and thy power have fitted me
> The holiness and grace to recognize.
> (*Para.* 31.82–4, trans. Reynolds)

And there is something still stranger and more wonderful The supreme point of the *Paradiso* is the supreme integration of reality, in one universal 'form', *la forma universal di questo nodo* (*Para.* 33.91), the scattered leaves of all the universe bound into one volume within the abyss of light (*Para.* 33.85–7). And yet, paradoxically, in this abyssal in-one-ing of all reality in its ground, the reality of concrete, individual, historical being and experience is preserved. As with the human features of Christ, mysteriously limned in the Trinity (*Para.* 33.131), so with the Florentine girl and Dante's earthly experience of her. From the summit of the Earthly Paradise where Beatrice is first glimpsed again, an arc is thrown back over space and time to the original moment of his earthly vision of her. So that the whole original complex of experience is reactivated, resurrected we might say.

> And instantly, for all the years between
> Since her mere presence with a kind of fright
> Could awe me and make my spirit faint within,
>
> There came on me, needing no further sight,
> Just by that strange, outflowing power of hers,
> The old, old love in all its mastering might.
> (*Purg.* 30.34–39, trans. Sayers)

> *Guardami ben! Ben son, ben son Beatrice.*
> Look, look at me well! I really am the real Beatrice.
> (*Purg.* 30.73)

And when, in Paradise, she finally ascends to her place in the Sempiternal Rose, thus putting between the mortal Dante and herself a distance greater in earthly terms than that from the heights of the heavens to the deeps of the ocean, her image still comes down to him distinct (*Para.* 31.73ff). And in answer to his parting prayer to her, she still, though ascended so high, could be seen to smile and look on him once more (*Para.* 31.91–2).

In order to provide an over-all understanding of the Dantean pattern I have been giving a synoptic view of the three main stages of its development. It is time to return to the experience from which it started and try to trace in detail the logic of its unfolding within the single stage we shall have space to deal with, that is the stage unfolded in the *VN*. If there is a logic and rationale of the imagination the only illuminating place to start investigating it is in the place where imagination itself works, along the pulse of life. To *start*, I say, for I have not forgotten what we said about *il ben dello intelletto*, the organising, systematising, validating intellect. And behind the pattern I have already sketched there lies (as suggested earlier) not only experience but a strong intellectual structure of epistemology and ontology, and even specialised epistemological questions like the relative priority of will and intellect, love and knowledge, i.e. whether love depends on knowledge or vice versa. The answers to such questions did not just validate experience *post eventum*. They facilitated the *a priori* acceptance of experience *in eventu*. But for us these questions must wait till after we have studied the experience. As indeed they did for Dante, initially untutored in *filosofia*. They are among the questions we can watch him working out in the *Convivio*.

The Beatrician experience began in a kind of epiphany, with all the force of a revelation, and the immediate effect of a kind of 'conversion', with all the power over heart and intellect that 'conversion' implies. The event took place when the nine-year-old Dante first laid eyes on the eight-year-old Beatrice Portinari. What he saw and felt at that miraculous moment has to be described in his own words.

> She was dressed in a very noble colour, a decorous and delicate crimson, tied with a girdle and trimmed in a manner suited to her tender age. The moment I saw her I say in all truth that the vital spirit, which dwells in the innermost depths of the heart, began to tremble (*tremare*) so violently that I felt the vibration alarmingly in all my pulses, even the weakest of them. As it trembled it uttered these words: *Ecce deus fortior me, qui veniens dominabitur michi* [Behold a god stronger than I, who in his coming will rule over me—i.e. Love]. (*VN* 2, trans. Reynolds)

This is the effect upon the *heart*—let us say on the *imagination*. The account goes on to describe how the effect was carried from the heart to the intellect, which 'began to be greatly wonder-stricken' (*maravigliare*) and pronounced to the image-bearing senses its conviction that *apparuit iam beatitudo vestra*—the source of your blessedness has now appeared.

The lasting consequence must also be quoted *in extenso*.

> From that time onwards I declare that Love ruled my soul, which was wedded to him thus early in my life. And he began to exert such assurance and mastery over me through the power my imagination (*imaginazione*) gave him that I was obliged to fulfill all his wishes absolutely. Many a time he ordered me to seek out and see[8] this young angel . . . And in all her ways I saw her as so noble and praiseworthy that one could apply to her that verse of the poet Homer: She did not look like the daughter of a mortal man but of a god. (*VN* 2)

I have quoted those passages *in extenso* to enable us to identify more easily the essential elements of what happens in them. Let us see what those elements are.

At the most comprehensive level Dante discovers that his being and his faculties are in the power of a force beyond himself and his control—a power personified here in the conventional god of Love but later (*VN* 25) philosophically analysed and 'demythologised'. (And the deepening understanding of Love as a metaphysical, and ultimately theological and personal power in man and the universe will go on through the *Convivio* and the *Commedia*.)

What that most comprehensive power subsumes in the experience of it may be organised along two lines already mentioned, ontological levels in reality and epistemological levels in knowing. As regards levels of reality, Beatrice in the experience is the perfect example of an 'image' or 'symbol' in e.g. the Coleridgean sense. That is to say, a concrete, individual object, existing *in itself* but also *deriving* from something greater than itself, and *embodying* in itself that *nescio quid maius*, that greater something from which it derives. I mention Coleridge as being a familiar source of useful ideas. But of course well before Coleridge, Dante was heir to all the underpinning available in the medieval heritage of Platonist exemplarism, the Christian concept of incarnation, and the Scholastic theory of analogy. Whatever theory we use to validate it the experience itself adds up to the sense that Beatrice, as the *VN* later puts it, was a *miracolo*. A *miracolo*, moreover, in which has 'appeared' the beholder's highest fulfilment, *beatitudo*, that concept central to the ethical, philosophical and theological thought of the Greco-Roman-Christian tradition. (And in this respect what begins here in the *VN* is what culminated in the *Paradiso*.)

As regards modes and levels of knowing it is obvious *de iure* and *de facto* that this understanding of Beatrice could not and did not come from mere rational, conceptual analysis. The experience came first. And the experience was a given, an overwhelming given, given to the *whole* being of Dante at all levels, to the heart, to the intellect and (in a passage of *VN* 2 not quoted) to the instincts. Even Dante himself seems to use the word *imaginazione* in something like our own ill-defined but inclusive sense to cover this complex of cognitive experience.[9]

Unique, of course, as this experience of Dante's may appear to be—or perhaps *because* of its apparent uniqueness and the consequently possible questions about the authenticity of the experience—it is usual to indicate how much it owes to the tradition of courtly love within which he writes, though eventually far transcending it. I should like briefly to indicate some elements in Dante's experience that belong to a tradition much older than courtly love *à la lettre*. Not for the purpose of reducing Dante to a convention. On the contrary, to confirm his experience by relating it to age-old, permanent possibilities.

The 'epiphany' that Dante saw in Beatrice he sums up in a quotation from Homer. Dante scarcely knew Homer, and this verse, *Iliad* 24.258f (referring in fact to Hector), he probably borrows and adapts from an Aristotelian quotation of it. The point I wish to make is that had Dante known Homer he could have found *passim* the idea of the Lady as an epiphany of the divine. And most notably of all in the remarkable evocation of Nausicaa as she appeared to Odysseus in *Odyssey*, 6.149ff. 'Are you divine or mortal?' he asks her. 'Never have I laid eyes on such a mortal . . .' And he goes on to speak of the *reverence*, the *awe* he feels in her presence, and even of the *beatitudo* of those who experience her grace and presence now—thrice-blessed they, but most blessed of all the man who shall enjoy her presence as his bride.

Later (c.620–550 BC) there is the famous love-lyric of Sappho that begins: *Like to the gods he appears* . . . Sappho is early, but the felt relevance of her experience is confirmed centuries later by the fact that the Roman poet Catullus[10] translated her lyric to address it to his own Lesbia. Sappho's lyric starts from the same two basic elements as Homer, *beatitudo* in the presence of a quasi-divine epiphany. But then it moves into details of the 'pathology' of the experience which are remarkably parallel to those in Dante. Those parallels include specifically Dante's *tremare*, and in general a 'seizure' of the whole being and its faculties, up to the climactic experience of being 'all but dead'. This last item is not in the passages we quoted from the *VN* but it is implied in the early *canzone* I referred to (FB 32.57ff). And it does occur at later moments in the *VN* when the original experience was—as often—repeated, e.g. *VN* 14 and the sonnet of *VN* 15 (. . . *Moia, moia!* Die! die!).

Lastly there is Plato. Platonism, as everyone knows, is a whole metaphysic of *eros*, at the heart and summit of reality and in the heart of man. And the stages in its progress are the rungs on a ladder of ascent of the one to the other. Its diffused influence on later ages is incalculable, even in ages to which the Platonist *corpus* was not available. When we see the wood for the trees we have to see in it the far forerunner of the Dantean pattern. But what I am concerned with at this point is nothing as large as that. I wish merely to draw attention to a section of the *Phaedrus* (250E ff), in which analysis of experience reveals more or less exactly the same phenomena as in the Sapphic and Dantean moments. It will suffice to quote and leave those details to be recognised for what they are.

'He who is newly initiated [observe the mystagogical term], who beheld many of those realities [i.e. *transcendent* realities, 'imaged' in those of this world], when he sees a god-like face or form which is a good image of beauty, trembles at first, and something of the old awe comes over him,[11] then, as he gazes, he reveres the beautiful one as a god . . .' (251A, trans. Loeb).

Further, as separation is pain (*passim* in *VN*) so presence is *beatitudo*. 'Therefore the soul will not, if it can help it, be left alone by the beautiful one, but . . . it is ready to be a slave . . . as near as possible to the beloved; for it not only feels reverence for the one who has beauty, but finds in that one the only healer of its suffering' (252A).[12]

It will be noticed that with Plato we have introduced a notion that is wider than what we conventionally call romantic love. That notion is the love provoked by beauty in general. And in point of fact in the Platonist metaphysic as a whole it is this more universal occasion of eros that is operative. 'Surely we love only what is beautiful?' remarks St Augustine, steeped in this same Platonism (*Confessions* 4.13). The beauty that occasions romantic sexual love is only a particular instance of the more universal phenomenon. In Plato this can be seen to some extent even in the *Phaedrus* (e.g. 248D), but most obviously in the *Symposium* (especially 204ff).

What I wanted to do in this brief *excursus* was to set the 'way' of the Dantean imagination in a context. The Beatrician experience, and the consequent way, is but *one* of a whole *genre* which provides many other *analogous* possibilities. *Any* passionate, personal experience—in the domain of beauty or even beyond—could be the 'trigger'. St Augustine, for instance, is an example of a man for whom the aesthetic experience was an important starting-point—by temperament as well as Platonist influence (see e.g. *Confessions* 4.13, 15; 7.17; *De Musica* 6). This is a point made by Charles Williams, who is fond of the example of Wordsworth's experience of 'Nature'. Retaining the term 'Romantic', Williams insists that it 'includes other loves besides the sexual' (*The Figure of Beatrice*, p.14).

Now as a matter of fact this is exactly what we find Dante himself saying, in a striking passage in *Conv.* 4.25—by then, as we recall, he was complementing experience by *filosofia* and its quest for *sapienza*. *Conv.* 4 is devoted to ethical and moral matters,[13] in the course of which Dante, discussing the *vertudi* appropriate to each of the four ages of life, comes to consider those appropriate to the first age, *adolescenza*. Also necessary to this age is *la passione de la vergogna*—a quality actually shown by nature itself at this age in *la buona e nobile natura*. In fact in *adolescenza* it is 'the clearest mark . . . of *nobilitade*' (*Conv.* 4.25.3).

The first thing worth noting here is that Dante describes *la vergogna* as a 'passion'—worthy of noting because, unless things have changed (since my time, as it were), both our sense of 'virtue' and the pallid word itself have long since lost any connotation remotely approaching *la passione*. Of course Dante is translating the technical Scholastic term *passio*, but, as will presently appear, he is giving it a more positive meaning than his sources did.

The next question is the precise meaning of *vergogna*. It is clear from the sequel that no single English term will render it. The Latin *verecundia* in its Classical sense comes near it, combining 'modesty' with at least a suggestion of the more radical sense of 'reverence' and 'awe'. Dante goes on to explain that in his intention it subsumes three *passioni* that are the foundation of the moral life. These are *stupore*, *pudore* and *verecundia*. As he defines them *pudore* is the sense of *pudor*, modesty, that *preveniently* restrains from the dishonourable. *Verecundia* is the sense of shame after the event. There remains *stupore*, which is the focus of our interest.

Dante goes on to define it as 'a stunning (*stordimento*) of the soul through hearing, seeing or in any other way becoming aware of things sublime and wondrous (*grandi e maravigliose cose*). Things which in so far as they appear sublime generate reverence in him who perceives them, and in so far as they appear wondrous generate the desire to understand them'. It is clear that what is being described here is an emotional and imaginative capacity for wonder, awe, *admiratio, thaumazein*. An emotion not existing in a subjective void but generated by an objective reality—and therefore, we may add, positing the possibility of a pre-conceptual mode of perception. An emotion not static either, or destined to remain purely an emotion, but generating the desire for and the process of conceptual understanding of the reality that produced it. We are reminded of how Plato and Aristotle saw the condition of philosophy in the capacity for wonder. And indeed since we have used the term 'sublime' we are reminded of the two natural capacities in which Longinus placed its condition. Namely the capacity for grand *emotions* and the capacity for grand *conceptions* (*On the Sublime*, chapter 8).

Patently in *stupore* we have Dante's own 'theory' of his Beatrician experience and of the imagination. And it is also a theory original to himself—precisely, no doubt, because it is indebted to his own experience. We discover this originality when we check his Thomist and Aristotelian sources.[14] Dante's generic term *vergogna* derives from their *verecundia*. But in the sources this remains merely a negative virtue—in fact Aquinas will not allow that it is technically a virtue at all (*Summa Theologiae*, II. IIae, Q.144, art.1). It relates only to the avoidance or repentance of evil—at the level of Dante's *pudore* and *verecundia*. It does not include the positive element of *stupore*. And a striking thing is that in making *vergogna* include it Dante restored an early, original sense of both the Latin *verecundia* and its Greek equivalent, *aidōs*.

Further, in *stupore* we have not only the theory of Dante's initial experience. We have also the theory of its development. The experiences that produce *stupore* produce, as we saw, the desire to understand its occasion. This is the project announced at the end of the *VN*. It runs through the *Convivio* and comes to fulfillment in the *Commedia*. But observe that understanding is not a purely intellectual operation on the data of a once-for-all experience of *stupore*. Experience and the intellect continue together. In the *Convivio* there is a connection between love and understanding. The *Commedia*, as we know, is based on further and deeper experiences. And these often involve *stupore*, sometimes explicitly mentioned—e.g. *Purg.* 31.127, *Para.* 31.31–40. And at the base of the whole ascent the initial and initiating *stupore* is repeated and deepened throughout the *VN*, in ways we shall not have space to detail. One of the marked stages in that work is when those experiences already generate the desire to understand (*VN* 13). And, as already noted, the work is itself composed at a stage of retrospective understanding.

Thus does *stupore* become 'the beginning of wisdom'.[15] And we might venture the opinion that this is imagination (if we may so identify it) of a precious kind, and a corrective to some undesirable connotations of the word. It starts 'where all the ladders start'—in the concrete and individual, which then becomes the concrete universal. For the 'sublime and wondrous things' are at first perceived not above and beyond the particular but in and through it. At least this is the way of the imagination in Dante. To adapt the remark of Coleridge, he elevates our thoughts by first sending them down deeper.

II

In the preceding pages we have got little further than a kind of 'notes and commentary' to the single, initial experience of the *VN*. At such a pace through the Dante *corpus* we would be headed for a volume rather than an essay. And although we have occasionally looked towards higher dimensions we have concentrated on the first storey of the Dantean imagination in its sense of the transcendent, the *grandi e maravigliose cose*, in and behind the concrete and particular *cose*. We might call it the natural, or secular, dimension—*salva reverentia* to Dante in comparison with the more usual returns from this dimension in literature. That storey is a necessary foundation for the second storey that is the ultimate subject of this essay, the *religious* imagination. And even if it were not the subject, any treatment of the imagination that omitted it—even in a consideration of the *VN*—would be truncated. To that religious dimension we shall now turn.

It is necessary to anticipate that here too we shall get little further than notes and commentary to the same core material to which we have limited ourselves in the first part. That is indeed a limitation, but within our space it will also serve the interests of simplicity and clarity (such clarity, that is, as the subject permits!). Such concentration will also serve an ideal I mentioned early on, coming down from the 'high priori' to the close weave of the phenomena.

I anticipate also that in this paper I shall not, except incidentally, take up the epistemology of *how* the cognitive awareness of Dante's imagination gets from what I have called the natural, or secular, dimension to the *praeter-* or *super*natural religious dimension. *Can* it be explained? Or is it a kind of quantum leap? I have indeed indicated directions in the tradition along which we might look for a theory. But here we shall concentrate on showing the ways and the extent of the presence of that dimension.

Another necessary anticipation concerns mysticism. As I said earlier, mysticism is not the same as imagination. But I said on the same occasion that in Dante it would also seem to be in some sort of continuity with imagination, and of course with *intelletto*. It will figure in the following pages because much of what I say concerning the religious dimension of Dante's imagination will turn on the phenomena of mystical experience. They will be derived from the phenomena of authentic mysticism, or descriptions of it. But for shorthand's sake I shall be obliged to commit the (common) fault of using the term *mystical* in an elastic way to describe the religious dimension in Dante—without, however, begging the question of whether some things in the *VN* imply mystical experience in the strict sense or not. A question on which the most positive arguments are in C. S. Singleton.[16] Rejected, however, by Domenico de Robertis.[17]

I do not propose to pursue the argument on this question. It is the same question, at a different level, and as finally soluble or insoluble, as the old one of whether *any* experience of 'higher consciousness' can be authenticated as really being what it appears to be. One could also get distracted by failing to distinguish between the question of the nature and implications of Dante's *language* and the question of whether it is based on *personal* experience. It does not matter whether it is or not. What matters is that the *language* of the religious dimension, including the mystical, is there. And this is established by Singleton, and not denied by de Robertis.[18] At the very least, therefore, it represents Dante's *interpretation* of the meaning, or logical potential, of the experience he did have.[19]

The moment in the *VN* where the religious dimension is most explicitly present is at its culmination in chapters 41 and 42 where there is recounted, first a vision of Beatrice in glory,[20] and then the *mirabile visione* in which things were beheld which determined Dante to be silent until he could speak worthily of her. As we have seen, this was probably the moment of perception which begot the retrospective *VN* and the project which eventually became the *Commedia*. But here I wish to attend not to what is explicitly present at the climax but to what is implicitly present along the way to that climax. And along that way I do not wish to cover again such ground as has been covered by Singleton, e.g. the Christological dimension (in chapter 1) and the parallel to the stages of the mystical ascent in the stages of Dante's ascent from love to *caritas* (chapters 3–4). I have already indicated that I would stay with the same core material we considered in the first section. And that means looking again at the 'pathology' of Dante's experience to see what further dimension of significance it might have, this time at the religious level. The 'pathology' I have in mind is that contained in all the phenomena of *tremare*, *beatitudo*, etc. which we analysed from the initial experience of them in *VN* 2 but which recur at many later stages in the presence of Beatrice.

Before turning to them we might give ourselves some contextual room by glancing at some passages where we can see the presence of the religious dimension without the need for much analysis. Thus in *VN* 3 there is the famous greeting from Beatrice in her eighteenth year. Under its influence (itself *ineffabile*) Dante's experience is no longer merely of *beatitudo* but of the heights and extremes of it, *absolute* blessedness—*tutti li termini de la beatitudine*.

In *VN* 11, the blessed influence of this greeting is further elaborated. It produces an *intollerabile beatitudine*, which is often beyond the capacity of nature to endure—*molte volte passava e redundava la mia capacitade*. It further generates the Christian virtues of humility and the flame of charity. 'Whenever and wherever she appeared, in the hope of receiving her miraculous salutation (*mirabile salute*) I felt I had not an enemy in the world. Indeed I glowed with a flame of charity (*una fiamma di caritate*) which moved me to forgive all who had ever injured me; and if at that moment someone had asked me a question, about anything, my only reply would have been: "Love", with a countenance clothed in humility'[21] (trans. Reynolds—cf. *VN* 26–8).

All this crystallises into the feeling that she is a 'miracle'[22] (*uno miracolo*, 30.3). A miracle come down from heaven to earth (26, sonnet), a miracle whose effect on the beholder 'can neither be described nor held before the mind' (21, sonnet—recall *ineffabile* in 3.1). Of course this notion of her heavenly origin owes something to the courtly tradition of the *donna angelicata*. But there is a difference in what it means for Dante. One of the differences is quite simply the sensed difference between literary convention and intensely realised experience. An example of that particular difference is provided by the early canzone (FB 32) already cited as containing the germ of *VN* 2 although not included in the *VN*. 'The day that this lady came into the world ... my childish body felt a strange emotion (*una passion nova*) so that I was filled with fear (*di pauru pieno*); and suddenly a check was placed on all my faculties, so that I fell to the ground, from a light that struck me through to the heart (*sì ch'io caddi in terra, / per una luce che nel cuor percosse*).'

As regards the concluding phrases I do not know if anybody has noticed the echo of St Paul's conversion, in his meeting with Christ on the road to Damascus. *Subito circumfulsit eum lux de caelo. Et cadens in terram audivit vocem* ... (*Acts* 9.3–4, cf. 22.7, 26.13–14). And with Dante 'filled with fear'[23] we may compare Paul *tremens ac stupens* (*Acts* 9.5). We recall our earlier discussion of *tremare* and *stupore*. But here we see the 'other' dimension of their meaning, the experientially religious, the sacral fear and trembling in the presence of the numinous. That anticipates the essence of what we shall argue about the religious dimension implied in the initial Dantean experience. This phrase of an early canzone, then, contains *in nuce* not only the *VN* but its completion in the *Commedia* to the summit of the *Paradiso*.

As is indeed made clearer by another difference between Dante and the tradition of the *donna angelicata*. The logical complement of her descent from heaven is her eventual ascent whence she came. This of course is at the heart of the actual experience from the moment of her death in the *VN* through the subsequent studies, and into the *Commedia*. But the experience is anticipated from the start, in puzzling signs (*VN* 3), in logical implication (*VN* 19, canzone), and finally in the prevision of her death (*VN* 23).

But, after all, we are concerned not with what logic can *deduce* from experience, and not with 'signs and visions' which go *beyond* experience into the 'extraordinary'. We are concerned rather with dimensions of meaning, in object and event, felt in a way intrinsic to the actual experience of the object or event. So in the prevision of the death of Beatrice a detail is to be noticed which implies a felt analogy between the nature and 'ascension' of Beatrice and the nature and Ascension of the incarnate Christ. 'I thought I was looking up into the heavens, where I seemed to see a multitude of angels returning to their realm, and before them floated a little cloud of purest white' (*VN* 23, trans. Reynolds). To the Christological parallels noted by Singleton I think it is relevant here to add *Acts* 1.9: '... While they looked on he was lifted up, and a cloud received him out of their sight'. In Scripture the cloud goes with theophanies. And we recall that already in the experience of *VN* 3, which anticipates all this, a flame-coloured cloud is seen.

In this general *aperçu* we have found a fusion of levels of meaning, the religious dimension explicitly perceived in and through, as well as beyond, what we have called the natural or secular dimension of transcendence. Turning from the religious dimension in general to the particular dimension of the mystical we find the same fusion of levels of experience, through an analysis of the *tremare* complex of phenomena. We have already touched on a connection in Dante's echo of the Pauline experience, *tremens ac stupens*, of *Acts* 9.5.

The over-all situation is that in the mystical tradition there is a 'pathology' which is closely parallel, in the phenomena and in the language used to describe them, between the mystical tradition and Dante's repeated experience in the presence of Beatrice. And this is true of *two* mystical traditions, the Judeo-Christian and the ancient Greek—we shall have another look not only at Dante's language but also at the background of the lyric of Sappho that I cited earlier.

The general parallel lies in the phenomena of fear, awe, trembling, pain, suspension of the faculties, even to a point resembling a kind of death, a sense of being 'blasted with ecstasy'. In a word, all the phenomena that Dante sums up in the expression: *distrutti ... spiriti* (*VN* 14.5).[24] In the Judeo-Christian mystical tradition these phenomena are summed up in the 'fear and trembling' of Biblical theophanies. 'My whole being trembles before you' (*Psalms* 119.120). A

striking example is *Job* 4.14ff:
> A shiver of horror ran through me,
> and my bones quaked with fear.
> A breath slid over my face,
> the hairs of my body bristled.
> Someone stood there . . .

Early in the Christian mystical tradition there is St Augustine, describing his first such experience. 'You beat back the weakness of my gaze with the beating of your radiance upon me, and I trembled with love and with dread—*contremui amore et horrore*' (*Confessions* 7.10.16).[25] 'At times', says St John of the Cross, 'the torture felt in such visits of rapture is so great that there is no torture which so wrenches asunder the bones and straitens the physical nature—so much so that unless God provided for the soul its life would come to an end' (*Spiritual Canticle*, Stanza XII.3, First Recension, trans. Peers).

Within this phenomenological complex certain specifics keep recurring. Numinous *fear* and *trembling* we have seen more than once already. Gregory the Great has this to say: 'The higher the realities glimpsed by the human soul when lifted up by the engine, as it were, of contemplation, the more it trembles with awe within itself (*eo in semetipso terribilius contremiscit*)'.[26] He is commenting on the theophany on Sinai (*Exodus* 19.16ff), in particular the statement there that 'inside the camp all the people trembled'.

Not only is there fear and trembling but what is beheld cannot long be endured by untransformed human nature. We have already seen Augustine to this effect. Later in the tradition there is Gregory once again. 'Because we are weighted down by the corruptible flesh we cannot possibly look at the brightness of the divine power in the mode in which in itself it stays immutably. The reason is that the weak eyes of our seeing cannot sustain the light that shines unbearably upon us from the ray of its eternity'.[27]

We may compare *VN* 14–16. And lines 35f and 55f of the canzone in *VN* 19: 'Were any . . . person to stay and regard her, he would either become noble[28] or die . . . You see Love depicted in her face, there where no one can fix his gaze'. We find a transcendent, unmediated version of the experience in, e.g. *Paradiso* 25.118ff. There, looking into the depths of the brightness of the soul of St John, Dante compares himself to
> one who squinnies and strains
> to look a while at the sun in eclipse,
> but by looking is bereft of sight,
> Such did I become in face of this final flame.

And the dichotomy of death-or-transfiguration reminds us of the motif in Scriptural theophanies, that no one can look on God and live. *Loci* are too numerous to list. But one, *Exodus* 33.18–23, became a *locus classicus* in the mystical tradition. The occasion comes as the climax to a series of theophanies in which God has been seen by Moses not as he is in himself but only with his glory veiled or in his awesome *effects*. Moses now makes bold to ask, 'Show me your glory' (*doxan, gloriam*). God agrees to let his splendour pass in front of Moses. But Moses must stand in the cleft of a rock and be shielded by God's hand until God has passed by and only his back may be looked upon. 'You cannot see my face', he said, 'for man cannot see me and live.'

Interestingly enough something like this motif is found also in Greek mythology. The story of Actaeon is well known.[29] He looked on Artemis in her undraped beauty. He was turned into a stag, filled with panic fear and torn to pieces by the dogs of the huntress deity. There is also the story of Anchises, who became the father of Aeneas with Aphrodite. But on realising her identity he was filled with fear and numinous awe. 'For he who lies with an immortal goddess is no hale man afterwards.'[30]

The last motif I shall illustrate is that of the *ineffability*[31] of what is felt and seen in mystical experience. It is, of course, a commonplace that it so far transcends normal experience and conceptual thinking as to be inexpressible in normal language and conceptual categories. Augustine again provides us with an instance. 'In the lightning-flash of a trembling glance the innermost intellect arrived at *That Which Is* . . . But I lacked the strength to fix my gaze, my weakness was beaten back and I came back down to my ordinary modes, bearing with me nothing but a memory of love and longing as for something of which I had caught the fragrance but had not yet the strength to eat' (*Confessions* 7.17.23).

There is, in fact, no better statement of the matter than in Dante himself.

> Henceforth my vision mounted to a height
> Where speech is vanquished and must lag behind,
> And memory surrenders in such plight.
> (*Para.* 33.55–7, trans. Reynolds)

A passage in the *Letter to Can Grande* gives the rationale. 'One must realise that because of the connaturality and affinity it has with separate intellectual substance, when the human intellect is raised in this life it is so far raised that on its return memory fails, because the measure of the human has been transcended' (28.78). And in support he goes on to cite instances from the whole tradition—beginning with the experience of St Paul (2 *Corinthians* 12.1ff).

We have been looking at the Judeo-Christian mystical tradition. There was also an ancient Greek one. And I said we would look again at Sappho's lyric, to see whether it too might not have a dimension of meaning beyond what meets the eye, and thus show that Dante's religious imagination is not absolutely unique, and therefore is that much more possible and credible. What that dimension would be is of course already obvious from the parallels in the poem to the complex of motifs we have been looking at in the Judeo-Christian tradition. What I wish to do is to confirm it from within its own Greek tradition. We can do it briefly with the aid of two or three pieces of evidence, taken from the domain of mystery religion and mystical experience, at least in the elastic sense in which I have permitted myself to use that term.

The first piece of evidence is from Plato's *Phaedrus*. In the first part of this essay I drew attention to the parallel between Sappho's 'pathology' of love and that of *Phaedrus* 250E ff. We left it at that level then. But of course context, process and language in the *Phaedrus* are those of 'enthusiasm', 'mystery', mystical initiation, divine possession, 'ascent' (244ff). Love is one form of that divinely-sent *mania* which is wiser than the wisdom of reason. To prove it we must learn the truth about soul, divine and human, by observing how it acts and is acted upon (245C). It is not necessary to labour the details.[32]

However, while this may be persuasive we cannot argue backwards in time, from Plato to Sappho. We need evidence from her own time, or earlier if possible. That is provided by the *Homeric Hymn to Demeter*, not later than the seventh century BC according to one estimate. It tells the story—the myth—of the origins of the Eleusinian Mysteries, from an episode in the wanderings of the goddess Demeter in search of her lost daughter Persephone.

She comes to Eleusis and the house of one Keleus—in the guise of an old woman. A theophany takes place as her divinity is revealed. And the details of that theophany parallel those of Sappho's poem.

> The goddess walked to the threshold: and her head reached the roof and she filled the doorway with a heavenly radiance. Then awe and reverence[33] and pale fear[34] took hold of Metaneira . . .
> (188-90, trans. Loeb)

> The goddess changed her stature and her looks, thrusting old age away from her: beauty spread round about her and a lovely fragrance was wafted from her sweet-smelling robes, and from the divine body of the goddess a light shone afar . . . And straightway Metaneira's knees were loosed[35] and she remained speechless[36] for a long while . . . (275ff)

Plutarch (c.46–120 AD) was right then to read Sappho's poem in the way I have been arguing towards. And his is our final and best statement of it. At one point in his Platonising Dialogue on Love (*Eroticos* or *Amatorius*) someone is asked to quote the verses in which 'the fair Sappho tells how at the epiphany of the beloved her voice fails and her body flames, and she is seized by pallor, derangement and swooning'. This being done,

> Then my father commenting said: By Zeus, is it not a clear case of

divine possession? Is this not a supernatural agitation of the soul. The transport of the Pythian priestess, when she touches her tripod, is it anything like this? Are any of those who are divinely possessed in the rites of Cybele so put beside themselves by the flute and tympanum and the chants to the Great Mother? (763A).

And so say we of Dante's Beatrician experience. *Quod erat demonstrandum*, or at least *tentandum*.

I have examined in any detail only the *VN*—and indeed only focal points even of it. I have omitted the epistemological question—what structure of knowing, and specifically of imaginative knowing, permits such perceptions? I have omitted the ontological question—what structure of reality permits the ascription of such dimensions to the reality of Beatrice? 'If, we are told, Beatrice was only a woman, Dante could not, "without blasphemy", have written about her what he did. To which we have to answer that we must resign ourselves to the facts: if that be the case Dante *was* a blasphemer.'[37]

Gilson does not accept that that *is* the case. But to enter into that question would take us into another essay. Let us conclude, however, with one point, inspired by some of Gilson's. It is this, that the author of *Genesis* 1.26 was the first 'blasphemer'! For it is he who tells us that 'God said, "Let us make man in our own image..."' *Man* here, we are told, is a common and collective noun. So it includes *woman* too—God bless her again.

At the other end of history we may quote a humble modern Irish poet—though not with all that much to be humble about. Without benefit of *più latinamente vedere* he lighted on the essential insights, or was lightened by them, out of the 'stony grey soil of Monaghan'.

Now I must search till I have found my God—
. . .
Surely my God is feminine, for Heaven
Is the generous impulse, is contented
With feeding praise to the good. And all
Of these that I have known have come from women.
While men the poet's tragic light resented,
The spirit that is Woman caressed his soul.
 (Patrick Kavanagh, *God in Woman*,
  in *Collected Poems*, MacGibbon & Kee, 1964)

In other words . . . *la sua ineffabile cortesia* (*VN* 3.1).

NOTES
1. Samuel Johnson speaking.
2. For the poems in the *VN* I use the translations of Kenelm Foster and Patrick Boyde, *Dante's Lyric Poetry* (2 vols), Oxford, Clarendon Press, 1967. Referred to as FB. References to 'Sayers' and 'Reynolds' are to their Penguin versions of the *Vita Nuova* and the *Commedia*.

3. Like St Augustine's *Confessions*—or even the Gospels?
4. The taste may be doubtful but 'beautiful is the *risqué*' that makes it irresistible to give the details of another of the replies that Dante got back, from one Dante da Maiano (6c in FB). It is something of a corrective against taking either ourselves or Dante with too precious a seriousness on these necessarily ambivalent matters: 'Having considered, my rather ignorant friend, the matter you ask me about, I answer briefly and explain its true significance. With your needs in mind I say this: if you are well and in your right mind, *che lavi la tua coglia largamente*, so that the vapours that make you talk nonsense be extinguished and dispersed; but if you are suffering from a serious illness, then, believe me, the only thing I understand from your words is that you were raving. Such is my opinion, duly returned; nor will I ever alter my judgement *fin che tua acqua al medico no stendo.*' Dante was to 'put down' a lot of people in his time. I don't know if he ever gave better than he got here—who knows but he may even have deserved it at the priggish age of eighteen. And apparently the put-down was not just witty but 'scientific' as well—see FB note *ad loc. cit.*
5. That, however, is an exaggeration of a truth. For 'touch' is indeed sightless, and so in 'touches of God'; yet shall we say that as a 'percept' and no concept, touch is blind *tout court*?
6. We shall consider this in the second part of this essay.
7. As an instance of what I mean see St Augustine, *Confessions*, 3.4.
8. Cf. Plato's *Phaedrus*, 251E, in view of the mention we shall later make of that work.
9. It cannot be our business here to go into the question of how far the prose of the *VN* retrospectively modifies the original experience. But as a gesture it is worth remarking that the essentials are already in an early *canzone* not included in the *VN*—see FB 32.57ff.
10. Forerunner of that unusual and important moment in the literature of love, the Augustan Elegists, in whose experience there is much of courtly love *avant la lettre*. Lattimore's translation of Catullus' Sappho lyric tries to render the rhythm of the original:

> Like[1] the very gods in my sight is he who
> sits where he can look in your eyes, who listens
> close to you, to hear the soft voice, its sweetness
>   murmur in love and
>
> laughter, all for him. But it breaks my spirit;
> underneath my breast all the heart is shaken.
> Let me only glance where you are, the voice dies,
>   I can say nothing,
>
> but my lips are stricken to silence,[2] under-
> neath my skin the tenuous flame suffuses;
> nothing shows in front of my eyes,[3] my ears are
>   muted in thunder.[4]
>
> And the sweat breaks running upon me, fever
> shakes my body,[5] paler I turn than grass is;
> I can feel that I have been changed, I feel that
>   death has come near me.[6]

1. Literally *the equal of* . . . 2. Literally *my tongue is frozen*, or *paralysed*. 3. Literally *I cannot see with my eyes*. 4. Literally *have a whirring* or *thunderous noise in them*. 5. Literally *a trembling* (tromos) *seizes me totally*. 6. Literally *I seem to be all but dead*.

11. Cf. *Purg.* 30.39 (quoted earlier), and Virgil, *Aen.* 4.23.
12. This line of the 'epiphany' is sometimes continued by reference to Joyce, with whom in fact it was an early theme—'the supreme quality of beauty being a light from some other world' (*Portrait of the Artist*, p.219 of Penguin *The Essential James Joyce*). See the episode of the girl on Dollymount strand. 'Her image had passed into his soul for ever . . . A wild angel had appeared to him . . . an envoy from the fair courts of life, to throw open before him in an instant of ecstasy the gates of all the ways of error and glory' (*op. cit.*, p.186f).
13. Specifically the quality of *nobilitade*—the sun-like source of all the other moral qualities, itself put by God in the soul, and being the 'seed of *beatitudo*' (see e.g. 4.20.9). The feeling for it is very Dantean, and after understanding it we might expect *a priori* to find it among the qualities that actuate the Beatrician experience. We are not surprised to find that that is the case again and again. From the very first moment in fact, when Beatrice appeared *vestita di nobilissimo colore* (*VN* 2.3).
14. See references *ad loc.* in G. Busnelli and G. Vandelli, *Il Convivio* (2 vols), Florence, Felice Le Monnier, 1934 and 1937.
15. C. Williams, *The Figure of Beatrice*, Faber and Faber, London, successive impressions from 1st edn 1943, p.80.
16. C. S. Singleton, *An Essay on the Vita Nuova*, Johns Hopkins University Press, Baltimore and London (1949, reprint 1977), especially chapters 3 and 4.
17. D. de Robertis, *Il libro della 'Vita Nuova'*, Florence, G. C. Sansoni (1961). 'Ma la *Vita Nuova* testo di esperienza mistica non è . . .' (p.121). See also p.123.
18. On the contrary in chapter v (*La Nuova Materia*) he brings in a greater wealth of background material.
19. As de Robertis also seems to admit on p.121. That is if I read him correctly and if he is not rather engaged in the reductionism of interpreting Dante's language as the mere hyperbole (*una capacità d'entusiasmo*) of an introverted and 'modernist' concern with the status and development of his 'art'. With that possibility I do not wish to have an argument here.
20. Both Singleton (p.102) and de Robertis (p.123) rightly deny the term 'mystical' to this experience, in as much as it is an experience not of God but only of Beatrice. But de Robertis sounds more radically reductionist—'in realtà è *solo* un "sospiro", un "pensero" . . .' (italics mine). In any case what are we to make of chapter 41 of the *VN*? (I.e. the penultimate chapter—numberings vary.)
21. Charles Williams would probably compare the Wordsworthian
    eye made quiet by the power
    Of harmony and the deep power of joy,
    which *see*(s) *into the life of things.*
    Possibly also *Measure for Measure*—see his essay on *Forgiveness in Shakespeare*, in the collection *He Came Down from Heaven*, Faber and Faber, London, 1950.
22. On this theme see also *Conv.* 3.7.16f.
23. Fear (*era molto pauroso*) is also part of Dante's experience of her greeting in his eighteenth year, on the ninth anniversary of their first meeting (*VN* 3). Again in the vision of Love in *VN* 4 he is a lord of fearsome appearance, *uno segnore di pauroso aspetto*.
24. The first appearance of the phrase (constant in Cavalcanti), as distinct from the experience. See further on the loss of faculties, to the

point of quasi-death, *VN* 15, 16, 22 (canzone, 37f). On death see also *VN* 19 (canzone), 22 (canzone, 42).
25. Behind this passage there is Plotinus, 'flooded with awe . . . stricken by a salutary terror' (*Enneads*, 1.6.7). With *horrore* compare *orrore* in *VN* 3 (sonnet, 11). Cf. the *Life* of St Teresa of Avila, in a section of chapter 29.
26. *Moralia*, 5.31.55; cf. 5.30.53 (*PL* 75.710 and 707).
27. *Ibid.* 5.29.52.
28. I.e. be transformed, transfigured, in view of both the meaning of *nobilitade* and the repeated experience of Dante in the *VN*, described as *trasfiguramento* and *trasfigurazione* in 14.10 and 15.1.
29. Told in Ovid, *Metam.* 3.
30. *Homeric Hymns*, 5 (*To Aphrodite*) 182ff.
31. For the motif in the *VN*, in addition to 3 and 21 (sonnet), already cited, see 26.3, 32 (canzone, 35f), 41.6. The last is climactic and anticipates the importance of the theme in the *Conv.*—3.3.12 into 3.4, 3.8.14ff. In *VN* 41 (sonnet) note also the mention of *intelligenza nova*, given by Love and drawing upwards.
32. We find the same 'enthusiastic' language at the end of the *Symposium* (215ff), in Alcibiades' description of the strange effect of Socrates upon him.
33. Recall *Odyssey* 6.149ff on Odysseus in face of Nausicaa.
34. Detail paralleled in Sappho.
35. Detail paralleled in Sappho.
36. Detail paralleled in Sappho.
37. E. Gilson, *Dante et la philosophie*, Paris, Vrin, 1939, p.74.

« 4 »

PATRICK GRANT: IMAGINATION IN THE RENAISSANCE

Humanism and the Literary Imagination in the English Renaissance

It is generally known that during the later Renaissance a strong English empirical tradition in philosophy, extending from Bacon through Hobbes to Locke, insisted so firmly on the exact description of things that it held imagination gravely in suspicion as a distorter of clear knowledge. It is less well understood how the transmission of European Humanism into England during the Renaissance contributed to this new philosophical climate, while also helping to force upon literature a new self-consciousness about the epistemological status of imagination. With this in mind, I would like to look mainly at three Renaissance works in order to suggest how they pertain to the development of a certain crisis of confidence in the cognitive function of the literary imagination. These are Juan Luis Vives' *Against the Pseudo-dialecticians* (Louvain, 1519), Erasmus' *Praise of Folly* (written 1509, published 1511), and Shakespeare's *Hamlet* (c.1600).

Drawing on Kristeller,[1] I take Humanism to be a broad cultural movement beginning in Italy in the fourteenth century, and linked to a revival of interest in a set of subjects associated with the term *studia humanitatis*. Humanism emphasised the study of Greek and Latin, proclaiming how knowledge of these languages and their ancient literatures affected morality, and it stressed the uniqueness of the individual.

Italian Humanism is often especially associated with Marsilio Ficino (1433–99), doyen of the Platonic Academy in Florence, and with his mercurial disciple, Pico della Mirandola (1463–94), who challenged the learned world with his 900 theses and his famous *Oration on the Dignity of Man* (1486). The *Oration* is a soaring display of learning and eloquence, full of a sense of impassioned discovery and wild aspiration to master all knowledge. Indeed, Pico comes close to suggesting that he had already done just that: 'I have ranged through all the masters of philosophy, investigated all books, and come to know all schools'.[2] Consequently, he proposes a synthesis of the best and highest of human wisdom, and sets his sights on bringing 'into the open the miracles concealed in the recesses of the world . . . even so does the *magus* wed earth to heaven, that is, he weds lower things to the endowments and powers of higher things' (249).

Pico, in short, placed great store on the human mind. He felt that the ancient philosophers, with whose names he so lovingly and showily studs his *Oration*, contained a secret wisdom and powerful intelligence now made available for the free play and synthesising imaginative designs of the thinkers of a new age, such as himself. Here is a famous passage in which he describes God's first address to humanity:

> ... The nature of all other beings is limited and constrained within the bounds of laws prescribed by Us. Thou, constrained by no limits, in accordance with thine own free will, in whose hand We have placed thee, shalt ordain for thyself the limits of thy nature. We have set thee at the world's center that thou mayest from thence more easily observe whatever is in the world. We have made thee neither of heaven nor of earth, neither mortal nor immortal, so that with freedom of choice and with honor, as though the maker and molder of thyself, thou mayest fashion thyself in whatever shape thou shalt prefer. Thou shalt have the power to degenerate into the lower forms of life, which are brutish. Thou shalt have the power, out of thy soul's judgement, to be reborn into the higher forms, which are divine. (225)

Alone among the hierarchies, among the specifically formed and determined degrees of angels, animals, and vegetative life, man is a 'chameleon', a 'self-transforming nature' free to make of himself what he wishes, a glorious lord of creation, a 'Proteus' in whom lie the 'germs of every way of life' (225) to be cultivated and brought to maturity according to his own pleasure. This extraordinary picture of man as self-creator rather than interpreter of his ordained place in the scheme of things, of man as synthesiser and pattern maker rather than analyst and classifier, has the singular effect of casting speculative philosophy itself in the mould of an imaginative, creative play.

It is quite clear that the first of my three authors, the Spanish Humanist Juan Luis Vives, had read Pico's *Oration*.[3] We can see this from his little treatise *A Fable About Man* (Louvain, 1518), which takes over the central conception of the human creature's ability to choose a place in the hierarchies of creation, and even to become Godlike. Vives describes how Jupiter entertains the other Gods by creating the world as a stage on which the master-player is man. Although man has something in him of Jupiter's own immortality, he wears a mask of flesh to play his part which, as in Pico, is undetermined. But at the height of his power he is free even to transform himself into Jupiter's nature, and is able to act, as it were, almost as his own providence:

> From religion and memory, foreknowledge is almost obtained, with the prophecy of the future, evidently a spark of that divine and immense science which perceives all future events as if they were present.[4]

The spirit of Pico's Florentine Humanism thus passes into the *Fable*,[5] unmodified except for Vives' depiction of man as the master-player at a game of perpetual, imaginatively free making-up.

In this context, Vives' treatise *Against the Pseudodialecticians*[6] is interesting because it shows that he well knew there were philosophical consequences to such a depiction of man's imaginative freedom. As is clear even in the brief passages already cited from the *Fable* and the *Oration*, Vives, like Pico, relies heavily on rhetoric rather than logic to communicate a sense of what distinctively constitutes the human predicament. Indeed, both authors assume that attempts to classify man's place in nature lead merely to sterile logic chopping, which is what Vives means by 'Pseudodialecticians'. Man's freedom within the cosmic hierarchies is thus analogous to his freedom from certain scholastic ('pseudodialectical') habits of mind attempting to construct a systematic, logical order for human thought to inhabit. For Vives, such academic schemes are not just misguided, but perverse, and he complains about 'monstrous' (95) abuses of language, and of jargon among logicians which ignores 'time, work, language, custom and common sense' (95). He scorns at their inflexible arbitrariness and garrulous ignorance, claiming that their abstruse technical language breeds unhealthy elitism: 'They dream and devise for themselves absurdities and a kind of new language that they alone understand' (49); 'So, when their opponent has been confused by strange and unusual meanings and word-order, by wondrous suppositions, wondrous ampliations, restrictions, appellations, they then decree for themselves, with no public decision or sentence, a triumph over an adversary not conquered but confused by new feats of verbal legerdemain' (58–9). Logicians, in short, play at an empty game to mask their arrogation of power, and such is always the danger of institutionalised obscurantism.

Against all this, Vives recommends 'common sense and normal human speech' (79), calling for the adjudication of plain meaning by 'the whole crowd of workmen' (55). 'Every language', he argues, has its own common sense, 'which the Greeks call *idioma*' (69), and we should respect such 'old and familiar meaning' (79). Too intricate a pursuit of the exact definition of words soon leads to abstract confusions which become especially misleading and destructive when applied, for instance, to the basic truths of faith:

> although the Nicene Creed and the consensus of the whole Church deny that there is more than one God . . . these men still, in their invincible disputations, strenuously maintain that there are three Gods, three uncreated, omnipotent, external, and immense creators, and this over loud protests of all the Church Fathers and the resistance of Christian piety, and in spite of all the angels and of God Himself, while the very devils wonder at their impudent

temerity. (83)

Vives is deft in defending his orthodoxy: academics, he maintains, constitute the real threat to plain, old-fashioned truth because they are so over-developed technically, and so proud of their expertise that they refuse the general consensus. The new Humanism is thus presented as wanting basically to return to old-fashioned orthodoxy, and already we can feel the drift of an argument which blew up into the Reformation.

These brief observations can serve now to suggest a series of strong tendencies characteristic of Humanism's attitude to literary language, which can be summarised as follows:

(1) an optimistic conviction about the creative power of human imagination and will.

(2) rhetorical persuasion of the reader, the important thing being to awaken a change of attitude.

(3) an attack on obscurantist jargon which would divide and classify human action, rather than affirm its synthesising, creative freedom.

(4) a persuasion that common sense and usage tell us enough about language for us to behave morally; demands for too much consistency lead only to undesirable deviations from well-tried truths, the *consensus gentium*.

These tendencies are all quite clear in Vives' *Against the Pseudo-dialecticians*, and yet we ought to notice how, in some respects, his actual arguments are unsatisfactory. His general case against philosophy, for instance, is that of any person of bluff but narrow common sense against any kind of specialist vocabulary. In our own day, mathematicians often do not understand learned papers by one another, and I certainly do not understand the working vocabulary of my doctor friend who is in internal medicine. But I would not be without our mathematicians and doctors, despite what appears to be their obscurantism, and although I am pleased to see the ordinary citizen vote, I would not want any ordinary citizen doing surgery on my brain. Besides, the Humanists themselves were far from being as populist as they suggest, for they were in fact a kind of international club of Latin-speaking specialists who spent a great deal of time writing congratulatory notices to one another: an elite if ever there was one. Finally, Vives' confident suggestion that we should be content with the plain sense of the Nicene Creed stands in uneasy relationship to a set of teachings stressing the flexibility of language and the soft focus of words upon meaning. On the one hand, we cannot follow Vives' main argument all the way without abjuring exact theological definition; on the other, exact definition constitutes the 'consensus' on which Vives himself relies. I shall return to this point by and by.

Meanwhile, let us look briefly at Erasmus' *Praise of Folly*,[7] for its famous irony and fun are in a sense intimated by Vives' arguments against the pseudodialecticians. Vives, we recall, takes the logicians to task for treating their word-games too earnestly. Erasmus responds to this same issue by treating the logicians with an ironic and witty satire which serves as a lightning rod to earth, rendering harmless their pretentious self-importance. Erasmian wit and imagination, combining levity with underlying seriousness, were of course much imitated in frequent displays throughout Renaissance literature of paradoxically serious foolishness, or wise foolishness, or foolishness which opens revealingly onto the complex reaches of human desire and ambition, hope and fear.

Basically, the *Praise of Folly* is an extended pronouncement, or *declamatio*, by Folly herself: she shows us how full the world is of her devotees, and how she is necessary to make the world go round. What could be more foolish, after all, than the process of human generation: 'So if you owe your existence to wedlock, you owe the fact of wedlock to madness'. 'Thus', Folly continues, 'from that amusement of mine, drunken and absurd as it is, spring haughty philosophers and their present-day successors who are popularly called monks, kings in their purple, pious priests and thrice-holy pontiffs' (76–7). Without Folly, that is, there would be no human world at all, a fact which makes human pretension all the more amusing, all the more foolish. The touch here is playful, and yet the comedy swiftly veers into satire as monks, kings, priests and pontiffs are revealed as Folly's malicious, inadvertent worshippers, prey to their own vanity and duped, mainly, by taking themselves too seriously. But the satire is then itself refracted when we recall it is Folly who speaks, and so we must not heed a word that she says. Under the multiple refractions of irony, Erasmus thus protects himself from accusations of irreverence, and indeed Folly sees life as a play wherein we do best if we assume many masks:

> To destroy the illusion is to ruin the whole play, for it's really the characterization and make-up which hold the audience's eye. Now, what else is the whole life of man but a sort of play? Actors come on wearing their different masks and all play their parts until the producer orders them off the stage, and he can often tell the same man to appear in different costume, so that now he plays a king in purple and now a humble slave in rags. It's all a sort of pretence, but it's the only way to act out this farce. (104)

Join in, participate in the illusion and accept the nonsense, for 'this is the way to play the comedy of life' (105). The metaphor of theatrical disguise and the emphasis on performance help to confirm how imaginative language best teaches Folly's lesson that a clever exhibition is the important thing. Even so, the concluding section of her declamation is not at all frivolous in recommending Christ's 'divine foolishness' as a means of leading us away from mere worldliness towards 'the supreme mind which alone they call the *summum bonum*' (204). There 'the spirit will itself be absorbed by the supreme Mind' which 'draws everything into itself' (207). In the world's eyes, this 'transformation' may be foolish indeed, but it is also wisdom. And it is, of course, the very same transformation of the synthesising, imaginatively free-ranging mind into God as is described in Pico's *Oration* and Vives' *Fable*.

At this point it is worth mentioning a difficulty noticed frequently by readers of the *Praise of Folly*, arising from the fact that Erasmus does not consistently succeed in masking his own authorial voice when Folly speaks, so that the wit and irony sometimes spill over into straightforward social commentary. I do not wish to dwell on this issue, other than to say how it makes clear that, despite Folly's insistence on the kaleidoscopic and illusory, Erasmus himself remains a conventional moralist. Indeed, he is free to take such lighthearted, elegant pleasure in Folly, such a quickwitted, intelligent delight in her games, precisely because he believes something certain. For, broadly speaking, Erasmus was still able to experience Christendom[8] as a living, single fabric: the consensus of the Fathers and the Councils, the unity of a civilisation based on a shared creed. And for practical purposes Erasmus was prepared to reduce this consensus to what he calls the 'philosophia Christi', a kind of openness to the plain teachings of Christ in the spirit of a shared, common truth.[9] No less than Vives, Erasmus also singles out the hide-bound, pedantic logicians for distorting such generally accepted truth by their obscurantist games and elitist institutions and sterile word-mongering.[10] Indeed, for Erasmus, word-mongering, power-mongering, and war-mongering are closely allied. The vested interests of the ruling elite, he held, are protected by an obscurantism enabling the free exercise of power, which leads inevitably to war.[11] Erasmus therefore holds that the destruction of Christendom (guaranteed by protracted war) would be a consequence of abused language, and he did not hesitate to lay this charge squarely at the door of philosophers who refused to acknowledge the primacy of rhetoric and *bonae litterae* for a humane education.[12]

It follows that, despite the emphasis on imaginative transformation and on the free play of improvised meaning and corrective wit, imagination for Erasmus preserves a fairly strict cognitive function related to the objective order of 'Christendom', within which safe anchorage his wit moves with a merry, naive freedom. His attacks on the logicians, equating their abstract language with elitism and then with violence, do warn us effectively against one possible distortion of learning, and insofar as Erasmus shows how imagination humanises by teaching us to avoid such extremes, we can be thankful. But, as with Vives, Erasmus' method is less than thoroughgoing, for he still assumes the definitions of an ancient faith as the very bastion of the corporate and public truth of Christendom, to which he is devoted. It seems that however firmly imagination insists upon particulars and individuals, it does not achieve the kind of humanising freedom Erasmus desires if it is entirely divorced from the kind of general truth which the patient pursuit of an adequate abstract language provides. The *Praise of Folly* offers little explicit awareness that this is the case. Into the elegant fretwork building of Erasmian wit and imagination, however, Martin Luther entered like a flaming torch.

Luther, quite simply, insisted upon a rigorous interpretation of the critical issue which Erasmus, like Vives and many Humanists, was content to fudge: if words, the mirror of human intelligence, are indeed fickle we cannot discover through them any reliable body of authority, or any objective hierarchy serving as a ladder for our creative spirits to mount towards God. Why, Luther might ask, should Pico's vision of a stable chain of being not be yet another fiction of the free-ranging imagination he extols? Reason is a whore, Luther roughly concludes—seductive, unreliable, exploitable. Our will is bound, not free to effect any self-transformation into God, and Christ is in us by a gift of grace, unmediated by any design of human reason, intent, or *tour de force* of imagination.

Quite correctly, Erasmus was accused of having encouraged the Lutheran reform (he was said to have laid the egg that Luther hatched),[13] but when forced to take sides, he could not follow Luther all the way. The two men exchanged treatises defining their central differences, and the subject they chose was, significantly, free will.[14] In affirming it, Erasmus held to his allegiance with traditional Humanism, but the break with Luther distressed him profoundly, for the movements of reform and counter-reform now turned violent, and the war-mongering, bigotry and hatred which Erasmus all his life opposed, seemed somehow to have sprung up from the centre of his own best efforts to defend against them. Christendom had indeed fragmented from within, and the Humanist ship of fools, so gaily decked with wit and ingenuity, was forced to weigh anchor, to cast off from the old cognitive bedrock, to venture into strange seas, driven before the winds of mere unregenerate will, among the treacherous currents of a profane world.

It is highly likely that Shakespeare knew something both of Erasmus and Vives, not least because their writings were used as school textbooks. Certainly, the example of an Erasmian wise foolishness seems clear in *King Lear*, and traces of Vives' *Satellitum animae* have been located in *Hamlet* and elsewhere.[15] We might recall too that Erasmus' *Praise of Folly* was written for Thomas More, whose *History of King Richard the Third* is the source of Shakespeare's play on the same subject. Also, More wrote a defence of the *Praise of Folly*, and in a letter commends Vives' *Against the Pseudodialecticians* for having constructed an argument exactly in the spirit of his own defence of Erasmus.[16] It is of interest too that an early work of More's is entitled *The Life of Picus, Earl of Mirandula*, and in the web of such connections

IMAGINATION IN THE RENAISSANCE

between texts, we can observe something of the transmission of Humanism into Shakespeare's England.

I prefer, however, not to speculate about details of Shakespeare's Humanist affiliations, but rather to talk briefly about *Hamlet* in the context of my remarks about the *Praise of Folly* and the encounter between Erasmian Humanism and Lutheran reform. For if *Hamlet* is a Humanist document at all, it has the disturbed, saturnine caste of a late, exhausted Humanism tainted by disappointment and unsure of its bearings, not least because of an unsettling sense of the dizzying gap between imagination and truth precipitated by late developments within the movement itself, which we see also reflected in the Reformation.

It is as if Shakespeare created Hamlet in part to celebrate the free play of language. Certainly, Hamlet's main advantage is his ability to see more things in words, and do more with them than his interlocutors, who are slow and shallow compared to him. They take refuge in the conventional, while he has a thrilling, lively sense of the particular in all its wild peculiarity and bizarre impingements upon experience, so that language becomes a way of disarming and of dismaying his adversaries. Language at times is even a way of protecting himself from himself, as, for instance, when he plays at verbal games and riddles to temper his nerves after seeing the ghost: 'Hic et ubique: Then we'll shift our ground' (I, v, 156).[17]

Typically, Hamlet sees the abstract as an evasion of the real, so that his own penetrating irony and surprising metaphors are tokens for him of authenticity. Here, for instance, is Claudius early in the play giving the young Prince advice on mourning the death of his father, Hamlet senior:

> Though yet of Hamlet our dear brother's death
> The memory be green, and that it us befitted
> To bear our hearts in grief, and our whole kingdom
> To be contracted in one brow of woe,
> Yet so far hath discretion fought with nature
> That we with wisest sorrow think on him
> Together with remembrance of ourselves.
> Therefore our sometime sister, now our queen,
> Th' imperial jointress to this warlike state,
> Have we, as 'twere, with a defeated joy,
> With an auspicious and a dropping eye,
> With mirth in funeral, and with dirge in marriage,
> In equal scale weighing delight and dole,
> Taken to wife.   (I, ii, 1–14)

And, a little later:

> 'Tis sweet and commendable in your nature, Hamlet,
> To give these mourning duties to your father,

> But you must know your father lost a father,
> That father lost, lost his . . .   (I, ii, 87–90)

Consequently, Claudius argues, too much grief is unnatural:

> . . . fie, 'tis a fault to heaven,
> A fault against the dead, a fault to nature,
> To reason most absurd, whose common theme
> Is death of fathers.   (I, ii, 101–4)

Claudius' speech is full of balance and reserve. It is formal, well-turned, and largely conventional. It also gives the impression of cool deduction, and the particles binding it together suggest logical sequence: 'Though yet', 'yet', 'That we', 'therefore'. Moreover, the advice against excessive mourning makes good sense: everybody has a father, and to survive your father is in the normal course of events. Ironically, Claudius is quite right, even though as a murderer and usurper he is wrong. And yet the consolation he offers is glib, and the more so because so confidently formal, wearing the garb of received authority and proceeding through a series of public consolations and easy deductions.

Hamlet of course sees through Claudius in a flash, and detests him for assuming the veneer of such trite sententiousness. Consequently, when Hamlet's mother, Gertrude, comes in on Claudius' side and asks her son reprovingly, 'Why seems it so particular with thee', Hamlet turns on her:

> Seems, madam? Nay, it is. I know not 'seems'.
> 'Tis not alone my inky cloak, good mother,
> Nor customary suits of solemn black,
> Nor windy suspiration of forced breath,
> No, nor the fruitful river in the eye,
> Nor the dejected havior of the visage,
> Together with all forms, moods, shapes of grief,
> That can denote me truly. These indeed seem,
> For they are actions that a man might play,
> But I have that within which passes show;
> These but the trappings and the suits of woe.
>   (I, ii, 76–86)

Hamlet picks almost maniacally on the word 'seems', for 'seeming' and reality are incommensurate, and he is especially intolerant of the kind of hypocrisy that settles for a 'seemly' show—such as we have just been given by Claudius. Hamlet is even consistent enough to know that for authenticity's sake he must turn his argument against himself: his 'inky cloak', tears, sighs, and so on are superficial, mere conventional hints, imperfect signs of grief, and he does not want Gertrude to be mistaken: these things too only 'seem'; they are 'actions that a man might play'. He draws here upon the language of the stage: human behaviour, he implies, is a kind of drama, a mask of words and deeds, of ingenuity and imagination by which we endlessly conceal the truth. But it is essential also to notice that Hamlet is not so stand-offish as to refuse to play the game: after all, he stages a play to catch the conscience of the king, and he plays at madness, though it may well be that he becomes mad in doing so, and he plays at swordplay at the end, and at elaborate verbal games throughout. Far from refusing society's game, Hamlet plays it much *more* ferociously, elaborately, ingeniously, than all the others, so that he ends up turning the game itself inside out. The critical cliché depicting him as a malcontent brooding on the edges of society is therefore too simple: he is much more threatening as the enemy within, a fact clearly enough realised by Claudius when he packs Hamlet off in a hurry to England with Rosencrantz and Guildenstern.

Hamlet's speech to his mother is thus turned against himself as a token of his uncompromising truthfulness. But Hamlet's truth, as it were, has here broken loose from the consensus, for it is intolerant of the merely conventional. It is as if the logic of Folly's perpetual parade of masks is pushed to the limit, for if language is a performance, a false front, it can never come to rest securely on any general statement, any idea which another might share.

Let us consider in this light the soliloquy which then follows, 'O that this too too sullied flesh would melt', in which Hamlet thinks about the funeral in private, counterpointing, as it were, Claudius' public recitation on the subject. In the middle of the speech, Hamlet asks himself:

Must I remember? Why, she would hang on him
As if increase of appetite had grown
By what if fed on; and yet within a month—
Let me not think on't; frailty, thy name is woman—
A little month, or ere those shoes were old
With which she followed my poor father's body
Like Niobe, all tears, why she, even she—
O God, a beast that wants discourse of reason
Would have mourned longer—married with my uncle,
My father's brother, but no more like my father
Than I to Hercules. Within a month,
Ere yet the salt of most unrighteous tears
Had left the flushing in her gallèd eyes,
She married. O, most wicked speed, to post
With such dexterity to incestuous sheets!
It is not, nor it cannot come to good.
But break my heart, for I must hold my tongue.
(I, ii, 143–59)

Hamlet is, as his mother says, 'particular'. Here he dwells on the particular time ('within a month', 'a little month', and again, 'within a month'), then fixing on the shoes, the 'salt', 'gallèd eyes' and 'incestuous sheets'. He does not ask himself about the conventional meaning of funeral processions or about grief or impropriety with the aim of understanding man's common lot, but he seizes instead on the inane physical trappings of the precise event to express his disgust and bitterness. We notice also how quickly his opening question, 'Must I remember?' is followed by 'Let me not think on't'. The tone is urgent, for quite clearly Hamlet is not free *not* to think about it. Although his astounding fertility of language, his ability to cut wittily through the conventional hypocrisies of others is a marvellous gift, this gift itself preys on him. His speech progresses by brilliant fits of association, metaphor and allusion. And he cannot stop it. When he does generalise ('frailty, thy name is woman'), it is by way of a perverse inference in the teeth of common sense, releasing the taint of misogyny, the stain of an infection detected in his mother's marriage and which spreads in the contagion of his imagination, threatening to blight his relation with all women whatsoever, as Ophelia is soon to discover. Although Hamlet sees through Claudius' hypocrisies and Gertrude's evasions, and although he is able to outplay others playing at power and deception, the very volatility of his imagination therefore threatens to undermine not only his own certainties, but also his common sense.

Shakespeare's play, we can now surmise, resembles Erasmus' *Praise of Folly* insofar as hidebound authoritarian formalities are subjected to scrutiny in both works by a witty deployment of irony, paradox, and a play of masks. And yet the fact that *Hamlet* was written after the Reformation reflects everywhere in a certain deadly weight upon the wit and brilliance, imposed by the kind of question Luther asked, and which Erasmus fudged: On what public consensus can we rely if the relationship between language and reality, imagination and truth, is, indeed, perpetually elusive? Hamlet, as we see, is plagued by this problem, and his departure from the mood of such Humanists as Pico and Vives and Erasmus on the self-transforming potential of the human being and his godlike power to scale the heavens, is caught in the speech to Rosencrantz and Guildenstern where Hamlet gives his version of the cosmic scheme:

> I will tell you why; so shall my anticipation prevent your discovery, and your secrecy to the king and queen moult no feather. I have of late, but wherefore I know not, lost all my mirth, forgone all custom of exercises; and indeed, it goes so heavily with my disposition that this goodly frame, the earth, seems to me a sterile promontory; this most excellent canopy, the air, look you, this brave o'erhanging firmament, this majestical roof fretted with golden fire: why, it appeareth nothing to me but a foul and pestilent congregation of vapors. What a piece of work is a man, how noble in reason, how infinite in faculties, in form and moving how express and admirable, in action how like an angel, in

apprehension how like a god: the beauty of the world, the paragon of animals; and yet to me, what is this quintessence of dust? Man delights not me; nor woman neither, though by your smiling you seem to say so. (II, ii, 301–18)

At face value, Hamlet lets them know that he has become malcontent and cynical, out of step with the world. He can no longer take pleasure in the 'goodly frame', and the spiritual potential of man ('how like an angel') means nothing to him. God's grand design is all very admirable, but if man is free within it, he is free to be a misfit, to turn his back on it all, and Hamlet claims to have done just that. The angel is diseased, but likes it. And yet we cannot take his speech at face value, for Hamlet is clearly playing with Rosencrantz and Guildenstern, as he does throughout. His words have a tone of mock bonhomie ('Listen, and I'll tell you what they are really thinking of me'), and are touched with contemptuous playfulness. The conventional cosmic picture is too ornate, too frivolously overdrawn ('excellent canopy', 'the air, look you', 'fretted with golden fire', 'What a piece of work is a man', and so on). Just so, his own disaffection is touched with an exaggerated posturing which mocks at those who would depict him thus ('Why, it appeareth nothing to me . . .'). Hamlet deliberately makes it hard for Rosencrantz and Guildenstern to know how to take him. The pose of openness and complicity among old friends is really the vehicle for ironic wariness. In fact a good deal of what he tells them about his malcontent disposition is true, but he is so conscious of conventional description that he undercuts it continually, holding it at ironic distance. Hamlet is not merely disenchanted with man the great wonder set free to transform himself within the scale of nature: the whole concept of a scale of nature itself is treated as just another metaphor, another mask for the hypocrites to hide behind, another false image posing as a true idea. And Hamlet isn't falling for any of it.

At this point a larger question looms into view: how does Hamlet's language-game affect his religious beliefs, his attitudes to questions of absolute significance? We recall that Pico thought man free to shape his destiny and to aspire to know God, whose providence has ordained man's unique status among creatures. Vives' *Fable* also declares man almost a providence unto himself, and extols man's ability to participate in the divine nature. Erasmus likewise recommends a kind of divine foolishness which leads to mystical union. In each case, a soaring declaration about human freedom is held on the rails, as it were, of an objective order, providentially designed and revealed as reasonable and acceptable to common sense (the scale of nature, the plain sense of the creeds, the consensus of Christendom). Alone among these examples, however, Hamlet takes to its end term the suggestion that man might indeed act as his own providence, and if that is so, man of course does not really need an objectively created, guiding design. The deepest strains of Shakespeare's tragedy arise from just such a presumption on the hero's part of complete human autonomy.

The standard model of a tragic fall inherited by the Renaissance from the Middle Ages, was Boethius' *Consolation of Philosophy*. The rise and fall of a king was held to follow the course, described by Boethius, of a rise and fall on Fortune's wheel, which represents time, and which turns continually. By contrast, at the centre of the wheel is the still point of eternity, which cannot be described in terms of time, and which is the seat of providence. The usurping king who takes his chance and rides to glory on the wheel therefore places himself in Fortune's hands, and is always deceived, always let down.

As Maynard Mack points out,[18] *Hamlet* is based on this model, but with the crucial difference that, by a typical stroke of genius, Shakespeare applies the Boethian scheme in reverse. Hamlet does not ride on Fortune's wheel; Claudius does that, and, by contrast, Hamlet vilifies Fortune at every opportunity. Hamlet, however, makes the opposite error of usurping providence; of wanting, as it were, to play God. Thus he decides not to stab Claudius at prayer, for it would be better to kill him in some more compromising situation, so that his soul would burn in hell. Thus he toys with suicide and tells Ophelia it would be better if she did not have children, and despite the ghost's warning him to leave Gertrude's soul to heaven, he does not. Thus he tends to diagnose the entire world's sickness, and to feel it, somehow, his own responsibility: 'The time is out of joint. O cursed spite, / That ever I was born to set it right!' (I, v, 188–9). Not surprisingly, he is crushed by the burden of all this, and only at the end of the play, with tragedy upon him, does he realise, 'There's a divinity that shapes our ends, / Rough-hew them how we will' (V, ii, 10–11); 'There is special providence in the fall of a sparrow' (V, ii, 221).

I have now come close to saying that Hamlet's usurpation of providence is one consequence of his attitude to language. He regards language, that is, as a set of satiric and ironic devices, of masks for expressing the force of a desire imaginatively, and within which the individual is free to move, transforming whatever resists him into a vehicle for his own will. But if this is so, there are no public certainties, only the shaping force of individual aspiration. On this model, the gap between imagination and ideas, between poetry and theology, is clearly chasmic and unbridgeable. To Luther's credit, he saw the true dimensions of this chasm, and declared that we believe in God despite the gap that exists between our fickle manipulations of deceptive, image-bound language, and God's truth. Our faith is a gift of grace, unmediated, and efficacious beyond any human means. Without it, we are condemned to march towards damnation along the splendid highway of our imagined self-sufficiency.

It is not too much to claim that Hamlet peers into this same chasm between imagination and higher truth, but draws the opposite conclusions to Luther, namely that for all practical purposes man is in charge of shaping his own life on earth. Shakespeare's special distinction consequently is to record not only the sense of brilliant liberation in Hamlet's use of imaginative language, but also the derangement that follows upon the ensuing usurpation of providence mirrored in nature's objective order. Shakespeare of course does not recommend going back to the simpler confidence of Pico, for he displays his hero's sceptical energy altogether too vigorously and sympathetically. But he also shows us how destructive is a thoroughly free-ranging imagination. A world constituted merely of masks within masks, of play and counterplay, of seeming and appearance, ultimately stultifies purposeful action, and public meaning itself.[19] Shakespeare's own imagination thus differs from Hamlet's in that Shakespeare grasps and expresses this truth, while Hamlet suffers it.

It seems, then, as the Humanists assumed, that we may not deny to imagination a cognitive rôle, for it gives us insight into complex human experience (Hamlet's 'particulars'). It is the case, as history readily enough confirms, that we frequently do violence to one another under the guise of general principles and high-minded causes. By enlivening us to the living, human complexities of situations which we might otherwise oversimplify, imagination educates our judgement in a manner that may enable us to resist the potential dangers of our own ideals. Imagination then operates as our great corrector of over-reaching generalisation (Hamlet's 'actions that a man might play'). Thus, it functions very much as Shakespeare so brilliantly depicts it, counterpointing our freedom to believe, which it helps us to proclaim, against our responsibilities to humanity, which it helps us to understand. And yet it is important not to deny to imagination some real relationship to the world which we investigate by abstract thinking. Hamlet, after all, is not Shakespeare, and the tragedy of a wholly liberated imagination is, as we see in the case of the hapless prince, that it threatens our humanity by divorcing us from a shared world and from one another. Analogously, any theological assessment of our human predicament ought to require of imagination a humanising 'translation' as it were, of the truths of faith; but it will demand also an acknowledgement that imagination itself may not humanise but only distort, if it loses contact altogether with the kind of thinking which seeks for exactness, clarity and shared understanding.

NOTES
1. For Kristeller's influential interpretation, see *Renaissance Thought. The Classic, Scholastic, and Humanist Strains* (New York: Harper and Row, 1961), pp.3ff. See also Paul Oskar Kristeller and John Herman

Randall, Jr., 'General Introduction', in *The Renaissance Philosophy of Man*, ed. Ernst Cassirer, *et al.* (Chicago: University of Chicago Press, 1948), pp.1-20. For a direct application of his views to England see Kristeller, 'Thomas More as a Renaissance Humanist', *Moreana*, vol.xvii, no.65-6 (1980), pp.5-22. By *studia humanitatis* Kristeller means a broad cycle of disciplines—grammar, rhetoric, history, poetry, and moral philosophy—which replaced a typical medieval emphasis on logic, natural philosophy, metaphysics, theology and law.

2. Giovanni Pico Della Mirandola, *Oration on the Dignity of Man*, trans. Elizabeth Livermore Forbes, ed. Cassirer *et al.*, *The Renaissance Philosophy of Man*, p.242. All quotations are from this translation, and page numbers are cited in the text.

3. Vives never visited Italy, and seems to have held a slightly disparaging view of Italian Humanism, preferring what he found in France and the Lowlands. He might have been stimulated to imitate the *Oration* because of the good opinion Pico had established in Paris, which he visited in 1485-6, and where Vives emigrated in 1509. See Carlos Norena, *Juan Luis Vives* (The Hague: Martinus Nijhoff, 1970), pp.25ff.

4. Juan Luis Vives, *A Fable About Man*, trans. Nancy Lenkeith, ed. Cassirer *et al.*, *The Renaissance Philosophy of Man*, p.392.

5. See Lenkeith, *Introduction*, p.385.

6. Juan Luis Vives *Against the Pseudodialecticians. A Humanist Attack on Medieval Logic*, trans. Rita Guerlac (London: D. Riedel, 1978). Page numbers are cited in the text.

7. *Erasmus. Praise of Folly, and Letter to Martin Dorp, 1515*, trans. Betty Radice (Harmondworth: Penguin Books, 1971). Page numbers are cited in the text. To some readers, the order of this discussion might seem back to front, for Erasmus was twenty-six years older than Vives, and the *Fable* was written after Vives had met Erasmus in 1516, and in imitation of the older man. Yet, in another sense, back to front is the right way round: Vives comes from the south, imitating Pico's *Oration* in the *Fable*, into which he introduces Erasmus' characteristic irony and fun, and in the *Praise of Folly* we can detect all the major Humanist tendencies. In these various intertextual bindings we grasp something of Humanism's development northward.

8. See Robert P. Adams, *The Better Part of Valor. More, Erasmus, Colet, and Vives on Humanism, War, and Peace* (Seattle: University of Washington Press, 1962), pp.166ff, *et passim*, for an account of Erasmus' concern for a united Christendom. Also, R. J. Schoeck, 'The Place of Erasmus Today', ed. Richard L. de Molen, *Erasmus of Rotterdam. A Quincentennial Symposium* (New York: Twayne, 1971) pp.83ff, for Erasmus' flexible use of tradition.

9. Erasmus' thoughts on the 'philosophia Christi' are conveniently plain in the *Paraclesis*, trans. John C. Olin, *Desiderius Erasmus. Christian Humanism and the Reformation* (Gloucester, Mass.: Peter Smith, 1973), pp.92ff.

10. Such arguments run through Erasmus' writings, and are present for instance in the *Praise of Folly*, 151, 153, 158, 172.

11. See *Praise of Folly*, 97, 98, 161, 193.

12. See *Praise of Folly*, 94, 96, 97, 161; Letter to Dorp, 68-9, 80-2. The connections between Humanist education and peace are fundamental to Erasmus' thinking: see Adams, *The Better Part of Valor*, *passim*.

13. Erasmus attributes the charge to Franciscans, in a letter dated December 1524, ed. P. S. Allen, H. M. Allen, H. W. Garrod, *Opus epistolarum Des. Erasmi Roterodami*, 12 vols (Oxford: Clarendon Press, 1906-58), vol.v, p.609.
14. Translated by Ernst F. Winter, *Erasmus-Luther. Discourse on Free Will* (New York: Frederick Ungar, 1961).
15. For details, see *Vives' Introduction to Wisdom. A Renaissance Textbook*, ed. Marian Leona Tobriner (New York: Teachers College Press, 1968), pp.38-9.
16. Letter of More to Erasmus, 26 May 1520, ed. Allen, *Opus epistolarum*, vol.IV, pp.266-9, trans. Rita Guerlac, *Vives Against the Pseudo-dialecticians*, pp.163ff.
17. *Hamlet*, ed. Edward Hubler, *The Complete Signet Classic Shakespeare*, ed. Sylvan Barnet (New York: Harcourt, Brace, Jovanovich, 1972). All quotations are from this edition, and are indicated in the text.
18. Maynard Mack, 'The World of Hamlet', *The Yale Review*, XLI (1952), pp.502-23, points to Hamlet's 'encroaching on the role of providence' and assuming responsibility for the evil he sees everywhere. I summarise Mack's argument here.
19. This is a main argument in A. D. Nuttall, *A New Mimesis. Shakespeare and the Representation of Reality* (London: Methuen, 1983), a study maintaining that literature gives us knowledge of the objective world, and that attempts to divorce literature from public meaning are self-destructive. Although I read Professor Nuttall's book after writing the present essay, it has helped me to clarify this conclusion. I also acknowledge an indebtedness extending over several years, deriving from conversations and comments on earlier manuscripts of mine dealing with images and ideas in Renaissance literature.

« 5 »

JOHN MCINTYRE : NEW HELP FROM KANT;
THEOLOGY AND HUMAN IMAGINATION

Any attempt to establish relationships between imagination and theology or religion must seem either excessively optimistic or simply forgetful of the bad record which imagination has had in the history of theology. At a popular level, difficulty arises over the simple matter of the use of the word 'imagination' used in the Authorised Version of the Bible to translate Hebrew and Greek words describing unattractive and even immoral aspects of human psychology featuring in the original texts. More frequently, however, the difficulty for any serious attempt to associate imagination with religion and through it with theology has been the depreciatory analysis given to imagination in philosophy and psychology. The critics of religion have not been slow to take advantage of such analysis to promote serious de-bunking of religion as being the expression of human fantasy or the compensatory delusion of an insecure or unstable personality. Admittedly, that is only one side of the case, for there are other voices, notably that of George MacDonald (*A Dish of Orts*, Essay, 'The Imagination: Its Function and Its Culture' 1907) who places imagination at the heart of his doctrine of the nature of God, or Richard Kroner (*The Religious Function of the Imagination*, 1941) who ranks religious imagination even above thought as the means of penetration into the heart of the divine mystery. Generally, however, the omens are not encouraging for any attempt to find a place for imagination within religion or theology, particularly if we are thinking of a constructive part that it might play, rather than proposing an internally located instrument of demolition. Optimism in face of such odds would be rather unjustified.

On the other hand, if we were looking for help in such an enterprise, Kant would seem to be an unlikely direction in which to turn. For his contributions to theology are somewhat different, varied and considerable though they may be. His extended criticism of speculative theology in the *Critique of Pure Reason*, where he seeks to demonstrate the invalidity of all metaphysical proofs of divine existence, provided the forum for the examination of the subject by all subsequent enquirers, particularly in the years since the Second World War, when there has been such a revived interest in the proofs. Generations of Gifford Lecturers, interested in the question of the relation of morality to religion, have been obliged to treat Kant's *Critique of Practical Reason* as prescribed reading, and have drawn heavily upon the moral affirmations of the *Fundamental Principles of a Metaphysic of Morals*. Ethical issues were never far from his mind in his writing on philosophy of religion in *Religion Within the Bounds of Reason*, when he is dealing with revealed religion, or faith and reason, or the grace of God. Kant, then, can not be regarded as one who has demonstrated to us the place of imagination in theology. Yet he is the philosopher in the modern era most relevant to our enquiries into that subject, for two reasons.

First, Kantian epistemology, rather than any other, has dominated the study of the nature of our knowledge of God, and even extended beyond epistemology to influence the analysis of the nature of interpretation, of faith and even of the *imago Dei*, though it is an influence which has not always been acceptable. In 1946 Cornelius Van Til in his book *The New Modernism* (James Clarke & Co., London) used this title to high-light the way in which Barth and Brunner failed to achieve a pure orthodox Protestant expression of any of the major Christian doctrines as a result of their use of Kantian epistemology and metaphysics. Their Kantian sympathies, so it was argued, had prevented them from breaking with the Liberalism, which shared these sympathies and against which they thought they were in revolt. In any case, Kant's view that all knowledge is an amalgam of the form prescribed by the mind and the matter contributed by the object will be unacceptable to those who claim that knowledge of God is direct and veridical, or that the Object so known is revealed to the believer without any human contribution. It is interesting, however, that even in this latter case there is often a lingering Kantian suggestion that a receptive structure has been placed, in the human mind or soul, by the Holy Spirit to enable it to appropriate the revelation. In other words, even knowledge of God conforms to Kantian requirements, that knowledge is an amalgam of matter supplied by the object and form imposed by the mind. In fact, that is where the Kantian epistemological reference to the *imago Dei* applies: Barth holding that since the *imago* has been destroyed in fallen man, God intervenes to restore it and to supply the faith to appropriate the Revelation, Brunner holding that only a formal *imago* which might yield knowledge of God's judgement, remains, and it is supplemented, again by the Spirit, so that it can apprehend God's grace also.

That is a very rough-and-ready application of the Kantian epistemology to the question of religious knowledge, but there are others. For example, Kant's presentation may be extended to the explanation of the varieties of religious and non-religious interpretations of the universe and of history. We are all confronted by a manifold of diverse objects and events and we all seek to impose upon them our own interpretations, some of which may be religious, others naturalistic, and yet others plainly sceptical. Such an account of the matter yields us the fashionable doctrine of Pluralism, whether we meet it in metaphysics, or Christian doctrine, or again in comparative religion, and it often is thought to remove such differences to a sphere of ambiguity where truth-claims no longer obtain. Such a view does seem to conform to the required procedure which Kant formulated for his new method of philosophy, and which he thought reflected his considerably misunderstood 'Copernican hypothesis'—the procedure, namely, that objects must be taken to conform to human thought, and not that thought should conform to objects presented to the human mind.

While this view has a *prima facie* connection with Kant's epistemology, it has to be urged that, despite its popular acceptance, in fact it bears little evidence of right understanding of the subtlety of Kant's thought. Thus, it fails to notice that according to Kant the form prescribed by the mind to the objects known derives, in part at least, from the categories of the understanding. So far is the knowing mind from being free to select whatever concepts it pleases for the interpretation of a chaotic manifold, it operates under limits imposed by the understanding. What we perceive, moreover, has already in ordinary experience been determined by thought, so that the object now carries its interpretation and its meaning with it. The given is never a simple datum as such, isolated and uninterpreted, to which we may subsequently attach some significance; but if we intend to use the term 'given' we shall have to be careful to distinguish the matter presented by what Kant calls 'intuition' supplied by the object, from the object as apprehended at the first point of our beginning to know it. The former is never intuited separately according to Kant. We do not therefore have a paradigm structure for interpretation giving meaning to an otherwise neutral and uninterpreted given, and in such a process being free to choose among options of meanings.

This use, or abuse as it is, of Kant's dictum concerning knowledge being a joint product of intuition and understanding draws attention to a more serious error, namely, a failure to understand Kant's philosophical method which he entitles 'transcendental'. Taking the given in the sense of the interpreted given of ordinary experience, the transcendental method sets out to establish the existence of the *a priori* principles which condition the possibility of experience as we know it, and to demonstrate their objective validity in that capacity. Accordingly, Kant comes to apply the term 'transcendental' not only to the method, but also to these *a priori* principles or conceptions which underlie experience as its necessary conditions; and he even goes as far at times as attributing the term to the faculty or the process from which they derive. (N. Kemp Smith, *A Commentary to Kant's Critique of Pure Reason*, Macmillan, London. 1930. pp.75ff). Kant's interest in epistemology, then, is not in the relation of subjective interpretations to allegedly objective data, but rather in the conditioning principles which make possible knowledge that begins by being complex, and which are involved in the objectivity of that knowledge. It is in the unfolding of these conditions that Kant develops a subject, his view of imagination, which is neglected by those who interpret his theory of knowledge as dealing only with given and interpretation. To omit such a view from an account of his theory is to misrepresent it, and to sell it short.

So we come to our second reason for turning to Kant for help in the examination of the place of imagination in religion and theology. If, as we have given as our first reason for turning to Kant for such help, it is the case that Kantian epistemology has been very influential in religious epistemology in the nineteenth and twentieth centuries, then it is most important that we take advantage of the whole of what Kant has to say, and not be put off with a fraction of it. Central to such epistemology is Kant's doctrine of imagination. As Professor W. H. Walsh (*Kant's Criticism of Metaphysics*, Edinburgh University Press, Edinburgh. 1975. p.75) says, 'It would certainly be necessary to re-write the entire (First) *Critique* if the present references to imagination were excised.' The point had been put in an even more dramatic way some forty years earlier by A. D. Lindsay (*Kant*, Benn, London. 1934. p.275). 'One of the most revolutionary, though perhaps least remarked, features of Kant's new theory of knowledge is the part which it assigns to imagination.' What, then, is that part? Without engaging in detailed exposition of Kant's theory, for that has been recently twice executed with clarity and precision (in W. H. Walsh, *op. cit.*, pp.53f, 72–7, and Mary Warnock, *Imagination*, Faber, London. 1976. pp.26–34, 137–41), we shall concentrate on those aspects of his theory which may assist us in our enquiry into the possible place of imagination in religion and theology.

We have to begin by correcting the earlier statement that for Kant all knowledge is an amalgamation of matter supplied by the object to the senses and form prescribed by the mind, and by adding that Kant affirms that imagination is the very important third factor in the knowing situation. It performs a mediating function between sense and understanding in a number of different ways, to which Kant has given the names 'transcendental' and 'empirical', yielding the titles 'productive imagination' and 'reproductive imagination'. Taking the productive imagination first, we note that the manifold which is presented to us in sense lacks the unity of any kind of ordered world, and it does not even evince any structure of succession in time. Thought which operates with pure concepts can not itself effect the synthesis of the manifold of intuitions, but it achieves this end through imagination. So imagination imposes upon the manifold a synthetic unity which Kant says is an *a priori* condition of the possibility of all knowledge. This synthesis is not one special sort of unity, determined by the kinds of intuitions received, so that it does not differentiate one object from another; how that is accomplished we shall see later. For the present, what Kant is speaking of is an *a priori* unity imposed upon the given manifold which is the condition of the possibility of any object being apprehended as an object. In fact this synthetic unity imposed by the imagination, or the transcendental synthesis of imagination, is inter-dependent with another unity, the unity of apperception, the one consciousness of which any intuition has to be an experience in order to be an intuition, and within which it exists with other intuitions in a variety of relations. Nor is the unity of apperception a unity of our minds only, for ideas are ideas of objects, and the relations which the mind affirms are relations which exist between objects in the world. But it is with the transcendental synthesis of imagination that we are concerned, and pursuing Kant farther we learn that the imagination synthesises the manifold under rules prescribed by the understanding, namely, the categories. But since the categories are pure concepts of the understanding, they can not be applied *tout court* to intuitions of sense. The categories and such intuitions are heterogeneous. There has, as Kant says, to be a third thing which must be both intellectual and sensible, something which performs the service of making pure concepts applicable to appearance in time and space. The agent effecting this application is called the transcendental schema, and it is the product of the imagination. In this process, the categories are realised or given significance in objects and their relations to one another; but they are also limited by being restricted to conditions which sensibility imposes upon them.

But Kant acknowledges that there are concepts other than the pure concepts of the understanding, namely, sensible concepts; and they too, require the mediating agency of schemata to connect them with the images which have been formed by 'the empirical faculty of reproductive imagination' (B181), imagination having previously been defined as 'the faculty of representing in intuition an object that is not itself present' (B152). So in the context of sensible concepts, Kant is propounding three entities: the concept itself, the schema and the image, and he is very insistent that the schema is not an image. Not only is the image an inadequate representation of the concept, but the concept which is general is no clue to the identification of any specific image; and so the schema is introduced to connect the image and the concept. The schema is defined as the procedure to be followed in the proliferation of images in accordance with the concept 'to which they belong'. This range of images which the imagination produces spontaneously and creatively, of course within the definition of the concept, enables the mind to identify and apprehend objects within our environment.

An interesting point arises when Kant contrasts the schema of the pure concept of the understanding with the schema of the sensible concept by saying that the transcendental schema does not yield any images. The question arises: why does he say so? A number of answers suggest themselves. First, the answer proposed by Professor Walsh (*Kant's Criticism of Metaphysics*, p.74) is that 'we cannot literally envisage the circumstances in which such a concept would apply' and so would be unable to proliferate a series of occasions which would instantiate the concept. He adds that since we can *see* the transcendental schema in certain cases, for example, we can see regular succession whereas we cannot see ground and consequent—therefore, there is no call for a corresponding image. Secondly, we could suggest that since it is the role of the transcendental imagination to effect a synthesis of the manifold through the application of the transcendental schemata, the end-term of such an application will be not an image but unity in the object. It is only when that has happened that objects will appear as objects. It is only then also that they are, as we might say, eligible to be recognised and identified as this or that object instantiating some sensible concept, eligible, also, to become the images produced by the reproductive imagination. In other words, the transcendental schemata are part of the conditions which combine to make experience of the kind that we have possible, and as such are not themselves the objects of experience in the form of images.

Thirdly, it might, on the other hand, be said that what Kant is denying is the possibility of transcendental schemata yielding visual images; reference to the lists of transcendental schemata which we find at B182–B185 confirms this point. But if we revert to Kant's notion that the schema is a universal procedure of the imagination, then we might conclude that the transcendental schema is a rule for the proliferation of a range of instances of the pure concept. That is exactly what we would expect, since the imagination will be exercising this rôle in many cases. Besides, where the pure concept, or the category concerned is a relation, or some such abstract concept such as substance, actuality or necessity, we could not properly expect its instantiation to take the form of an image; but the imagination would nevertheless apply it in the appropriate cases.

It would be wrong, even in such a brief résumé as the present account of the part assigned by Kant to imagination in his epistemology, to ignore his *Critique of Judgement*, though we have to be careful and remember that for him a statement about the beauty of an object carries with it *prima facie*, no epistemological claim. Two aspects of his account of aesthetic judgements may be noted. First, the aesthetic pleasure asserted in the aesthetic judgement arises in a very special way. Kant employs the distinction between the determinant judgement which subsumes the particular intuition under a universal rule, law or principle, and the reflective judgement, where the universal rule is not derived from experience, rather has the judgement to begin with the particular and find a universal rule or concept upon which to proceed. When he applies this notion to natural science, he says that the scientist works with reflective judgements, and makes use of the concept of the 'finality of nature', the principle that the phenomena to be explained fall into some orderliness or system. When this principle operates successfully, and several heterogeneous laws of nature are embraced within the one principle, a feeling of pleasure is experienced and so associated with the notion of finality. Kant extends this analysis to aesthetic statements, where the principle which the reflective judgement uses is described as 'finality without end' or 'purposiveness without purpose'. The phrase refers to the pattern, or structure, or form, that is internal to the beautiful object, the interdependence and interlocking of its components to give it its 'point' and its significance. Kant is denying that such a beautiful object serves any utilitarian purpose outside of itself. He does mention also that it is imagination which employs the reflective judgement to apprehend the form which gives the object its beauty. Pleasure once again is experienced, said this time to be due to the fact that imagination has been able to comply with the requirement of the understanding for conformity to law (*Critique of Judgement*, 190).

The second point that is to be noted concerning aesthetic judgements is that despite the subjective character of the pleasure accompanying them, the claim is made for the universal validity of such judgements. So although there is what Kant calls a state of free play of the cognitive faculties, imagination and cognition, nevertheless the description of the aesthetic object must be universally communicable (*CJ* 217f), and have universal subjective validity. The argumentation which Kant employs to establish his case is extremely obscure, but the thread of it is his contention that in aesthetic judgements as in ordinary cognitive judgements there is a common involvement of imagination and understanding, and a single process of conceptualisation, even though the method of conceptualisation is different in the two cases. Professor Schaper (*Studies in Kant's Aesthetics*, Edinburgh University Press, Edinburgh. 1979) argues convincingly for the view that, since empirical judgements are normative for any experience of objects in that they prescribe the conditions that apply to any such experiences, those judgements, namely, aesthetic, which describe the experience of form must conform to the same conditions 'which make coherent sense of experience', that is, of anyone's experience (Schaper, p.76). By thus relating aesthetic judgements to perceptual judgements, Kant is thought to secure the communicability of these judgements, and to preserve his very important claim for subjectivity of the aesthetic estimate of the object.

As we turn now to the purpose of this study, which is to investigate what help is to be obtained from Kant in exploring the place of imagination in religion and theology, we shall not expect such help to be of a direct kind. For Kant had much to say that was critical of speculative theology, though such criticism had as its target the endeavour to establish God's existence by means of metaphysical proofs. Also, if we are thinking that knowledge of God is a process of direct experience, then equally we find him totally unsympathetic—though that in itself will not greatly upset those of us who have been brought up on the view that knowledge of God is a process of mediated immediacy. On the contrary, our expectation of the exploration will be to learn from Kant what imagination is and how it contributes to the process of knowing, what insights we can achieve through an analogical extension of the epistemological and evaluative rôles of imagination in empirical epistemology and aesthetic appraisal to the religious and theological scenes, and how by these uses of imagination in religion and theology, we may advance our understanding of theological content and method. Therefore if we are not so foolhardy as to suggest that what is proposed is a Kantian analysis of our subject and solution of its problems, our modesty will not prevent us from claiming the attribute 'Kantian-type' for our analyses and description.

1. Let us begin with a very general statement, the previously mentioned contention made by Professor Walsh (*Kant's Criticism of Metaphysics*, p.76) after he has been examining the role of the imagination in producing schemata and defending the view that envisaging a range of cases of a particular concept 'involves something more than the bare intellect', namely, that 'imagination is an indispensable and irreducible factor in human thinking'. The simple acknowledgement of such a claim, and it is in no sense an exaggeration as is easily seen from the above brief review of Kant's many references to it, would have made a profound difference to the kind of analysis to be given to the human soul's relationship to God. Into that analysis have been brought almost all of the activities of the human mind—knowing, feeling and willing, obeying, trusting and confessing, acknowledging, loving and worshipping, and so on. The list is almost endless, and it is clearly virtually co-terminous with the entire range of what the mind does. Yet with the almost singular exception of George MacDonald, and those writers in the last decade who have wakened up to the importance of imagination for the understanding of the whole of religious life and activity, it has gone ignored. Once that importance is admitted, there is practically no part of religion from which it can be excluded, and which is not greatly enhanced by such inclusion. The reasons for such exclusion are surely no longer valid, ranging as they do from the equation of imagination with image-making of a less savoury sort, which the intellect must suppress for the health of the person, to the attribution to imagination of the capacity to invent idols and images to misrepresent and even-

tually displace the one, true, and invisible God. The refutation of such implausible, if historically documented, reasons for the elimination of imagination from serious theology, is supplied by Kant's systematic introduction of the concept into his philosophy of mind.

2. One particular aspect of the acknowledgement of the part played by imagination in human thinking is Kant's emphasis upon its place in epistemological analysis. Because of the quite special status which Kant gives to the concept of God, as a regulative idea of Reason, we cannot look to him for the introduction of imagination into the analysis of our supposed knowledge of such a non-empirical existent. Other circumstances, however, may induce us to retain imagination in our epistemological analysis as it relates to our knowledge of God. First, as has been stated frequently in the exposition of Kant's views, imagination is the medium through which the understanding operates in conjunction with the senses to produce the kind of world that we experience. Now there has been a long tradition in theology which has affirmed that God is to be known *per ea quae facta sunt*, through the things that he has made. This dictum has admittedly been used by theologians who wished to establish inferential knowledge of God, derived by a variety of arguments from these things that God has made, and Kant's dismissal of the arguments is well-known. But it is possible also to see these things which God has made as media through which we know God, and so to entertain a theory of the non-inferential, mediated knowledge of God. A case for this kind of religious epistemology has been made by E. L. Mascall (*Words and Images*, Chapter 2 and in his later Gifford Lectures given in Edinburgh University, *The Openness of Being*, pp.98ff) that what we observe by sense is not the *objectum quod*, but the *objectum quo*, 'through which and in which the intellect grasps, in a direct but mediated activity, the intelligible extra-mental reality, which is the *being*, the real thing. It is this latter, intelligible being which is the *objectum quod*' (*op. cit.*, p.99). Because of the interpretative relationship which obtains between the *objectum quo* and the *objectum quod*, some consideration for the part played by imagination along the lines proposed by Kant would be helpful in expounding such a theory.

Secondly, within a rather different tradition, a strong claim is made that God is not known in himself, in his naked majesty if the phrase may be allowed; rather does he make himself known in and through the process of revelation. By definition such revelation takes place in the space-time world of ordinary experience; in fact, it occurs within ordinary experience to such a degree that the greatest expositor of this view, Karl Barth, suggests that the deep involvement of revelation in the ordinariness of human experience totally prevents it from being revelation of God for some people. Once again, because the knowledge of God occurs within the context of empirical situations, imagination is not to be excluded from our epistemological analysis. Indeed, because of the interpretative element in these situations, it could be claimed that it is all the more necessary to acknowledge the possible place of imagination in the knowing process. Thirdly, and as an extension of the previous point, if we accept something of what Oscar Cullmann intended by his saying that 'All Christian theology in its innermost essence is Biblical history' (*Christ and Time*, SCM Press, London. 1952. p.23), then we have to take account of the place which imagination has been assigned by a number of writers, such as, variously, Hume, George MacDonald and R.G.Collingwood, within historical knowledge, as being relevant to our religious epistemological investigation. Here, it would be wrong to be discouraged by the relatively scarce amount of philosophical enquiry into the nature of historical knowledge prior to the last three decades or so. It is a subject of immense importance to theology, as the long-standing controversy over faith and history has indicated. But equally, a study of the place of imagination in religious historical knowledge may have something to contribute to the general epistemological discussion. Fourthly, as has been mentioned above, there can be no question of the introduction of imagination into the analysis of our knowledge of God, if we remain within the limits which Kant set himself in the *Critique of Pure Reason*: the Ideas of Reason, God, freedom and immortality are regulative ideas, and in no way constitutive of the realities which they designate. Even in the *Critique of Practical Reason*, where as Professor Walsh shows (*op. cit.*, pp.229ff) the practical reason is obliged to affirm the existence of the objects of the Ideas of pure reason both for the possibility and the actual achievement of its own objective, namely, the highest good, such affirmation is not to be taken as an addition to the sum total of speculative or metaphysical knowledge. In paraphrase, 'I must not say that *it is* morally certain that there is a God, but only that *I am* morally certain' (ibid., p.239) What Kant is speaking of is belief in God which is a matter of personal conviction, and not a piece of communicable scientific knowledge. There are, however, assumptions made by Kant which we may not feel obliged to accept; for example, his premise that the concept of God is a regulative idea, which makes it impossible for him ever thereafter to recover the possibility of its being constitutive also; his norm of knowledge as being scientific, with its implication that our knowledge of God has to conform to that norm or be downgraded; his consequent failure to recognise that in the religious context, and even using Kant's terminology, it is no embarrassment to be speaking of belief rather than knowledge (though it is a convention that I do not intend to follow in this essay); and finally, the expectation that even if we did achieve such knowledge that God exists, the communication of it is a relatively simple additional step—an expectation which theologians have never dared to entertain with any confidence since Kierkegaard posed the problem of how the subjective thinker can communicate the truth which is subjectivity. Few if any of these assumptions would now be acceptable to theologians who see Kant's postulated limits of knowledge as ruling out the possibility of religious knowledge *a priori*, and who can see in Kant's wrestling with the idea of God in the context of moral action an indication of his own attempts to break through these limits. The rejection of these assumptions does not of itself substantiate the opposite propositions. But what we would want to claim is that the way is open to consider what is involved, for the understanding of our knowledge of God, in the worship of God, in active obedience to God in the practicalities of Christian living, and in the range of our emotional responses to God, all of which practices make sense only on the basis of the actual existence of God.

3. In fact, the relevance of Kant's method in his so-called transcendental philosophy to such a theological procedure is not without its importance. Given that the human mind appears to apprehend a world of independently and continuously existing objects related to one another in a variety of different ways, notably causal, what are the conditions of the possibility and actuality of such knowledge? Or, given that the moral agent is aware of the categorical imperative, what conditions must be affirmed if that moral obligation is to be fully explained and sustained? So I would see it as no illegitimate or unfair application of this same method to the subject-matter of religion to ask similar questions which in this case would relate to conditions of the possibility of certain people speaking of a God who for them has an independent and continuous existence, speaking to such a God in prayer and worship, and generally living their lives in the context of the reality of that God's being. It is in no way an attempt to structure some kind of inferential argument to God's existence on the basis of the religious or mystical experience of some people. Nor is it in any way invalidated as a method by the fact that some people can not lay claim to the kind of experience concerned, any more than it would be right to say that Kant's argument in *Second Critique* is stultified by the existence of amoral people who disclaim awareness of moral responsibility. Though it may sound as if we are making a virtue of necessity, I am inclined to think that is the only method upon which we can proceed in the analysis of religious experience. It would be idle to speculate upon some demonstration of divine existence which would carry as much conviction to the unbeliever as to the believer, or to hope to formulate a theory of religious language which met the criteria of non-religious verificationism, or to ignore the significance of the 'personal co-efficient' particularly in religious knowledge, when it is now being widely acknowledged as present in all knowledge. The purpose of this method is not to set theology 'six feet above contradiction' as proclamation

NEW HELP FROM KANT

from the pulpit is sometimes said to be. The religious experience is obviously open to other interpretations; the possibility of its occurrence, even in the forms specified by religionists themselves, may be described in other terms by its detractors; and religious language still remains human language, so that it is exposed to alternative semantic treatment, in which it may even be refuted. So a theological method based upon Kant's transcendental method is not an esoteric enquiry safe from criticism or attack, any more than Kant's use of the method provided him with immunity from denigrators or objectors. But equally the method is not apologetic, or designed to answer likely refutations of the validity of the religious experience and of its expression.

4. Turning now to some of the detail of Kant's account of the imagination, I should like to select, to begin with, his view that the imagination produces images that belong to a concept by following a procedure which Kant has called the schema. This activity of the imagination is interesting for a number of reasons. For example, it is a creative and a spontaneous activity of the imagination, in which it is distinguished from the senses which are passive. In its proliferation of images, it is controlled by the concept which it is schematising. That point is of considerable importance, in that it shows that the creative activity of the imagination, just mentioned, is not totally uninhibited. It has to follow rules prescribed by the concept, insofar as the images which it proliferates are rightly seen to be images of *that* concept and of no other. In other words the imagination is not free to fantasise; it is creative but it is so within specific limits. Further, the proliferation of the images by means of the schema serves the definitely epistemological purpose of making possible the identification and the description of an object in the external world. In this connection, it will be recalled that earlier we had a discussion concerning those concepts which are in fact categories of the understanding, which yield schemata for the imagination but not images; whereas the empirical concepts do provide images when the imagination follows the procedure of the appropriate schema. While Kant seems to suggest that we come by these empirical concepts through the activity of the reproductive imagination (somewhat in the manner in which Hume had said we achieve 'abstract concepts'), what is not clear is how the imagination could ensure recognition of an object on 'a first sighting' if it had no schema from which to produce the necessary image for identification. The answer may just lie in the suggestion that the understanding is in possession of the bare concept, which would be something like a definition. Only when apprised of the fact that the object presented is an instance of the concept, can the imagination embark on the schematising procedure which will lead to future occasions of recognition. The point that I am really after is that the understanding would appear to have access to so-called empirical concepts other than through the senses, and the

process of reproductive imagination; and it is a matter to which we shall return after considering the light that Kant's account of schematism throws upon a very important theological subject, namely, the nature of the parables of Jesus.

The parable as used by Jesus has been described by C. H. Dodd (*The Parables of the Kingdom*, London. 1934. p.16, quoted by Sallie McFague, *A New Dictionary of Christian Theology*, ed. Alan Richardson and John Bowden, 1983. p.425) in these terms: 'At its simplest the parable is a metaphor or simile drawn from nature or common life, arresting the hearer by its vividness or strangeness, and leaving the mind in sufficient doubt about its precise application to tease the mind into active thought' . . . 'and the imagination into participatory thinking'. The characteristics of parables are thus delineated for us by Sallie McFague: mundanity, for they employ descriptions of ordinary occasions and things; extravagance, for they embody polarisations and tensions between persons and groups; and indirection, in that their 'message' is not given literally but by means of the story. What might be added to this description is an observation which arises from Kant's account of the schema created by the imagination. For what we have in the parables is an activity of that very sort, and the imagination which Dodd requires for participatory thinking about the meaning of the parable is present at an earlier stage in its formulation in the mind of Jesus. Parabolic thinking could then be said to be a procedure which Jesus follows for the imaginative proliferation of images which represent a certain concept. In concrete terms, since the majority of the parables are parables of the Kingdom, the Kingdom is the concept which the imagination of Jesus relates to the idiosyncrasy of the detailed existence of his hearers, through a series of images, or extended images in the form of stories or briefer episodes, which are commonly called 'the parables'. The concept, the Kingdom, moreover, is to be understood and responded to, in terms of the several parables, and is not some universal epigram to be extracted logically from comparison of the parables. The Kingdom is, as it were, bodied forth in the parable, and encountered there by the listener, and it is not to be sought in some idea lying back of the parable or the series of parables. This construction is, I believe, borne out by the way in which Jesus extends his parables of the Kingdom across a whole spectrum of images—a man who sowed seed in different kinds of grounds with consequent varied results, a man who sowed good seed in a field in which his enemy subsequently sowed tares, a grain of mustard seed tiny in its beginnings but enormous in maturity, leaven working in a lump, a treasure hidden in a field, a merchant man seeking goodly pearls, a net gathering all kinds of fish in the catch, a king pardoning servants who owe him different sums of money, a king who invites guests to his son's wedding and their reactions to his invitations, the ten virgins with their lamps awaiting the arrival of the bridegroom, the king about to go on a journey to a foreign country, who entrusts varying sums of money to his servants until his return, and so on. The message of the parable in each case is what it has to say for the hearer as he applies it to his own existence, and not some theologoumenon, an eschatology, extracted from it, or from the series.

So central was the parable to Jesus' teaching method, and so unique was it to him in the form in which he practised it, that we may be justified in finding in it a clue to the way in which religious thought and expression operate. It is not new to see the parable as *the* form of religious language but in the past it has tended to be reduced to a form of analogy, with strong emphases upon the bases of comparison, and upon the positive and the negative analogies. What I am thinking of, rather, is the way in which the parabolic imagination proliferates the images in series, always under the control and prescription of the religious concept. It would not be unreasonable to interpret Ian Ramsey's widely popularised theme of models and qualifiers (*Religious Language*, SCM Press, London, 1957, pp.49ff), to regard the model as the concept which Kant has located in the understanding, and the qualifiers as the series of images which the imagination deploys, always in relation to and under the control of the model, but always proportioning it to the particularity and the peculiarity, what Ian Ramsey called 'the oddness', of the religious situation. As the imagination deploys these images, instantiating the model as it is limited by the religious situation, the intention is that thus disclosure will be achieved, and despite its 'odd logical placing' the idea of 'God' will come to have content and significance, as will the statements made by religious people, in which his being and actions are described. The discernment evoked as Ramsey himself says (*op. cit.*, p.46) through, for example, the telling of stories, leads to the act of total commitment 'when the penny drops'. Indeed, the procedure which Ramsey describes answers very closely to the technique employed by Jesus in his parabolic teaching and both, as has been suggested, may be construed in terms of something akin to Kant's schematism of the imagination, and both understood as forms of imaginative activity in a religious context, helpful at once in identifying and in describing the religious subject.

5. There is one description which Kant gives of the activity of the imagination which could prove of considerable help in the understanding of theological method. It is his account of the way in which the imagination synthesises the manifold of the intuitions. As will be recalled, Kant regards this synthetic unity of the imagination to be interdependent upon the unity of apperception, and I should like to explore one possible theological transcript of this relationship. On the one hand, there is a sense in which faith in one of its aspects could be

regarded as a religious unity of apperception. Admittedly, there is more to faith than that. It involves an explicit commitment to Jesus Christ, expressed in a specific and identifiable way of life, in an attitude of love and compassion to one's fellows and in obedience to the will of God. But these expressions of the faith, and the perceptions which the believer has of the world in which he lives and acts, are not single and isolated occurrences, passing in series through the consciousness. They have a unity in the consciousness of the believer, which is not just the unity of their empirical co-existence, but a unity which is conditioned *a priori* by faith, which in this connection fulfils a transcendental rôle in Kant's quite special use of that term. There is a judgement of St Paul's which illustrates this point, 'We know that all things work together for good to them that love God' (Romans, 8.28a). St Paul is not, I believe, there affirming that all the events that happen to the Christian somehow arrange themselves in a series which can clearly be designated as good in the sense that they are all positively advantageous and pleasurable in themselves, nothing of a contrary nature befalling him. Rather, is St Paul's meaning that faith, of which love for God is the expression, is the unifying condition of an overview of these events which construes them as being 'for good', even though some of them may have characteristics which on another reckoning would have to be regarded as evil. In Kant's terms faith is the transcendental unity of the apperception, while the unified overview would answer to his empirical unity of apperception.

But it is the unity of the manifold which derives from imagination that concerns us more particularly, and without adhering to the Kantian paradigm too closely, but using it rather as a guide-line and an indicator, I should like to explore ways in which the synthesising capacity of imagination so central to Kant's view, can be traced in biblical and dogmatic theology. One immediate starting-point is the theological construction of the presentation of the person of Christ, or of what is known in theology as his 'work', that is, his death. George MacDonald (*A Dish of Orts*, Essay 'The Imagination: Its Functions and Its Culture') wrote, 'Nowhere can the imagination be more healthily and rewardingly occupied than in endeavouring to construct the life of an individual out of the fragments which are all that reach us out of the history of even the noblest of our race. How this will apply to the reading of the gospel story we leave to the earnest thought of our readers'. Earlier in this same essay MacDonald had been speaking of the fact that it is 'when we turn to history (that) we find probably the greatest objective sphere of the intellectuo-constructive imagination.' This synthesising, intellectuo-constructive operation is carried out largely, if not altogether entirely, through the use by the imagination of what Professor Walsh calls 'colligatory concepts', a theme which he develops over the years after his adoption of it in 1958 in the course of his *Introduction to the Philosophy of History*, which he likens to the 'concrete universal' of Idealistic logic. The fragments of accounts of Jesus' actions and words, to which MacDonald referred, are synthesised and interpreted, through the application to them of a colligatory concept; and the history of Christology abounds in these. For example, one of the original concepts of this sort was that of the 'Messiah' which co-ordinated the material through the use of passages from the Old Testament, as well. The different actions and sayings of Jesus then find an integrated place within the concept, which in its turn develops ever increasing range and depth as the interpretation proceeds. It may be worth mentioning that this kind of concept differs from those mentioned above, the empirical concepts, in that the latter are plainly what would be called abstract universals, being instantiated in the cases subsumed under them, whereas the concrete universal, or colligatory concept, is single and unitary. Another such concept would be that of the 'teacher' with an emphasis upon the unique character and content of Jesus' teaching (cf. W. A. Curtis, *Jesus the Teacher*). The nineteenth century abounded in presentations of Jesus as the 'hero', while the second half of the twentieth has not been slow to follow with the equally popular concept of the 'revolutionary'. The point is fairly obvious and need not be laboured. Nor is the colligatory concept technique confined to biblical theology; it can be discovered in most systematic theology; for instance, in the employment by Karl Barth of the concept of 'the Word', which may be written, revealed, incarnate, proclaimed, bodied forth in sacrament, listened to, and obeyed; in Bultmann's preference for Heidegger's notion of *Existenz*, which becomes then a grouping for the parables, the miracles, the sayings, the mission, death and resurrection of Jesus, as well as the faith of the believer and the rôle of the Church; or farther back in time, the concept of 'dependence' in Schleiermacher, of 'value' in Ritschl, or of 'covenant' in the so-called federal theologians.

The characteristics of this synthesising activity of the imagination will repay examination. First, it should be clear that the choice of an appropriate colligatory concept presupposes a very thorough knowledge of the 'manifold' to which it is to be applied. There is no likelihood of 'beginner's luck' with its assumption of ignorance of the field. This kind of choice arises out of experience of concepts which have been acceptable to others, and an ability to judge where they may have proved inadequate, and are no longer acceptable. Secondly, the progression from the 'manifold' to the colligatory concept can not be said to be one of orderly logical progression, however much one would want it to be so. The method of proving its validity subsequently may, in very many cases, involve just such a process of logical deduction or inference, or still more probably hypothetico-deduction, with some kind of experimentation and verification thrown in for good measure.

But the choice of the concept in the first instance is more properly described as the *leap* of imagination, requiring its own qualities of insight, perception, creativity and originality. Thirdly, the success of the choice of the colligatory concept will be judged not only by its capacity to synthesise the 'manifold' here and now but also by the range of its extensibility into new and at present unpredictable occasions. In this respect, the colligatory concept will function somewhat as did Kant's schema, which it will be recalled was a procedure for proliferating images. The successful concept will provide the medium for the interpretation of other situations beyond that for which it was originally intended. The *unio hypostatica* of the Chalcedonian Creed has fulfilled this kind of rôle to a pre-eminent degree; having been devised originally for the definition of the relation of the two natures in Jesus Christ, it was extended beyond that base to describe the relationship of human and divine in the Bible, and the Church, and, with modifications, to the relation of the creature to the Redeemer in the Eucharist. C. H. Dodd, with his concept of 'realised eschatology', drew the doctrine of eschatology out from its confines in the Last Things to be applied across the whole gamut of the life and teaching of Jesus Christ.

There is another aspect of the synthesising activity of the imagination acting in a religious capacity in relation to the manifold which in a sense answers to the notion of faith serving as the transcendental unity of apperception. It is the unity which is produced in the manifold through the penetration of it by concepts of religion introduced by the imagination. For the religious imagination, the world in all its complexity consists of God's creatures, set within definable orders of creation, and governed by laws of providence; creatures who come under the influence of the redemptive power of God and whose lives are radically affected by such an influence; creatures whose relations to one another are normatively controlled by the commandments of that God; and so on. In Christian terms, such is the character of the objective world, the only real world the Christian knows. That claim which is central to this kind of method starts and ends with the acceptance of the objectivity of what is known and looks for subjectivity in the knowing mind; and the essence of the method is to explore the conditions of the possibility and the actuality of the knowledge which so exists.

Mention of the synthesis of the manifold of intuition of course stirs echoes of the notion of the 'finality' or 'purposiveness of nature' which is so important in the *Critique of Judgement*. Kant in that *Critique*, it will be recalled, did not regard this finality as something imposed upon nature by any external agent. It was in the first instance to be regarded as a regulative principle governing the mind's exploration of nature. In the event, however, the expectation was justified, and certain principles, hypotheses and structures were found to be operative within nature again without any implication of a prior designing mind or a divine Creator. Faith in the exploration of its manifold is governed by a not entirely dissimilar concept of finality, the chief and acknowledged difference being that faith has something positive to say about the source of the purposiveness. The reference to the *Critique of Judgement*, however, is intended to draw attention to two other points. First, in this *Critique* Kant emphasises the spontaneity and the creativity of imagination in its action of formulating reflective judgements, as opposed to the way in which, according to the *Critique of Pure Reason*, it is controlled in its activities by the limiting rules of the categories and concepts, even when the latter are empirical. Yet even though the principle of the finality of nature, in respect of the analysis of the natural world, and the principle of finality without purpose in the making of aesthetic judgements, may seem to regulate the imagination in these two areas, the imagination is not thought thereby to be diminished in spontaneity or creativity. On the contrary, the imagination with this freedom is able to establish results which could never have been reached had it been confined to the limits set for it in the *Critique of Pure Reason*. A strong case can be made for allowing imagination that same sort of charter for creativity and spontaneity in the field of religion, in its analysis of the world and of history, of human personality, and supremely in its reading of the life, person and work of Jesus Christ. We would have to remember that Kant recognises in the *Critique of Judgement* that imagination does operate within the over-all regulation of the principles he mentions; and acknowledge comparable limits in such concepts as, say, the providence of God, or the love of God. In fact, perhaps the situation would be more accurately described in another way, thus. For Kant, in the *Critique of Judgement*, the two principles named in the two parts of that *Critique*, namely, the finality of nature, and finality without purpose, are not so much limits to the operation of the imagination, as the inspiration of its creativity and spontaneity; so, comparably in the religious field, the imagination derives its stimulus to creativity and spontaneity from its understanding of these two concepts which I have mentioned, and these are only a selection from a longer list. Indeed, if creativity is to be regarded as essential to God's being, and in all the defections which we have witnessed in recent years from long-established doctrines, that attribute of God has not been denied, then creativity and spontaneity are the very qualities that we would look for in a mind exploring that God's creation, in nature, history and human personalities.

The second point to be noted in consequence of the references to the *Critique of Judgement* is the importance for religion of Kant's contention that the aesthetic judgement claims universal validity, while being based upon the person's feeling towards the object judged to be beautiful. Eva Schaper, in concluding one part of her singularly well-argued and in many ways original analysis of Kant's aesthetic (*Studies in Kant's Aesthetics*) makes a convincing case for the view that while Kant insists that aesthetic judgements are non-cognitive in character, they must not therefore be thought not to be about objects. 'It is just that in appraising the object aesthetically we make no *epistemological* claim' (*op. cit.*, 52).

While Professor Schaper seems here to be reflecting accurately what Kant intends, the question has to be asked whether Kant himself does full justice to his own position. Aesthetic judgements *qua* aesthetic may be making no epistemological *claim*. Agreed: but first they do presuppose a cognitive relationship between the experient and the aesthetic object, for they 'must not be thought not to be about objects', objects cognised as possessing certain other perceived characteristics. Secondly, the aesthetic perception, while based upon feelings which claim universal validity, relates to qualities of objects, which are thereby differentiated from other objects which do not possess them.

Thirdly, it is illogical not to follow through with this line of argument and conclude that aesthetic judgements in so far as they are describable as judgements must carry an epistemological reference to the objects they categorise, and it is an epistemological reference of this kind which is known as aesthetic.

A good deal of religious discourse contains references to attitudes, feelings and a wide range of other subjective states. So much is this so that Schleiermacher could construct a comprehensive dogmatic around the notion of 'the feeling of dependence'; and more recently Christian Existentialism, drawing upon Kierkegaard's theorem that 'subjectivity is truth', has had much to say about the importance of personal decision, and about the necessity to appropriate religious truth subjectively if it is to be understood, and more so, if it is to lead to salvation and to discipleship. In this, as it might be called, 'subjectivist drift', what Schaper says about Kant and aesthetic judgements is helpful. First, the fact that there is almost excessive emphasis upon the subjective component in religious statements, according to some modern theologians, does not exclude the claim that they refer to an object, or as the believer would say, to a Subject. By putting the matter in these terms, we avoid both the suggestion that a religious statement is a flat statement of fact, and the equally unacceptable reduction of religious statements to accounts of subjective feelings. Secondly, such is the Subject to whom reference is thus made, the Subject in relation to whom the imagination proliferates its images in spontaneous free-play, that these images, and the feelings and attitudes that accompany them command universal recognition and validity. Kant had said in respect of aesthetic judgements that while we may not expect everyone to share these feelings and adopt these attitudes, we judge that they ought to. That is where aesthetic judgements differ from accounts of what is agreeable to us. It is an indication, too, that such judgements involve the 'cognitive faculties' (*Critique of Judgement*, p.60) and 'accord with conditions of universality'. Such is the experience of the religious Subject that, on the one hand, such experience carries with it a reference to a cognised object; and yet, on the other hand, since it is the religious Subject to whom we refer, the feelings we have towards him, and the relations in which we stand to him, while essentially personal, as personal as love, trust and obedience, are nevertheless not peculiar to the experient or the believer, but are universalisable and applicable to all men and women in that they are the creatures of that Subject.

In conclusion, if I were to sum up the contribution which Kant by his own exposition and extensive use of the concept of imagination throughout his philosophy, makes to the understanding of the way in which it might be employed in theology, I would concentrate on two points. First, he establishes the credibility of the role which imagination may be thought to play in the epistemological situation, and in aesthetic appraisal. That analysis, as I have tried to show, has very important consequences for theology. Too often in the past has imagination been equated with fancy and fantasy, and so has been construed as the medium which religion employs to fabricate its illusions, and to distance its practitioners farther and farther from reality. Admittedly Kant had himself appeared to be entirely agnostic about the true nature of the imagination, saying of it that it is 'an art concealed in the depths of the human soul' (*Critique of Pure Reason*, p.183), but earlier, while remaining agnostic, nevertheless recognising its tremendous importance, thus, as 'a blind but indispensable function of the soul, without which we would have no knowledge whatsoever, but of which we are scarcely ever conscious' (ibid., p.112). While Kant seems here to be differing in his claims for imagination, his whole presentation of the case for acknowledging the rôle of imagination in epistemology is systematic and thorough., Professor Walsh has put the matter in this way: '(Imagination) is certainly a fundamental human ability, without which thought would be useless, or at least would have no grip on the world' (*op. cit.*, p.73). Kantian epistemology has exercised considerable influence upon the analysis of the nature of religious knowledge over the past two hundred years, and little place has been given to imagination in that analysis. Now that the reasons for such neglect have been exorcised, the way is open for the enrichment of our understanding of the nature of religion and theology, and of the kind of knowledge involved in both, through the admission of the place that imagination perhaps already occupies in all of them.

Secondly, in the works which have been considered in this study, Kant affirms, by implication, that imagination is one in all the very varied parts which he assigns to it, both in ordinary perception and in aesthetic appraisal. That assimilation would be in line with his general contention that it is 'a fundamental human activity'. It is by no means unusual, in philosophy of mind, to employ the same term to cover a wide range of mental activities, such as, for example, understanding, reason, experience or will. Mary Warnock, who in her book *Imagination* (Faber. 1976) gives us a comprehensive account of the many ways in the course of the history of philosophy, in which the term imagination has been used, and of the many situations to which it has been applied, nevertheless, in her conclusion, comes out strongly in support of the thesis that imagination is one as found in our perception of the world around us, in the meanings we discern in objects before us, diagrams, pictures, music, imagery or artistic creations. That discernment of meaning, which is directly in line with Kant's understanding of the way in which we know the world, is an essential feature of religious faith. For it seeks such meanings, not only in the world about us, in nature and history, but also in the lives of other people and their relationships to us and to one another, in valuational systems and moral behaviour; particularly in the records of the activities of God in the world, in human lives and supremely in the life, death and resurrection of Jesus Christ. To continue to exclude imagination from our epistemological analysis of the way in which such determination of meanings takes place is *a priori* to ensure the deficiency of such analysis. To include imagination is to begin to make good some of the most serious inadequacies which the theory of religious knowledge has evinced over many years.

THE PHILOSOPHICAL PART

« 6 »

A. D. NUTTALL : ADAM'S DREAM
AND MADELINE'S

On November 22, 1817, Keats wrote[1] to his stiff, clerical friend Benjamin Bailey. Bailey, it seems, was upset. The painter Haydon had offended him in some way and Keats, in a turbulent overflow of good feeling and excited speculation, sought, so to speak, to set his friend on his legs again. Haydon is one of the few private citizens in relatively recent history to consider putting up a plaque to his own glory.[2] His thoughts ran naturally and easily on his own genius and Keats was content to run alongside. Accordingly Keats' reassurance of Bailey turns without warning from ordinary comfort to a disquisition on genius. There is a kind of argument in this part of the letter: one cannot be offended by defects of character in a genius since it is the essence of artistic genius to have no character at all, to be open to all influences, all colours. Although Keats may well have taken his cue from the grandiose self-description of Haydon, this brief, anticipatory sketch of what is to become in other letters[3] the theory of Negative Capability really has little to do with Haydon and much with Shakespeare. It has still more to do, perhaps, with Keats' sense of his own amoral latitude of imaginative sympathy. But here Bailey, it seems, had Doubts (like Prendergast): is not the imagination, so far from being inaccessible to moral censure, an inauthentic thing, indeed a source of lies and self-deception? In response to these doubts Keats, generously anxious to share his joy with Bailey, redoubles his pace:

> O I wish I was certain of the end of all your troubles as that of your momentary start about the authenticity of the Imagination. I am certain of nothing but of the holiness of the Heart's affections and the Truth of Imagination—What Imagination seizes as Beauty must be truth—whether it existed before or not—for I have the same Idea of all our Passions as of Love they are all in their sublime, creative of essential Beauty—In a Word, you may know my favourite Speculation by my first Book and the little song I sent in my last—which is a representation from the fancy of the probable mode of operating in these Matters—The Imagination may be compared to Adam's dream—he awoke and found it truth. I am the more zealous in this affair because I have never yet been able to perceive how anything can be known for truth by consequitive reasoning—and yet it must be—Can it be that even

the greatest philosopher ever [when] arrived at his goal without putting aside numerous objections—However it may be, O for a Life of Sensations rather than Thoughts.[4]

Here Keats philosophises. The movement of his mind is hyperbolical, elliptical, hesitant, incoherent, but it is real philosophy. The philosophising of Keats (unlike that of Coleridge, say) is all home-made, cobbled together in the back yard of his mind. Where Coleridge cocooned his thought in self-protective tissues of learning, ancient and modish, Keats had neither time nor natural aptitude for such stratagems.

His first—thoroughly endearing—indiscretion is to protest too much. Just as the phrase, 'As a matter of fact', is commonly used to introduce a lie, so people say 'I am certain of nothing but . . .' when they are not, in fact, quite certain or when, as here, they are by an act of will substituting the certainty of faith for the ordinary certainty of rational conviction. But Keats' level of self-awareness is high. He is conscious of the apparent wildness of his thought and seeks to strengthen his position by getting behind the usual structures of rationality. And what he produces is in fact highly challenging: a sort of 'innocent eye' empiricism, utterly unlike the artificially reduced empiricism of the scientific revolution. His thought runs like this: what the imagination seizes as beauty must be truth even if the thing it seizes never existed before the act of seizure; for the passions create actual beauty; one awakes with a start and realises that the imagination is not a mere web of illusions but on the contrary provides the primary material of knowledge; meanwhile mere chains of deductive reasoning of themselves tell us nothing—they are as strong or as weak as their premises, and those premises are not themselves rational sequences.

The story of empiricism—the philosophy which says that all our knowledge must arise from experience—is a curious one. Empiricism is associated in England with the rise of science. But the scientists found that they could not work without certain pre-empirical restrictions on the matter of their enquiry. Controlled experiments are more informative than uncontrolled experiments. Bacon, early in the seventeenth century, had urged scientists to let the rain come in, to let the wind blow through the laboratory, since to do otherwise was to 'rig' the experiment, to point it towards a pre-selected result. But the scientists wanted specific answers to specific questions and therefore sought to exclude irrelevant variables. As their methods sharpened it became increasingly clear that science was not the child of experience alone, but of experience and mathematics (the English tradition of Locke infiltrated by the French tradition of Descartes). The mathematical imperative was to exclude all that is not exactly quantifiable or measurable and the impact of this imperative is nowhere so evident as in the strange doctrine of Primary and Secondary Qualities. According to this doctrine length, breadth and weight are real qualities of objects as they actually exist, whereas sounds, tastes, smells and colours are not. These were termed secondary qualities and were commonly understood to exist only in the mind of the perceiver (who, notice, becomes forthwith the inventor rather than the perceiver of such qualities). If no other living thing existed a rose would be as broad, as long and as heavy as it is, but, until someone or something with a nose comes along, it has no fragrance.

The doctrine is prominent (with certain curious hesitations) in Locke's great work,[5] but before the *Essay concerning Human Understanding* it had already crept into the consciousness of the age. Look, for example, at Galileo's *Il Saggiatore* of 1623.[6] Taken strictly, the doctrine scarcely licenses the inference that colours and smells are entirely subjective to the perceiver: the rose must be *such* that it affects the nose as fragrant rather than foul, *such* that it strikes the eye as red not blue, which is as much as to say that the Secondary Qualities may, at a microscopic level, prove to be *bene fundatae* in the Primary and hence, after all, a characteristic of the objective world. But most people were not so careful in their inferences. The measurable world alone was real and the world of colours, sounds and smells was abruptly crowded into tiny cells of illusion, within the human skull. Experiment and Experience, though etymologically cognate, shudder and move austerely apart. But meanwhile the flag of empiricism still flies over the fortress of science. Here we reach the heart of the paradox. For experience is made of Secondary Qualities, Poets had always been the experts on experience in this simple, fundamental sense of the word: on the way the world looks, feels, tastes, smells, sounds. And all this stood condemned—in the name of empiricism!

The story of English Romanticism is largely the story of the artists' reaction—in part hysterical, in part cogently destructive—to this intolerable reduction of experience. The reaction was indeed violent, but it scarcely occurred to any of the Romantics to re-capture the flag. Instead of offering real Experience to counter the artificially gutted Experience of the natural philosophers, they marshalled under the flag of Imagination, a word whose central reference is to the fiction of images, implying, therefore, a submission, before the battle has ever begun, to the arrogantly dismissive truth-claims of the opposition. Blake wrote,

> The atoms of Democritus
> And Newton's particles of light
> Are sands upon the Red Sea shore
> Where Israel's tents do shine so bright[7]

The scientist who felt himself momentarily threatened by these lines could recover as soon as he remembered the word 'imagination'; 'Ah', he might say with an indulgent smile, 'you are *imagining* this?' and he would turn again to his experiment.

Keats in the face of this challenge is a degree more radical than most Romantics. Note that, if colour and sound are Secondary, beauty must be *a fortiori* still more Secondary, or perhaps we need to say Tertiary. There are similar 'tough-minded' implications for ethics. But beauty certainly figures in real experience, fused with colour and fragrance. If one is a genuine empiricist that first experience has absolute authority. It is what we are given before we think, that without which we cannot think and therefore it is mere idiocy to attempt to encroach upon this primary gift with posterior distinctions of reason.

But like the other Romantics Keats speaks not only of sensation but also (and more prominently) of imagination. The ordinary distinction between the two, as long as it survives, is potentially embarrassing to his theory, but it may be that this commonplace contrast ('Sensation is of real objects, imagination of unreal') can be blurred or removed altogether if one's empiricism is radical enough. Unjudging, with a wise passiveness, the mind simply welcomes whatever is presented to it. Here Keats can almost touch hands with Hume; in the first part of the *Treatise* Hume refused to ground the difference between mental images and perceptions in the fact that the objects of perception are real while the objects of imagination are unreal. To make external reality a criterion in this way is to step outside experience, and that the good empiricist can never do. Accordingly Hume distinguished perceptions as having a greater *vivacity*. The mind of the reader can respond to this in two ways: either it will be acknowledged that reality has been simply surrendered, 'reduced out' and an implicitly solipsistic scheme substituted, or else it may be inferred that in some way mere vivacity can now guarantee reality in the old full-blooded sense of the term. But if more or less vivacity is the mark of a greater or lesser degree of reality it is now open to the Romantic to argue, on Hume's own ground, 'Since *my* images are more vivacious than my percepts, their title to reality is, in a manner, incontestable'. Keats' word for 'vivacity' is 'intensity'.

We are now in a position to see why it is that commentators on Keats often hesitate over the question whether his observations about beauty, imagination and sensation are to be referred to the world of subjective images or to the perceived world. To the radical, psychologising empiricist this distinction simply ceases to be important; the barriers between the two are dismantled, the passport office stands un-manned. The presentations are of varying intensity and that is all. In the most radical versions of the theory there is finally no implication even of subjectivism or solipsism, since the ego is as much a secondary construction as is the causally governed 'external world' of the scientist.

But Keats, as we have seen, stays with the *term* 'imagination', and as long as the term is used the implication of subjective fiction is not quite dead. 'Imaginary' and 'real' are natural opposites. The Romantics, most notably Coleridge, strove to abolish this opposition by making the imagination an organ of perception (think what it would be like explaining that to Dr Johnson). The fact, increasingly evident to nineteenth-century thinkers, that all perception involves an element of interpretation, that we bring to the act of perception certain expectant schemata which can be satisfied or disconfirmed by the real, seems, in part at least, to have been picked up by Coleridge. Here indeed, is a place where, perhaps, the imagination may be enlisted as an organ of truth. Bacon's dream that we can 'put our notions by' and proceed directly, without expectation or hypothesis, to 'the things themselves' is a philosophical nonsense. We operate through certain schemata of expectation which are corroborated or disconfirmed in specific experience. Some great figures in the history of mimetic realism work by re-activating schemata of expectation in the viewer. As we begin to look at a face painted by Rembrandt, certain mechanisms of perception are set in motion with an added energy and the result is that Rembrandt makes the ordinary world (other-real-faces in the gallery) look different for a time. The picture gives, not an extension of our factual knowledge but rather a deepening of our hypothetical awareness of what a face can be like, together with a temporary sharpening of associated perceptions. The knowledge which is deepened is *connaissance* rather than *savoir*, *Erleben* rather than *Wissen*. Literary art meanwhile, with its larger command of the temporal dimension, can focus hard on probable *sequences*, and in this way the intent imaginings of a great realistic novelist can even come to resemble the 'Thought Experiment' of the scientist. At this point, Aristotle's classic theory of hypothetical mimesis (the poet tells us 'what kind of things would happen', *Poetics*, 1451a) can be joined to Coleridge's defence of the imagination as the living agent of all perception. We know via a prior sense, which may be more or less intense, of possibilities and likelihoods.

Yet certain discomforts remain. The art I have just described is that generally known as realistic. The Romantics placed little emphasis on such skills and were concerned rather to redeem ideal or wildly improbable art. Moreover, 'imagination' is perhaps a misleading term to apply to the formation of probable schemata of the kind that work in close harness with the specificities of experience. Hume indeed invoked imagination to shore up his disintegrating epistemology but that was entirely deliberate on his part. For him, the stable shapes composed by the mind are not tested against the real but rather complete and fill out the ragged and discontinuous data of the senses. Thus he invokes the imagination, precisely, as a *fictive* power and not as an organ of veridical knowledge. In the last resort, says Hume, we *feign* the existence of ordinary public objects.[8] He is certainly providing an account of what is normally called 'knowledge' but his account is violently reductive. He offers only a way of arguing that what we took to be knowledge is not really knowledge at all. The reader may be forgiven for suspecting that the only difference, at bottom, between the petrifically reductive Hume on the one hand and the sanguine, inflationary Coleridge on the other lies in the fact that Hume knew what he had done. Certainly Coleridge seems to have had no precise notion of the way a Gestalt is put to work in Gestalt psychology.

The sense of strain persists. Of course, if we change the *meaning* of the word 'imagination' so that it is the same as the meaning of 'perception', the novel proposition 'Imagination is an organ of perception' will soon collapse into the inert tautology, 'Perception is perception'. If, on the other hand, a genuine synthetic proposition is being offered—either 'Perception is partly imagination' or 'Imagination is involved with our perceptions', the fictive character of imagination is allowed to remain and the ghost remains unexorcised. Indeed for most people statements of the second type have the flavour of scepticism, suggest that the truth-claims of perception are less absolute than we thought. This inference is drawn (once more) because the primary meaning of the term perception (which is of the real) has been infiltrated by imagination (which is of the unreal).

In Keats' letter to Bailey, the sentence starting with the words, 'What the imagination seizes . . .' begins in heady confidence, but before it is over this confidence is flawed. The root meaning of 'imagination' has begun to assert itself. The word 'seizes' implies a thoroughly cognitive imagination, grasping that which is other than itself. The verb 'must' is the first signal of an area of acknowledged ignorance or doubt (think of the way a mathematician will say, 'This proof has got to be right'). The words 'whether it existed before or not' make the doubt manifest. That which is grasped or seized is there before it is grasped or seized. That which is imagined begins and ends with the act of imagining. But, to be sure, we are in the world of the radical empiricist and so is Keats, at least as long as he holds to the highest pitch of excitement. Bishop Berkeley wrote *Esse est percipi*,[9] 'To be is to be perceived', which effectively eliminates any *separate* object of perception transcending the act of perception itself. The tree in the quad lapses into unbeing as we turn our heads away, just as images fade within our minds. The notion is notoriously counter-intuitive. It affronts the usual sense of what is required or implied in our notion of reality. That it could nevertheless fascinate the Romantic intelligence is clear from the axiom declared in Shelley's *Defence of Poetry*: 'All things exist as they are perceived'.[10] Keats, less stridently confident than Shelley, half-acknowledges the element of Berkleian paradox in his thought, but then drives on. By implication, however, he has shifted the meaning of 'imagination'. We move from the cognitive to the fictive imagination with the words 'creative of' (already quite different from 'seizes').

Of course things made are no less real than natural things. Artefacts exist as securely as cows. For that matter, mental images qua images certainly exist (though some philosophers have tried to deny the fact). But the parenthesis, 'qua images', is all-important. No one in Keats' time doubted—not even the hardest of the scientists—that dreams exist, as dreams. What was denied by common sense was the substantial reality of their contents. Last night, perhaps, I really did dream that there was a rhinoceros in the library but no rhinoceros was in the library. The dream itself, as is the way of dreams, was an illusion. Here Keats may be resorting to philosophical sleight of hand, trusting that we will not notice the fluid transition from tenor to vehicle (or indeed perhaps not noticing it himself). Clearly the imagination may form images of beauty and these creations, qua creations, are to be added to the fabric of reality. It may also be that the regular forming of such images may alert our perceptive powers to the presence of beauty in the real surrounding world. But none of this makes the imagination itself an organ of truth. All we have gained is the real existence in the world of imagined beauty (as well as real beauty) which is exactly the account the hardest reductionist would give.

The story I have told so far is, however, much too confident and misses entirely the glancing, vital movement of Keats' mind. The word 'creative' may carry a larger burden than I have so far allowed. Keats is indeed beset by doubt but at the same time he senses that he has almost within his grasp an overwhelmingly simple answer. Let us try, then, to give a stronger sense to 'creative'. When the mind intuits beauty it does not merely grasp that which is coldly external to itself, nor does it pretend that something is the case; it gives full being, by a miracle, to the category of beauty which forthwith leaps up in the world. If we ask how this is to be distinguished from mere feigning, the answer may lie with the irreducible substance and character of beauty. It cannot be stitched together from strands of consecutive reasoning. Sensation, indeed, is more conceivable as supplying the material, but only as long as sensation is allowed to be informed by aesthetic passion, by the full diapason of *feeling* (another favourite word of Keats). The excitement of this passage is like the excitement which some have found in Anselm's celebrated Ontological Proof of the Existence of God—the excitement of watching something which appeared to be merely conceptual turning real before one's very eyes.

Anselm in the eleventh century argued that, if we allow that God must be greater than we can conceive, it follows that he exists.[11] An island which actually exists is better (richer, stronger) than an imagined island. But if God did not exist we could immediately suppose him made better by mentally attributing existence to him. But *ex hypothesi* he is better than we can imagine and so must already possess all the virtues which we might attribute to him. So he must already have existence; that is, he exists.

Anselm says that any denial of this consequence generates a contradiction:

> Even a fool, then, must be convinced that a being than which none greater can be thought exists at least in his understanding, since when he hears this he understands it, and whatever is understood is in the understanding. But clearly that than which a greater cannot be thought cannot exist in the understanding alone. For if it is actually in the understanding alone, it can be thought of as existing also in reality, and this is greater. Therefore if that than which a greater cannot be thought is in the understanding alone, this same thing than which a greater cannot be thought is that than which a greater can be thought. But obviously this is impossible. Without doubt, therefore, there exists, both in the understanding and in reality, something than which a greater cannot be thought.

To most people in the twentieth century Anselm's argument carries no conviction at all. It continues, however, to fascinate philosophers although refutations of it abound. Anselm urges us to see that in this one case a logical necessity must also be an ontological or practical necessity: 'God would not be thus great if he lacked existence: the definition of God requires the real, not notional existence of God'. Someone who refuses to accept the shift from one sort of necessity to the other mght well reply, 'You have shown that if God did exist, in order to conform to the definition he would have to exist; meanwhile the definition need refer to no existent'.

In so far as Anselm's notion of greatness seems to be associated with 'richness of being', it may seem to approximate to the 'vivacity' of Hume and the 'intensity' of Keats. But Anselm does not psychologise his conception; the greatness to which he refers is a power of objective existence rather than a measure of the impact on the perceiver. He is, however, entirely willing to turn existence into a predicate, and this is sufficiently odd. It is as if one were to say that although Hamlet is on the whole a better person than Hitler, Hitler beats Hamlet hollow with his score on existence, since poor Hamlet has only a shadowy, fictional degree of being. Indeed, it can almost be said that Anselm fetishised existence and so became master of exactly the right potent magic to heal the solipistic wound of the Romantics. On the one hand we have a generation which has been authoritatively instructed that its most valued experiences are merely subjective and on the other we have a new version of the philosopher's stone: a device for turning mere concepts into reality. Keats, in his proper darkness stretches out his hand towards the Anselmian solution.

The difference meanwhile for the psychologising Hume is crucial. Anselm's fetish is credited with miraculous redemptive powers. Hume could have nothing to do with this. With Keats, however, it is otherwise. For all his radical empiricism, he continues to hope for a miracle by which the old transconceptual, truly independent reality might be restored, which is as much as to say, he retains the old, unreduced conception of reality. Hume could not permit himself to be excited by the miracle of the image brightening into reality, since there is no longer a chasm to be crossed: he has revised the very notion of reality so that it is itself no more than an image presentation. The transformation envisaged by Keats would appear in Hume's redaction as merely a further increase in the vivacity of the image. Thus Keats makes use of radical empiricism just long enough to establish that intensity alone may constitute a primary claim to reality but the fervour with which he then pursues his thought is eloquent of his refusal to go all the way with the empiricist reduction of reality. He employs the hard-won primary equivalence of presentation to an inflationary rather than a reductive end. Instead of saying, 'So called percepts are no more real than images: all you *have* is a flux of ideas', he says 'images, no less than percepts, may be images of truth'. Instead of saying 'reality comes down to vivacity', he says 'It is sensation, not argument, which gives us substances; therefore the stronger the sensation the stronger the substantial reality; it must be so because that is what reality *is*'. In the last clause the analogy with Anselm's thought is striking: 'That is what the word "God" means'. In radical empiricism the notion of existence seems to be knitted into the notion of experience at a pre-philosophical level; for Anselm the notion of existence, not notional existence but real existence, is built into the idea of God. Each glimpses the chance of showing that his highest value (God for Anselm, the world of beauty for Keats) might after all be self-authenticating. For Hume all this would be futile mumbo-jumbo.

But Keats' air of triumph in securing an equivalence which for Hume would have been merely analytic shows, as I have suggested, that he regards full existence as entailing more than mere presence-to-the-mind. If we ask 'What more?' we shall find the old requirements of independence and stability (in contrast with the flickering character of 'merely mental' images). I suspect that Keats begins to think in this way and then finds himself in difficulties. Intuitions of beauty, though intense, are notoriously evanescent. We find the thought about stability and independence peremptorily crushed in the words 'whether it existed before or not'. This leaves us with beauty as a matter of recurrent creation, its claim to independence still strong because of its transcendent, irreducible nature. Remember that the artist is himself colourless, without identity and could therefore never have spun such a thing as beauty from his own substance; once again there is a theological parallel: Descartes in his *Discourse on Method* found in the idea of God a richness which proved that it could not have been produced by the human mind and in his *Meditations* he advanced an ontological proof of God's existence which is substantially identical to that advanced by Anselm.[12] For Keats this combination of evanescence and transcendence naturally pushes his thought in the direction of religion. The effect of this can be seen in the words 'holiness', 'creative', and of course in the allusion to Adam's dream.

To be sure Keats had no learning in philosophy. The names of Anselm and Hume would have meant little or nothing to him. The line which runs from Hume to Coleridge, in which the imagination is invoked, in the face of the un-meaning flux of presentations, to feign (Hume's word) or else to compose the continuous identity of public objects cannot be traced in Keats, though it is likely that he listened to others talking about such things. But the profound Romantic imperative to blot out the hierarchical opposition of knowledge and imagination is obeyed by Keats, which is enough to show that we are dealing here with a need which is both simpler and more fundamental than the technical shifts of Coleridge's philosophy. But at the same time Keats is thinking very hard and it is of the nature of real philosophic thought that it connects with other philosophic thought, even where there is no contact by way of reading or direct influence. Keats, after an astonishing feat of honest intelligence, seemed to have won through to a marvellous conclusion: the reductionists are wrong; poetry and aesthetic experience are not an idle delusion; they are parts of reality.

But if Adam's dream proved to be truth, what are we to make of Madeline's dream in *The Eve of St Agnes*? It is a fallacy to suppose that the highest energies of thought will always appear in an author's prose-writings. *The Eve of St Agnes* is one of the most feeling-saturated, purely Romantic poems ever written, but at the same time the thought of the poem is more alive, more exquisitely tormented and divided than anything we found in the letters. The story told in the poem mirrors the story of Adam's dream of Milton, but the sexes are transposed. Adam dreamed of Eve, awoke and found that she was really there. Madeline dreamed of Porphyro, awoke and found that he was really there. The dominant effect of the poetry is to enforce the likeness of the two stories, the sense of miracle and joy. But there are other effects, of a less docile character. Keats warned us of the anarchic latitude of the poetic imagination. As soon as we begin to read *The Eve of St Agnes* we become strongly aware of a feature largely suppressed in the debate so far (that is, in the letter to Bailey), namely sexual love, though the letter does speak of 'the heart's affections' and Keats also wrote 'as of love'. Adam's dream in Milton, we should remember, was a love dream. When Milton writes in *Paradise Lost* viii, 463 how Adam 'saw the shape' of Eve, the great Latinising poet shows that he knows exactly when to use the native, Saxon word; had he used the Latinate equivalent, 'form', all the tenderness would have been lost. He then permits himself a Donne-like moment of near-surrealism when he describes how Eve was made from Adam's rib, drawn from a wound, 'with cordial spirits warm/And life blood streaming fast' (466–7). In the objective primal myth God simply does this while Adam sleeps. In Milton's version an eerie effect is obtained by having Adam dream of something which is actually happening, just as Madeline in Keats' poem dreams of consummation at the moment when it occurs. The idea of flesh transmuted has here the faintly licentious force of dream imagery. Some twenty lines later it is raised to the Miltonic sublime: 'Bone of my bone, flesh of my flesh', echoing the marriage service, pre-echoing the terrible moment of the Fall (ix, 914–15). Eve's looks breathe 'the spirit of love and amorous delight' (iv, 477), 'she would be wooed, and not unsought be won' (503) and Adam leads her to the nuptial bower 'blushing like the morn' (511). The whole passage in Milton is an essay in the new Protestant idiom of sanctified sexuality. God conducts Adam to Eve and oversees the marriage rite. Sex and religion are harmonised (though Eve's blushes worried C. S. Lewis).[13]

Keats followed Milton in many things but he did not reproduce the Miltonic harmonisation of sexuality. He knew as an artist that he must turn instead to an older tradition, in which sexuality and religion co-exist in a tense and uneasy relationship, the tradition of mediaeval Courtly Love, blurred by its transmission through the Elizabethans and the Gothic Novelists. The central empiricism of Keats' thought (remember 'proved upon our pulses')[14] is in fact subjected to restrictive pressure from two directions, from religion and from sexuality. This was something which Keats could not handle philosophically, but the organisation of poetry is not the organisation of a philosophical treatise and in *The Eve of St Agnes* he found a way to dramatise these polarities.

Courtly Love is laced with schizophrenia. When the lover in Chrétien's poem genuflects outside his lady's room[15] the action represents both an element of spiritual devotion in the love and, at the same time, hell-brink blasphemy. Aquinas had condemned passionate sexual love as a *ligamentum rationis*, a binding up of reason.[16] Profound love is worse, perhaps, than casual sexuality, since it carries with it the danger of idolatry. The cynical amorist, oddly enough, is in less danger of forgetting that God is the most valuable, most lovable thing. That this feeling could survive into the Romantic period is shown by Coleridge's note on *Romeo and Juliet*, 'All deep passions [are] a sort of atheists, that believe no future'.[17] As love is exalted through the language of religion the danger of blasphemous parody or even idolatry is increased. That is why the mediaeval writers again and again conclude their poems and treatises with pious recantations. Nor, by and large, do they pretend that love can be merged with the major system—say, by marriage. Sexual love remains the dangerous, beautiful obverse of true religion.

When Shakespeare's Romeo and Juliet speak of shrines, palmers, pilgrims and saints, profanity and gentle sin (I, v, 92–108) the starkness of the old conflict has gone but a certain tension remains. Similarly when Donne writes 'us Canonized for love' ('The Canonization', 36) the conceit is almost a joke, made from the security of love, but still with a consciousness of that latent unease which nourishes all jokes. With the rise of Gothic Romance this *frisson*, this illicit echoing of the sacred in the erotic, is made the vehicle of a mild pornography. Virginity at risk among murky Gothic buildings became the order of the day. Pope set the tone with the brilliant avant-garde bad taste of *Eloisa to Abelard* (castration and frustration in a Gothic setting). This, rather than the high moral tone of *Paradise Lost* supplied Keats with the tradition he needed. The result is that, even while the lyric power of the poem enforces the intuition of miracle, it simultaneously offers an erotic parody of the myth, which in itself implies the presence of an unsubdued scepticism towards the new, high-minded Romantic harmonisation of knowledge and imagination.

For Porphyro stage-manages the awakening of Madeline. The miraculous brightening of the dream to reality is a trick. Like all seducers Porphyro promises not to 'displace one of her soft ringlets' (148) and proceeds in due course to do rather more than that. Most important of all, when Madeline first wakes, her first reaction is horror:

Her eyes were open, but she still beheld,
Now wide awake, the vision of her sleep—
There was a painful change, that nigh expelled
The blisses of her dream, so pure and deep . . .
How changed thou art! How pallid, chill and drear . . .

(298–301, 311)

The high-minded love-myth of Romanticism is accompanied in this poem by a low-minded love-myth, and this low-minded strand is essential to the Gothic character of the whole. The low sexual sequence has been brilliantly analysed and documented by Jack Stillinger in his article, 'The Hoodwinking of Madeline'.[18] Stillinger points out that what Porphyro proposes is a 'stratagem' (139) variously characterised by Angela as 'cruel', 'impious' and 'wicked' (140, 143). Porphyro wishes, voyeur-like, to 'see (Madeline's) beauty unespied' (166). Critics since Swinburne have noted, with varying degrees of reluctance, the similarity between Porphyro and the vile Iachimo in *Cymbeline*, II, ii. At 340 we have the image of robbing a nest (denied, but also in a way, asserted). Stillinger notes that the 'tongueless nightingale' at 206 is an allusion to the ugly–elegant Ovidian story of the rape of Philomel. In *Cymbeline* Imogen had been reading this story before Iachimo found her sleeping. At 257 Porphyro wishes he had a 'Morphean amulet', that is a means of drugging Madeline. This, Stillinger observes, links him with Lovelace in *Clarissa* (and also one might add, with Humbert Humbert in *Lolita*). Most tellingly of all, he finds such allusions as there are to *Paradise Lost* tend to associate Porphyro with Satan. At 224 Porphyro grows faint before the beauty of Madeline. Keats wrote in his copy of Burton's *Anatomy of Melancholy*, beside a passage describing how the Barbarians stood silent before a fair woman, 'Abash't the devil stood'. Here the reference is to *Paradise Lost*, iv, 846 (Satan before Zephon). There is a similar moment at ix, 463 where Satan is momentarily arrested in his evil design by the beauty of Eve. At one point in the revision of 314–22 which Keats made in September, 1819 (Woodhouse and Taylor, Keats' publisher, found the revised version too sexually explicit and induced him to change it almost completely) the phrasing recalls Satan at the ear of the sleeping Eve (*Paradise Lost*, iv, 800). Keats wrote that Porphyro's 'close rejoinder flows/into her burning ear'.

I have said that the story of *The Eve of St Agnes* mirrors the story of Adam's dream but that the sexes are transposed. Now we begin to see what can flow from that transposition. There are two important dreams in *Paradise Lost*, Adam's and Eve's. In Keats' poem the second dream, that planted in the mind of Eve by Satan, is allowed to infiltrate the first. Indeed the dream which Eve relates (v, 31–92) has an oddly Keatsian flavour. She tells how she was drawn into the moonlit garden and there urged to eat the apple of the tree 'with fruit surcharg'd', to ease its load and taste its sweet (v, 58–9). Perhaps all *Romantic* poets really are of the Devil's party without knowing it?

When Adam's dream ends in *Paradise Lost* there is a moment of chill dereliction: 'she disappeared, and left me dark' (viii, 478). Just as *The Eve of St Agnes* may be related to the 'happy understanding' Keats reached with Fanny Brawne on Christmas Day, 1818,[19] so, in a darker manner, Adam's dream may be related to the death of Milton's beloved second wife, Katherine Woodcock, in February, 1658, Milton having already embarked upon the composition of *Paradise Lost*. The terrible sonnet[20] on the dream which followed that death ends with the words, 'I woke, she fled, and day brought back my night'. Keats' knight at arms in 'La Belle Dame Sans Merci' awoke to find himself 'on the cold hillside' (44). In Milton the natural trauma of waking from a wish-fulfillment dream is healed by God's gift of Eve. In *The Eve of St Agnes* it is healed by the amorous prowess of Porphyro himself, lover, redeemer of fallen reality, ravisher.

At the lowest level of Gothic Romance Madeline's horrified reaction is needed for the sheer base excitement it can provide. At a slightly higher level some suspense is needed if the miracle is to be felt as truly miraculous. But the very efficacy of these literary mechanisms betrays the original philosophical insight of the letter to Bailey. Even there, indeed, all was not well. What I have called the radical empiricist argument insists that the reality-claim of any experience should be measured, quite simply, by the presentational intensity of that experience. Dreams, mental images and the feigned worlds of romance can be exceedingly vivid and may therefore be as real as anything else. But if we then use the language of change: 'The image *brightens* into reality', we implicitly concede that the image (dream, poem) was itself less than real; otherwise there would be nothing to applaud in its unlooked-for transformation. Of course the brief period of suspense necessary to our sense of miracle could be supplied from a mere failure of comprehension: it is not that Adam's dream gradually became real but that *we* find—gradually—that the dream was real all the time. To adjust the sentence in this way is to save the philosophy at the expense of the myth (for myth naturally deals in objective events disposed in time). But poetry operates at the mythic end of the spectrum and myth has a way of remaining obstinately linked to commonsense notions: Adam dreamed and when Eve came along in person reality replaced delusion. The whole effect is dependent on our not confusing the categories.

So too in *The Eve of St Agnes* the common sanity of the inherited story pattern impedes the blurring of the distinction between dream and ordinary reality, although philosophically Keats urgently requires that this line should be blurred. One must grant indeed that there are certain moments of exciting confusion in the poem. For example, we are given contradictory indications of the nature of Madeline's dream. In the brutal jargon of the 1980s we may ask our question directly: is it a sex dream? At 301 we are told of 'the blisses of her dream' but, in the same breath, that they were 'pure'. In the cancelled revision of 314–22, though Madeline's repose is 'serene', her dream is 'wild'. Moreover the revision stresses the slightly perverse idea that when Porphyro consummates the union Madeline is still dreaming hèr (presumably congruent?) dream.

Intensity alone is not enough to guarantee reality. The other requirement we make, that a thing should be stable, should be there still when we go back to look again, is met neither by dreams nor by the visionary heights of passion: the very drama of the poem implicitly acknowledges this commonplace truth. When the Romantics sought to beat back the 'hard reality' of the scientists, their shrillness in debate again and again betrayed their cause. The imagination is invoked as an organ of truth but, as we saw, the very word 'imagination' implies something other than ordinary perception, some creative activity of the mind. It is at this point that Romantic Platonism can come in, with what may seem to be a saving effect. Using the neo-Platonic shift whereby the artist, instead of being doubly removed from reality as he is in Plato's

Republic (597), is allowed direct access to the Forms,[21] all the base empirical requirements of stability and the like can be referred to the transcendent realm (where, indeed, they assume the exaggerated form of eternity). What this world calls imagination may in fact be perception of transcendent ideal forms, which are conceived as having an independent existence. Blake wrote in his *Jerusalem*, 'Imagination is the Real and Eternal World of which the Vegetable Universe is but a faint shadow, and in which we shall live in our Eternal or Imaginative Bodies when these Vegetable Mortal Bodies are no more'.[22] Such Platonism is really a postponed empiricism, guarded from falsification by the terms of the postponement. If it is pressed hard, this idea can come to oust ordinary experience (think of Blake's remark that 'Natural Objects always did and now do deaden, weaken and obliterate Imagination' in him).[23] What is inescapable is that the primary opposition between imagination and common perception has reasserted itself. The gap Coleridge sought to close has opened once more. Thus one finds an other-worldly reference in Romantic poetry which is tantamount to a confession that common reality is, after all, not to be sought from poets.

And yet—irony of ironies—*The Eve of St Agnes*, with a strange candour, dramatises all these tensions and is therefore startingly *true*— true, that is, to the divided mind and heart of the age. Many critics have sensed a transcendent or even a religious direction in the poem. E. R. Wasserman says it teaches us that it is only in heaven that empyreal imaginings are true.[24] W. W. Beyer suggests that the poem is rooted not in the senses but in our dream of God.[25] R. A. Foakes sees in the union of Madeline and Porphyro a 'Sacramental image of all that is good, as through their love they are made immortal'.[26] Newell F. Ford in his excellent study, *The Prefigurative Imagination of John Keats*[27] finds clear evidence that Keats sometimes construed the deliverances of imagination as a foretaste of some eternal joy to come.

All these things figure in the writing. But the *poem* is sure of none of them. In his *'Ode on a Grecian Urn'* Keats makes lyric use of the idea that the requirement of stability is met by the marble stillness of a work of art; only the notoriously affirmative words, 'Beauty is truth, truth beauty', fall with desperate crassness in a poem which is elsewhere marvellously alive to all the real ironies involved. To find an unequivocal immortality at the end of *The Eve of St Agnes* is surely very strained. Prospero in *The Tempest* says that we are such stuff as dreams are made on and that at the last we leave not a rack behind. The commentators laboriously interpret this as meaning the exact reverse, that we are eternal. So at the end of *The Eve of St Agnes* Porphyro and Madeline dislimn before our eyes. 'Like phantoms' (361) they pass through the hall and then, with that marvellous modulation of tense, 'they are gone' (370). In all this story it was the higher intelligence which fell victim to enchantments, never the lower modes of understanding. The rich, amoral interplay of sex and ideality, stratagem and magic, dream and waking is mistaken for the desired fusion of these things, for the long-withheld healing of the Romantic wound. Even the Grecian Urn, once one had entered the world of its fictive forms, proved live and mobile in its stillness. A poem may achieve a kind of palpable reality by the very force of its impact—that is implied in the letter to Bailey. But poems may also by stressing poignancy or irony, confess the frailty of those same moments of vision. The narrow Romantic theory which sees poetry as concerned only with glory is affronted by this. Coleridge's 'Dejection', a successful imaginative expression of the failure of the glory-giving imagination, shows how the practice of the Romantic poets could on occasion transcend their theories. In like manner Keats' poem is not only a larger thing than the critics allow, but also a larger thing than Keats himself, who wrote the best of all literary letters, could ever have explained. I am pleading, notice, for the presence of a kind of realism in both 'Dejection' and *The Eve of St Agnes*. The term 'realism' is now out of favour, but if the imagination really is to convey truth, what else should we expect but realism?

I have a sense that this essay has probably failed signally to produce the result which many of its readers will have desired and expected from it. The anxieties of Romanticism are still with us and we look eagerly for authoritative voices (from Coleridge to Barfield, from Barfield to Mary Warnock) telling us that the imagination gives truth. Keats in his letter to Bailey enforced the doctrine with as much authority as anyone could well produce, but the poem in which the idea is acted out is both ravishingly enchanting and mercilessly sceptical. No critic in his right mind could claim that *The Eve of St Agnes* is a cynical poem. To find beauty and wonder poignant because fugitive and involved with illusion is not cynical but only profoundly humane. But, in Keats' case at least, one has to say that the philosophic *credo* of the letter to Bailey does not survive when tested in the fire of a real poem.

NOTES
1. Letter No.43 in H. E. Rollins (ed.), *The Letters of Keats, 1814-1821*. (Cambridge, Mass.: Harvard University Press, 1958), Vol.i, pp.183-7.
2. See Ian Jack, *Keats and the Mirror of Art* (Oxford: Clarendon Press, 1967), p.23. The plaque was to read, 'Here Haydon painted his Solomon, 1813'.
3. See, 'To George and Thomas Keats', 21, 27 (?) December 1817 and 'To Richard Woodhouse', 27 October 1818, in Rollins' edn, Nos 45 and 118, vol.i, pp.191-4 and pp.386-8.
4. In Rollins' edn, vol.i, p.184-5.

5. *Essay Concerning Human Understanding*, II, viii, 7-10, in the edn by A. C. Fraser (New York: Dover Publications, 1959), vol.i, pp.168-71.
6. See *Discoveries and Opinions of Galileo*, trans. Stillman Drake (New York: Doubleday, 1957), pp.273-5.
7. 'Mock on, Mock on, Voltaire, Rousseau', in *Poetry and Prose of William Blake*, ed. Geoffrey Keynes (London: the Nonesuch Press, 1956), p.107.
8. *A Treatise of Human Nature*, 1.iv.6, in the edn by L. A. Selby-Bigge (Oxford: Clarendon Press, the 1964 reprint of the edn of 1888), p.254.
9. *Of the Principles of Human Knowledge*, i, 3, in *The Works of George Berkeley, Bishop of Cloyne*, ed. A. A. Luce and T. E. Jessup (London: Thomas Nelson and Sons, 1948-57), vol.ii, p.42.
10. *A Defence of Poetry*, in *The Prose Works of Percy Bysshe Shelley*, ed. R. H. Shepherd (London: Chatto and Windus, 1906), vol.ii, p.34.
11. *Proslogion*, ch.ii, in *Anselm to Ockham*, ed. and trans. E. R. Fairweather, vol.x (1956) of the *Library of Christian Classics*, pp.73-4.
12. *Discours de la Méthode*, iv and *Méditation Cinquième* in *Oeuvres et lettres de Descartes*, ed. A. Bridoux (Paris: Gallimard, 1953), pp.149 and 312-13.
13. See his *A Preface to Paradise Lost* (London: Oxford University Press, 1960), p.123.
14. 'To Reynolds', 3 May, 1818, in Rollins' edn, vol.i, p.279.
15. Chrétien de Troyes, *Lancelot*, 4716-7, in the edn with an English translation by W. W. Kibles (New York and London: Garland Publishing, 1981), p.196.
16. *Summa Theologiae, Prima Secundae*, Quaest, 34, Art.1.
17. *Coleridge's Shakespearean Criticism*, ed. T. M. Raysor (London: Constable, 1930), vol.i, p.10.
18. *Studies in Philology*, LVIII (1961), pp.533-55.
19. See Aileen Ward, 'Christian Day, 1818', *Keats and Shelley Journal*, x (1961), pp.15-27.
20. 'Methought I saw my late-espoused saint.'
21. See for example, Plotinus, *Enneads*, v, viii, 1 (32-36) in *Plotini Opera*, ed. P. Henry and H-R. Schwyzer (Oxford: Clarendon Press, 1964), vol.ii, p.269.
22. *Poetry and Prose of William Blake*, ed. Keynes, p.535.
23. *Ibid*, p.821.
24. See his *The Finer Tone* (Baltimore: Johns Hopkins Press, 1953), p.107.
25. See his *Keats and the Daemon King* (New York: Oxford University Press, 1947), pp.124-5.
26. See his *The Romantic Assertion* (London: Methuen, 1958), p.94.
27. Stanford: Stanford University Press; London: Oxford University Press, 1951.

« 7 »

MARY WARNOCK : RELIGIOUS IMAGINATION

The heyday of faculty psychology is long behind us; we no longer believe in the functions of the mind compartmentalised, segregated, each with its own sphere. Nevertheless, as we approach the twenty-first century and should know better, it is still remarkably difficult to avoid dropping into the language of faculties, and talking about Reason, Emotion, Imagination, each with its own part to play. Indeed there seems no other language available to us. I firmly believe that it is impossible to make a precise conceptual distinction between reason and the emotions, and that imagination, often rightly taken to be the supreme property of the human animal, cannot be separated from either. Yet we have to attempt to think of the imagination and its essential characteristics alone, even if this is a fiction. For to think or to perceive imaginatively, as we use those words, is one of the crucial functions, and the most valuable, of the human brain. So it is worth seeking a central meaning for the term 'imagination' which will make clear both its importance and its wide scope.

Sartre with his usual salad mixture of the obvious with the profound, defined imagination as *the ability to think of what is not*:[1] the non-existent, the non-present, the merely possible, as opposed to the actual. And this certainly fits with many of our ordinary assumptions. 'It's all in his imagination' we may say, when someone fancies himself ill, or persecuted. 'She's an imaginative child' we say, of one who treats a broom-handle as a horse, or lives in a palatial house under the dining-room table.

Sartre went on to identify the imagination with human freedom; and he meant not only that the imagination would remain free even if its owner was in prison, but, more profoundly, that without the ability to envisage what is not present, the past, the future, the absent and the unreal, human endeavour and human thought would be impossible. Other animals express immediate pains or pleasures; they purr, growl, squeal if in pain, and so on. Only humans, as far as we know, go in for the intelligent and sophisticated communication that results from thinking about things, and referring to them, when they are not available in any way to the senses. Certainly warnings, threats, promises, regrets, prognostications all turn on the ability to refer coherently to that which is past, absent, or yet to be.

Language is the clearest means of reference to the absent, and, with its nouns and verbs of general application, has developed largely with this purpose. But there are other ways to refer. An object that is present to us may be taken to stand for one that is not. One material thing may become *symbolic* of something other than itself. We need imagination to use or to interpret symbols. This is indeed the defining function of the imaginative mind. And so we may start the search for the peculiarly religious imagination, if there is such a thing, by a consideration of the nature of symbols.

In the Statesman's Manual, Appendix B, Coleridge wrote as follows: 'Now an allegory is nothing but a translation of abstract notions into picture language, which is itself nothing but an abstraction from objects of the senses. On the other hand a Symbol is characterised by a translucence of the special in the individual, of the general in the special, of the universal in the general: above all by the translucence of the eternal through and in the temporal'. A symbol, that is to say, is something we already see and know; we do not have to invent it or think it up, like a picture, out of our experience. It is there before us; but we see *in* it something other than itself. The symbolic object becomes significant both on account of what it is and at the same time on account of what else it means. Coleridge goes on to elaborate this thought. In this roughly Kantian use of the term it is the Understanding which forms general ideas for the purposes of classification and comparison. But Understanding, by itself, can give us only clarity, not depth. 'The completing power which unites clearness with depth, the plenitude of sense with the comprehensibility of the understanding is the imagination, impregnated with which understanding itself becomes intuitive and a living power.' There are numerous examples in Coleridge's writings of his own theory of the imagination in use. The 'depth' provided by imagination is an increase in the intelligibility of what is perceived and at the same time an intensity of feeling not just accidentally associated with the object of perception, but somehow a necessary part of perceiving it. I must content myself with just two examples.

My first is from a notebook entry for February 1805, where the necessary connection between image and emotion is illustrated. Here that which is perceived imaginatively is a mental image, a dream, rather than an object of ordinary perception. Coleridge is describing a dream: 'On Friday night 8th February 1805 my feeling in sleep of exceeding great love for my infant seen by me in the dream, yet so that it might be Sara, Derwent or Berkeley, and still it was an individual babe and mine. Of love in sleep . . . a sort of universal-in-particularness of Form seems necessary . . . will not this prove (Love) to be a deeper feeling, with such intimate affinity with ideas, so to modify them and become one with them; whereas the appetites and the feelings of revenge and anger coexist with ideas, not combine with them; and alter the apparent effect of the forms, not the forms themselves. Certain modifications of fear seem to approach near to this love-sense in its manner of acting'.

It must be remembered that Coleridge seldom wrote very clearly in his notebooks and that he was often under the influence of opium when he wrote. Nevertheless he often wrote truly. It seems to me here what he suggests is both true and of great importance, that in his dream-image, which might be Sara, Derwent, or Berkeley, but was still an individual love, there is a necessary connection between the feeling of love combined with the perception of the image, and the recognition of this as standing for something universal, something beyond itself.

My second example is simpler. This time the object experienced, the symbol of something other than itself, is an actual sight, not a dream-image. In a notebook entry for December 1804, Coleridge wrote 'O that sky, that soft blue mighty arch resting on the mountains of solid sea-like plain, what an *aweful adorable omneity in unity*'. A symbol, in this case the sky, the interpretation of which requires imagination, enables us to see individual things as universally significant. A symbol carries with it more than particular significance, and, recognising this, we feel both love and fear.

Before pursuing these ideas further, I want to turn to Coleridge's half-understood but greatly revered master, Kant, whom he read with growing excitement at the turn of the nineteenth century. In the *Critique of Judgement*, Kant wrote 'All our knowledge of God is symbolic'.[2] To think otherwise would not only be to 'fall into anthropomorphism', but it would also be to mistake the nature of knowledge itself. For knowledge must necessarily be a matter of applying the concepts of the understanding to the materials afforded us through the senses and we have no sense-experience of God.

Where our perceptions are concerned, not with scientific knowledge, but with aesthetic enjoyment, Kant has a further distinction to make. This distinction was borrowed by him from English and Scottish aestheticians such as Addison, Burke and Blair, but adapted to and enriched by his system as a whole. When we perceive an object as *beautiful* we perceive it as a form, whose pattern (or finality, or *point*) is a perceptible conformity to a law or limit, even if this is supplied by the imagination itself, independently of any law of nature. So, for example, we may feel an inevitability about the music we find beautiful, even if there is no *natural law* to determine that the melody must proceed in the way it does, or the cadence be completed as it was. In presenting us with an object as beautiful, Kant says, imagination brings the object under a concept, though an indeterminate concept of the understanding. When, on the other hand, the imagination presents us with an object as *sublime* it is different. 'We observe' he says[3] 'that whereas natural beauty conveys a finality in its form, making the object appear as it were pre-adapted to our powers of judgement, so that it thus forms of itself an object of delight, that which . . . in our apprehension of it excites the feeling of the *sublime* may appear in point of form to contravene the ends of our powers of judgement, to be ill-adapted to our faculty of presentation and to be as it were an outrage on the imagination, and yet is judged all the more sublime on that account.' The point is this: in our apprehension of beauty, understanding and imagination work together in that we see the finality or pattern in the beautiful object, and this is the source of our satisfaction with it. But we experience a different emotion when we contemplate something which cannot be so reduced to order. We cannot form any neat image of that which is presented as sublime. There is no form or pattern to be grasped in the object, or if there is, it does not exhaust the full content of the object; and so we cannot wholly reproduce it as an image. The explanation is that the sublime suggests to us an idea which, in Kant's terminology, is an *Idea of Reason*, an idea which cannot be derived from any sensory experience nor embodied in any sensory form. The great Ideas of Reason are God, Freedom and Immortality. We cannot scientifically understand any of these, since they are not part of the world of phenomena with which science is exclusively concerned. Yet they serve as Ideals, goals or touchstones according to which our life may be lived.

The great phenomena of nature may convey for our imagination *suggestions* of sublimity; of ideas, that is, which can never be fully comprehended in human concepts. Similarly the works of writers, artists or musicians of genius, may convey to us symbolically what Kant calls Aesthetic Ideas, the counterparts of Ideas of Reason. He defines an aesthetic idea thus: 'it is a representation of the imagination which induces much thought; yet without the possibility of any definite thought whatever, i.e. concept, being adequate to it, and which language can never get quite on level terms with, or render completely intelligible'.

The objects in nature that we call sublime, or the great works of art, music, literature or painting, which induce in us the sense of sublimity, become, according to Kant, symbols standing for something other than themselves. Symbols are intended to present ideas, but they cannot wholly succeed in doing so. They are of necessity substitutes, stand-ins for what cannot be embodied entirely in sensible objects or those concepts with the help of which sensible objects are classified and compared. What we perceive as sublime in nature, or what we appreciate or create in the highest art, are symbols of something forever beyond them. And thus it seems natural enough that Kant should say of our knowledge of God that all of it is symbolic. To think that it could be direct or scientific would be to reduce God to the level of the world of appearances with which scientific knowledge is concerned.

The concept of the imagination working through symbols, and enabling us to understand these symbols as significant of something beyond themselves is at the heart of the romantic theory of imagination and of art. It is particularly and essentially associated with Wordsworth. But it would be a mistake to think Wordsworth's theory of imagination as *simply* an aesthetic theory, relevant only to a certain taste or high style of poetry. On the contrary, *The Prelude*, in which the theory is best both expounded and exemplified, is an exercise not only in poetry but in autobiography. It is the story of an actual life, given meaning by the natural symbols recollected and mixed inextricably with the emotions of awe and love, as Coleridge knew. Wordsworth himself, it is true, thought that poets were in some sense singled out, through their heightened imagination, to experience the universality and significance of individual experiences.

> Like angels stopped upon the wing by sound
> Of harmony from Heaven's remotest spheres.
> Them the enduring and the transient both
> Serve to exalt; they build up greatest things
> From least suggestions . . .[4]

He was also aware of a need in himself to expound, to render not only permanent, but as far as possible intelligible, the visionary power of certain moments of experience, of things experienced, that is, as symbolic. The purpose of such explanation is universal, *for everyone*:

> That men, least sensitive, see, hear, perceive,
> And cannot choose but feel.[5]

For Wordsworth the grasping of some aspect of nature as symbolic entails not an intellectual but an essentially emotional response, which has, in turn, to be conveyed.

> . . . to fear and love,
> To love as prime and chief, for there fear ends,
> Be this ascribed: to early intercourse,
> In presence of sublime or beautiful forms,
> With the adverse principles of pain and joy . . .
>
> This spiritual Love acts not nor can exist
> Without Imagination, which, in truth,
> Is but another name for absolute power
> And clearest insight, amplitude of mind,
> And Reason in her most exalted mood.[6]

Imagination, then, working through symbols is the highest and deepest aspect of man's connection with nature. For Coleridge, equally, we know that the loss of imagination is the greatest and most irreparable loss. He describes, in *Dejection: an Ode*, in terms which I believe everyone can understand, what happens when he can look at

the stars behind the clouds and the crescent moon and 'see, not feel, how beautiful they are' . . .
> I may not hope from outward forms to win
> The passion and the life, whose fountains are within.

What he has lost is *joy*: 'joy is the sweet voice, joy the luminous cloud'. And elsewhere in the Ode he explicitly identifies this lost joy with the loss of
> What nature gave me at my birth
> My shaping spirit of imagination.

The loss, then, is the loss of ability to see *through* objects in the natural world to what lies behind them. For the joyless, each thing is what it is and it suggests nothing further, no intimations of immortality or infinity. It is the imagination which supplies such hints, which treats the objects of sense as *potential symbols*.

There is no reason to doubt that ordinary people, not just Wordsworth and Coleridge, are familiar with such powers of the imagination. Michael Paffard has written two books designed to show how widespread are these imaginative powers. In the first, *Inglorious Wordsworths*[7] he published the results of a questionnaire sent out to sixth-formers and undergraduates asking them to describe moments that have been variously named 'spots of time' or 'epiphanies'; moments where the natural world, or a room, or a church service seemed suddenly and luminously symbolic and important, signifying something beyond itself. In the second book, *The Unattended Moment*[8] he collected passages from autobiographies and memoirs which recorded such experiences. The results strongly suggest that what we may call 'Wordsworthian' feelings of awe and love in the face of some natural phenomenon, intuition of the infinite and inexpressible significance of the ordinary world, are, though for each individual rare, yet in general frequent. Many people, not only poets or artists of genius, sometimes feel intensely the huge significance of the present moment, of some landscape or seascape or townscape in which momentarily they see a sublimity, from which their imagination takes off though resting on it still. Perhaps the most frequent feelings expressed are feelings of unity with the universe, an understanding of the whole of life. I will quote just one example of such a 'spot of time', Willa Muir, the wife of the poet Edwin Muir, wrote as follows:[9] 'One evening when I was sixteen it broke over me so strongly . . . that I was awed into giving it a name. I was sitting alone in a boat beached at the back of the island . . . Except for a distant curlew's call there was no living sound. The feeling came upon me like a tide floating me out and up into the wide greening sky . . . into the universe, I told myself. That was the secret name I gave it: Belonging to the Universe. Like Thoreau I felt myself "grandly related".' Such experiences can have, as they did for Willa Muir, an enormous importance in life. As Wordsworth believed that his visionary spots of time changed his life, made him more understanding and loving of other people, so countless other, inglorious, Wordsworths have felt their whole lives given sense by moments of imaginative illumination, when the universe appears intelligible and seems to belong to them, and they to it.

If it is the function of the imagination to see more in an object than meets the regular eye of sense; if it is by imagination that we can regard one thing as symbolic of another and as holding a meaning apart from itself, then these moments of illumination are undoubtedly moments in which the imagination is heightened. Such experiences are ways of perceiving the world imaginatively. The question must then be asked whether they are in any way connected with religion. Certainly, not all of those who experience such moments of heightened awareness would think of them as specifically religious. C. S. Lewis, for example, whose descriptions of such 'epiphanies' in his autobiography, *Surprised by Joy*,[10] are among the most vivid and memorable, distinguishes the joy of the imaginative moment from anything that he would call religion. His account in the last chapters of his book of his conversion, first to theism, and then to Christianity is the most moving story; and his understanding that what he was in search of, once he had recognised the existence of a god, was next the place where religion, all religions, had reached maturity, is in my view illuminating and astute. Nevertheless, when he found where that place was, in Christianity, he adopted, it seems, an oddly literalist and rigid religion. And so his concluding words are these:[11] 'But what of joy? . . . To tell you the truth the subject has lost nearly all interest for me since I became a Christian . . . I believe . . . that the old stab, the old bitter-sweet, has come to me as often and as sharply since my conversion as at any time of my life whatever. But I now know that the experience, considered as a state of my own mind, had never had the importance I once gave it. It was valuable only as a pointer to something other and outer. While that other was in doubt, the pointer naturally loomed large in my thoughts. When we are lost in the woods the sight of a sign-post is a great matter . . . But when we have found the road and are passing sign-posts every few miles we shall not stop and stare.'

It seems to me that Lewis seriously undervalues what he once rightly saw to be of intense value. Let us consider, for example, his own description of the first stab of joy that he experienced.[12] 'As I stood beside a flowering currant bush on a summer day there suddenly arose in me without warning, and as if from a depth not of years but of centuries, the memory of that earlier morning . . . when my brother had brought his toy garden into the nursery. It is difficult to find words strong enough for the sensation which came over me: Milton's "enormous bliss" of Eden . . . comes somewhere near it. It was a sensation of course of desire; but desire for what? Not, certainly, for a biscuit tin

filled with moss, nor even (though that came into it) for my own past
... and before I knew what I desired, the desire itself was gone, the
whole glimpse withdrawn, the world turned commonplace again or
only stirred by a longing for the longing that had just ceased. It had
taken only a moment of time, and in a certain sense everything else that
had ever happened to me was insignificant in comparison.'

This was an experience of memory, and is therefore comparable to
Proust's great revelation, when he tasted the madeleine soaked in tea,
or set his foot on the uneven paving-stone outside the Guermantes'
door. Proust used the same word as Lewis, 'le joie' as the mark of the
creative power revealed in his experiences; and it was the word also
used, as we have seen, by Coleridge, to describe that imaginative
power which he felt himself to have lost when he wrote the *Dejection:
an Ode.* Proust like Coleridge thought that he had discovered in
himself a final and total lack of talent. Towards the end of his novel he
describes how, on the way back from a 'cure', no better in health and
full of depression, he observed in himself a total absence of joy when he
noticed the effect of light on the line of trees that ran along beside the
railway. '"Trees" I thought "you have nothing more to tell me; my
cold heart hears you no more ... If ever I believed myself a poet I now
know that I am not one".'[13] The next day he roused himself to go to a
party, and on the way reflected again on his lack of joy, his absence of
imaginative power. Suddenly everything changed. Waiting at the door
to be admitted he stumbled, and, recovering himself, stepped with one
foot on a flagstone that was lower than the one beside it. At the feeling
of the uneven stones he was immediately filled with an amazing
delight, the same delight as he had felt once before, when he tasted the
madeleine. This time, by causing in himself again the sensation of
uneven stones, he managed to track down the memory. It was of
Venice, and he was recalling not just a similar pair of uneven stones in
the Bapistry of St Mark, but all the sensations and emotions which had
then accompanied his standing on them. The joy, the indescribable
happiness that this recollection brought came from the recognition
that we can know, absolutely certainly, how things were. We can grasp
a complete truth and suddenly it is clear to us that how things *were* and
how they *are* are one. For we are seeing into the timeless nature of
things.

Proust had no doubt that the creative imagination can work only on
what is not immediately present to it. Therefore, insofar as the imagination is engaged with present experience, it must take the present as
referring to something other than itself, something beyond or behind
itself, a meaning which experience has, but which is not identical with
experience. Coleridge sometimes records in his notebooks a search for
the meaning of a particular shape or colour. ('O that I could but *explain*
these concentric wrinkles in my spectra'). So the narrator in Proust's

novel recalls that 'as far back as Combray I was attempting to concentrate my mind on a compelling image, a cloud, a triangle, a belfry, a flower, a pebble, believing that there was perhaps *something else under those symbols* which I perhaps ought to try to discover, a thought which these objects were expressing, like hieroglyphic characters'. And he recognised that the impulse that led him to try to interpret experience then, and his present probing into the happiness he felt in reliving the past, was the same impulse. It was a desire to know the nature of things. When he realised that the creative imagination, the joy he could experience, was essentially connected with memory of the past, he recognised in things 'something which, being common to past and present, is more essential than both' . . . 'Let a sound, a scent already heard and breathed in the past be heard and breathed now, simultaneously in the present and the past, real without being actual, ideal without being abstract, then instantly the permanent and characteristic essence hidden in things is freed, and our true being . . . awakes and revives. An instant liberated from the order of time has recreated in us man liberated from the same order, so that he should be conscious of it. We understand that the name of death is meaningless to him, for, placed beyond Time, how can he fear the future?'

Though Proust, and for that matter Coleridge, think of the joy which is imaginative power as essentially creative, there is as I have already suggested, no reason to confine the visionary power of imagination to those who will try to express these moments of illumination in works of original art (though as we know from Wordsworth the urge to do so may be very strong). Such imaginative powers may be possessed by anyone; and the moments of illumination may come from nature, from personal memories, or from great works of art, music or literature. What is common to them is the feeling of infinity, of depth or height without end. Wordsworth once again expresses this exactly:

>   . . . the soul
> Remembering how she felt, but what she felt
> Remembering not, retains an obscure sense
> Of possible sublimity, to which,
>   With growing faculties she doth aspire
> With faculties still growing, feelings till
> That whatsoever point they gain, they still
> Have something to pursue.[14]

The sense that there is something more, that there is never an end, is the sense generated, I believe, by imagination, whether exercised on something apparently trivial, as when a child has an overwhelming passion for cars or for birds' eggs; or in the mysterious powers of memory, nature or art. It is a sense akin to the Christian quality (whether virtue or natural gift) of Hope. I can find no reason to suppose that the human imagination cannot function as much in the sphere of religion as in any other; nor do I see any reason to believe that the religious imagination is different in any essential way from the imagination we have so far been considering. If it is true, as I believe it is, that all knowledge of God must be symbolic, there is indeed every reason to treat the aesthetic and the religious imagination as one, since it is the use of symbols that is central to the imagination.

But it may be thought that it is a dangerous and subversive doctrine to assert that we come to what knowledge we have of Christianity (because after all this is knowledge of God) through the imagination, and that the imagination involved is no different from the aesthetic imagination. For is this not tantamount to saying that religion is fiction; that the imagination here as elsewhere, concerns itself with 'that which is not'; and that if religion brings pleasures or consolations, these are not different from the pleasures and consolations of art? It may be very agreeable to think of religion in terms of the common human capacity to imagine, but does this not at once and inevitably detract from its *truth*?

Such questions are natural enough, but they display I think, a narrow and naive view of truth, a view based on the supposition that all propositions are either scientifically true or scientifically false, that history is a series of hard facts, to grasp which we need only to be told, not to imagine, or reflect or interpret. Christianity is much the worse for such crudities (and for all I know other religions are too). They arose partly out of the rise of science, when, in the nineteenth century, Christians felt that they had to defend their faith as a system of truths on equal terms with the supposedly unquestionable and demonstrable truths of science. But I do not want to pursue that part of the story.

Instead I would like to look, doubtless in an equally crude and simple way, at the subject matter of religious beliefs. Religion, any religion, it seems to me, is concerned with the relation between man and nature, with the permanent difference between the good and the bad, with the contrast in human beings between their ultimate solitude and their superficial sociability, with the longings they have for things they can never apparently attain, with the awe they feel towards those aspects of the world which remain mysterious or beyond their control; with the love, and something akin to gratitude they may feel for being alive and part of such a universe beyond themselves. They feel, in religion, that they are 'grandly related'. But, above all, religion is concerned with the temporal nature of life, with birth and death, and the passage of time. Other animals, as far as we know, live from one hour to the next, and have no need to comprehend the whole of a life, or the whole of a section or chunk of a life, as a unity. Insofar as they remember, their memory is practical: they can learn to do things they couldn't do before. They do not recall for the sake of recollection, nor, as far as we can tell, do they tell each other stories with a beginning, a middle and an end.

Now within the concept of the story it seems to me that the distinction between history and fiction has been greatly exaggerated, to the detriment of each. To take a simple case of the supposed factual kind of story, let us suppose that someone is telling the story of his own life ... writing his autobiography. In order to do this he must shape his memories, and turn his life, actually lived, as every life is, from one moment to the next, into something with a clear pattern, if not a plot. And he does this (unless like some autobiographers he is simply boasting, or giving himself a task for his retirement) in order to make something clear. Storm Jamieson, for example, justifies the writing of her marvellous autobiography, *Journey from the North*, in two ways.[15] First she says she has a good memory and happens to have lived for a long time in a period of many changes. But, she writes, 'The second and stronger reason, no more and no less egotistical than the impulse to write a novel, is the wish to discover before it is too late what sort of a person I have been, without allowing vanity or cleverness to soften the outline of the creature ... I have tried to write with perfect sincerity, without malice to others or to myself. A degree of failure was implicit in the effort from the start and a degree of distortion, however many precautions I took not to lie. But if I had not thought the effort worth while to others besides myself I should not have made it. It is improbable that the glass I have been looking into for the last four or five years reflects only my own mind and heart'. The reflection in the glass which is herself, which in itself requires an imaginative effort to locate and to describe, is seen also to be other people. To perceive in this way the universal in the particular is, as I have argued, the very central function of the imagination. Storm Jamieson, moreover, likens the impulse to write autobiography with the impulse to write a novel. The difference between 'fact' and 'fiction' no longer seems vast. In the same way Rousseau, writing about his own Confessions, defied anyone to controvert their truth by adducing mere historical facts. And Sartre, writing the life of Flaubert which was intended to be biography, nevertheless spoke of his book as a 'true novel'. What we learn from memory, our own or other people's, may, though concerned with particulars, be general and universal.

The universal understanding that may come from memory comes essentially through the medium of the story itself. The very nature of memory is temporal. We recall *now* what happened *then*. But the power that memory is to bring together the past and the present constitutes, as Proust saw, its victory over time. It *is* the power to perceive the timeless in the temporal. In this way memory is only a special case of the imagination at work. And, further, the shaping power of the imagination is often strongest in the act of bringing order out of temporal chaos, turning events which follow one another in time into a *plot*, and thus into a significant whole. Aristotle's distinction between tragedy and history makes this very point. He thinks of history as simply an account of what happened; tragedy is 'more philosophical' precisely because the plot, the order, has been imposed and it is from the plot that the characters arise and show the universal qualities that they have. Aristotle undoubtedly claimed a sense in which tragedy, being more philosophical, was more *true* than history. The very limitations imposed on events by plot or story, the inevitability with which one event issues in another allow us to think of the events as a whole. The whole story becomes symbolic. Each time we hear it, we grasp its significance. I am not saying, neither was Aristotle, that every story is an allegory. Let us remember Coleridge's distinction. An allegory is deliberately sought out, to be illustrative of a previously understood concept. What is symbolic, on the other hand, is something already existing, an individual object of possible contemplation with characteristics all its own, which yet can be seen by the eye of imagination to mean something which is not individual only, but general, and, I would add, timeless.

I am not competent to enter into any of the theological arguments which centre on questions about the historical nature of the Gospels. But I suppose that there is none who would deny that Christianity is a religion of history. It turns on events, not simply on concepts. For the ordinary churchgoer, who is aware of the unfolding of the Christian year, the story aspect of the Christian religion must be central. The story is in itself particular, concerned, that is, with a particular life at a particular place and time; but, as we have seen, particularity in a story is not incompatible with universality. The individual stands for more than itself, to the imaginative understanding.

To return to C. S. Lewis: of all critics he perhaps had the greatest and simplest understanding of the aesthetic imagination, as far as it may be exercised on literature. Writing in an essay on stories, concerned not with great literature but with children's books, he wrote, by way of example, of the concept of fear.[16] He argued that there are certain stories, for instance Jack the Giant-Killer, which appeal to the imagination essentially embodying fear, and fear directed towards a particular kind of object. He is right, it seems to me, to suggest that emotions, such as fear and love, and indeed awe, cannot be defined or described separately from their appropriate object. It is by virtue of the nature of the object that we can give a name to the emotion. (Think, for instance, of the emotion jealousy. This could not be described without a description of the circumstances which gave rise to it.) In the case of the children's story, the peculiar fear embodied is the fear of the gigantic, its heaviness, monstrosity, uncouthness, unpredictability. 'Nature' he says 'has that in her which compels us to invent giants, and only giants will do.' The whole quality of the response to this particular story is determined by the fact that the enemy are giants. The test of whether a reader's imagination has been touched by the idea within the story is how often he rereads it or asks for it to be told again. Mere anticipation, the tension of waiting to find out what happens next, as the story unfolds for the first time, and one event follows another, is not identical with the deep imaginative effect that a story may have. Indeed it may sometimes be an obstacle to such an effect. 'Not until the curiosity, the sheer narrative lust has been given its sop and laid to sleep are we at leisure to savour the real beauties. Till then it is like wasting a great wine on a ravening natural thirst.' Surprise, paradox, denouement in a plot is best if you know what it is that is coming. Then the point of it, the meaning of the whole, can be understood. The purpose of a story, according to Lewis is to catch an idea, and convey it in terms of the concrete, the temporal and the transitory. 'In life and in art both' he said 'we are always trying to catch in our net of successive moments something that is not successive'. He is right. And it is imagination which reaches the story, which interprets it so that its successive moments yield the non-temporal truth.

Lewis himself would not apply this profound insight to his reading of the Gospels. Determined as he was to separate the non-religious imagination from religious knowledge of truth, he insisted, in considering the story of Christ's life, on an absolute distinction between fiction and fact, between myth and history. Writing about his own conversion he said:[17] 'I was by now too experienced in literary criticism to regard the Gospels as myths. They had not the mythical taste. And yet the very matter which they set down in their artless historical fashion . . . was precisely the matter of great myths. If ever a myth had become fact, had been incarnated, it would be just like this. And nothing else in all literature was just like this. Myths were like it in one way. Histories were like it in another. But nothing was simply like it.'

So he was determined to overlook in the Gospels all those aspects of story which he himself understood so well in connection with the rest of literature. He could not allow himself to take seriously the nature of our response, that the life of Christ itself as recorded in the Gospels is a symbol, a universal-in-particular standing for something, we cannot say exactly what, but speaking to us of infinity, eternity and the triumph over time. Lewis' literalism leaves out of account the obvious fact that incorporated in the Gospels is a whole background of story and Messianic myth, a tradition looking, it is true, to the future not the past, but an object for the imagination, nonetheless. He also overlooked the fact that the Christian's response to the Gospels is, in part at least, like a child's response to a fairy-story. We must hear it again and again, and every time, though well-known, it may appeal to us anew; and not just to us, but to our forebears, and, as I hope, our descendants too. For us religious imagination is peculiarly dependent on apprehended continuity. Since religion itself, any religion, is so centrally concerned with the contrast between time and eternity, between the transitory and the abiding, anything which can be fastened on by the imagination as a symbol of endurance is likely to be central to religion, and to religious belief. This is the crucial role of the Christian church. It is the rock, the unmoved centre, the vehicle of belief from one generation to another. An apprehension of continuity, whether geological, biological or, in terms of human artefacts, archaeological is itself accompanied by awe and sometimes by a passionate interest akin to love, the very emotion, as we have seen, central both to the imagination itself and to religion.

The continuity of the Liturgy has a double symbolic importance. It is that which conveys the repeated Christian story; and it is itself a signal of the continuity of the Church since its foundation. But the Church has always been ambivalent in its attitude to the imagination, and especially to what may be thought of as the aesthetic imagination. C. S. Lewis, in becoming Christian, in this respect followed a long tradition, in demoting 'joy'. For it has often seemed that the pleasures of the imagination, however deep, must be set in contrast to the different more practical response demanded by the true reading of the Gospel story, which, properly understood, is supposed to change people's lives; no one's life was ever changed, except perhaps for the worse, by the beautiful, even by the sublime. Wordsworth's testimony is discounted. He was not, after all, a theologian. And so there have been repeated efforts to cut out the aesthetic from the centre of worship; to return to the *facts*. Christianity must be rendered intelligible and plain, poetry and music must be banished, unless they are somehow shown to be the only vehicle for the historic truth.

Such movements within the Christian religion seem to me to stem mainly from two sources. One is a kind of egalitarianism. The Church must not seem to exist for the élite, the chosen, Wordsworthian few, the finer spirits. This might be a respectable motive, if it could be shown that only a few could experience the joy of the interpretation of symbols. But I do not believe that this can be shown. I would argue, on the contrary, that the imagination, the way of thinking of one thing as signifying something beyond it, is common to all human beings, though some may think in this way more, or more reflectingly, than others. Everyone, I believe, is capable of, and indeed seeks for, an imaginative response to the immediate and the present in terms of that which is neither immediate nor present, and which cannot be precisely stated in plain terms.

The second source of the anti-aesthetic movement is the exaggerated dichtotomy, of which I have spoken already, within the category of story, between the fictional and the historical, between myth and fact. The insistent demand to be told whether or not someone believes the

Gospel story to be true or not, yes or no, does he or doesn't he believe in the resurrection, or the virgin birth, seems to me to show a failure to understand the full part that imagination plays not only in religion, but in literature, history and in life itself, lived as it is through time, yet demanding a constant effort to make sense of time, to turn events into stories. Dennis Nineham, in the introduction to his first book of *Explorations in Theology*[18] says this: 'The characteristic religious difficulty to-day is a metaphysical difficulty, at any rate in this sense: where men seem to need help above all is at the level of the *imagination*; they need some way of envisaging realities such as God, creation and providence imaginatively, in a way which does no violence to the rest of what they know to be true. They need to be able to mesh in their religious symbols with the rest of their sensibility . . .' This seems to me profoundly true, and such meshing in will not come about as long as the religious imagination is held to be totally different, because of its different subject-matter, from the imagination we can all of us exercise on the natural world, the world of literature, music and art. Again, in an essay entitled 'History and the Gospel',[19] Nineham speaks of the need to regard the Gospels as part of the earliest disciples' response to the events they record, their reconstruction, their attempt to turn mere events into story. 'If we could look at them' he says 'from that perspective perhaps we could be more relaxed about them and they would reveal truth we are at present missing . . . If we were thus relaxed, perhaps we could sometimes let go of the historian's hand, and call in the psychologist, the poet and the literary critic, who could help us to unpack the profound truth, often layer after layer of it, which stories of this sort can yield.' I would not argue that religion *depends* on story. The religious imagination could, I suppose, work through the visible and the audible in nature, leading to thoughts of continuity, mystery, and the place of the transient, in the permanent continuity of nature. But to work through story is to relate these concepts of time and eternity to human life and human behaviour, to what people *do*, as well as to what they *are*. In this way the imagination humanises the otherwise impersonal. A *personal* God must have a history. It is in this direction then, that I believe our understanding of the religious imagination must lie. We must consider seriously the nature of those symbols which can be interpreted by us as conveying the profoundest truths. And we must see the need for such interpretations as part of our common humanity.

NOTES
1. J-P. Sartre, *The Psychology of the Imagination*, Methuen 1972.
2. Immanuel Kant, *The Critique of Judgement*, translated J. C. Meredith.
3. *Op. cit.*
4. Wordsworth, *Prelude*, Book XIV, 98.

5. *Op. cit.*, XIV, 85.
6. *Op. cit.*, XIV, 162.
7. *Inglorious Wordsworths*, Michael Paffard, Hodder and Stoughton, 1973.
8. *The Unattended Moment*, Michael Paffard, SCM Press, 1976.
9. Willa Muir, *Belonging*, The Hogarth Press, 1968.
10. C. S. Lewis, *Surprised by Joy*, Geoffrey Bles, 1955.
11. *Op. cit.*, ch.XV.
12. *Op. cit.*, ch.I.
13. *Remembrance of Things Past*, translated Scott Moncrieff, volume XII.
14. Wordsworth, *Prelude*, Book II, 312.
15. Storm Jamieson, *Journey from the North*, Collins, 1969.
16. C. S. Lewis in *Essays Presented to Charles Williams*.
17. C. S. Lewis, *Surprised by Joy*, ch.IV.
18. Dennis Nineham, *Explorations in Theology* I, SCM Press, 1977.
19. *Op. cit.*

THE EXEMPLARY PART

« 8 »

DAVIS MCCAUGHEY : IMAGINATION IN THE UNDERSTANDING OF THE PROPHETS

Mary Warnock expresses some impatience with Coleridge. 'Coleridge,' she says, 'treated philosophical theories as friends. You may love many friends who do not agree among themselves, and you may get crazes for people because you see in them some qualities which may not, in truth, be their most obvious qualities. It is because of this unintellectual attitude to philosophy that Coleridge can never be taken seriously by professionals.'[1]

A similar impatience must greet anyone who from another discipline of Christian theology makes an excursion into Old Testament studies. He is likely to find at work there a number of friends who do not agree with each other, but each of whom seems to be saying interesting things. If in addition the outsider dares to suggest that contemporary literary theory may cast some light on the ways in which the imagination operates in the prophetic writings of the Old Testament and that that theory may help to elucidate the texts, he is immediately confronted with the question 'Which theory?' Certainly not everything which is being said about the processes of interpretation is consistent with everything else said with equal force and learning. It is only given to a few, among whom must be named the one in whose honour these essays are written, to maintain a steady, consistent and systematic approach to major theological questions while remaining open in mind to the contribution of so many and so many diverse thinkers. Life was simpler, or seemed so, when we were students.

I

How and where do we begin a fresh engagement with the prophets? And first, how do we think that the prophetic imagination works?

The place most congenial to us today is with the written texts, the writing prophets. In the writing of these texts and in their transmission, we may assume, imagination operates in a manner similar to that in other creative writers. That at least is a starting-point. The prophet must sooner or later express himself in words if he is to fulfil his calling to communicate with those who lack the charisma of prophecy. It is only through those words that we can perceive something of his inspiration. We cannot probe the prophetic inspiration except through what the prophets wrote, or what survives of their writings, or what is represented as their writings. Information about the writing prophets, in narrative form, is relatively slight.

So we begin not with a theological discussion of the nature of inspiration, nor with biographical or psychological accounts of individual prophets but with the texts which flow from them, with their so-called writings. This is not to deny the value of such theological or biographical enquiries: our search is for a proper starting-point.

St Thomas in his discussion of prophecy[2] insists that prophecy is not a *habitus*, a steady disposition, but that

> the prophetical light inheres in the soul of a prophet by way of a transient passion or impression . . . So just as the atmosphere ever needs to be newly lighted up, so too the prophet's mind ever needs new revelation, just as a pupil who has not mastered the principles of his art needs instruction about each single point. Isaiah says, *Morning by morning he awakens . . . he wakens my ear*. So too the very wording of Scripture is descriptive of prophecy, as when we read 'the Lord has spoken' to one or other prophet, or that 'the word of the Lord' was heard, or that 'the hand of the Lord was upon him'

So even for St Thomas with his preoccupation with the vision of God the particular points of inspiration which issued in oracles are definitive of prophecy. In the process of inspiration he distinguishes between intellectual and imaginative vision, and asks 'whether prophecy which has intellective and imaginative vision is more excellent than that which is intellectual only', and against St Augustine comes to the conclusion 'that a prophecy which enables some supernatural truth to be perceived, starkly, in terms of intellective vision, is more to be prized than that in which supernatural truth is manifested by likenesses of bodily things in terms of imaginative vision' (174.2). Nevertheless, for St Thomas the prophetic message is characteristically conveyed by similitudes, by the use of images: 'prophetic vision is not a vision of the divine essence itself. When the prophets see what they do see, it is not in the divine essence but in certain similitudes lighted up by a God-given light' (173.1).

We need not describe the ways in which, according to St Thomas, the prophetic knowledge of God and his will comes about through various operations of the divine-controlled imagination. Whether through the infusion of new images or through a heightened awareness of existing images, the mind is able to express and the tongue declare that which would not otherwise be available to it.

A very different thinker from a different period also sees in prophetic inspiration and utterance something akin to poetry. In his discussion of 'the pathetic fallacy' John Ruskin wrote:

> And thus, in full, there are four classes: the men who feel nothing, and therefore see truly; the men who feel strongly, think weakly,

and see untruly (second order of poets); the men who feel strongly, think strongly, and see truly (first order of poets); and the men who, strong as human creatures can be, are yet submitted to influences stronger than they, and see in a sort untruly, because what they see is inconceivably above them. This last is the usual condition of prophetic inspiration.[3]

For Ruskin, it would appear, prophetic inspiration is inaccessible. Presumably this being 'submitted to influences stronger than they' may refer to the dreams and strange images through which prophetic inspiration was supposed to have come. Yet, a few paragraphs later Ruskin relates the work of a poet who is great to the inspiration of the prophet in such a way as to acknowledge the latter as a fundamentally reasonable activity comparable to that of his first order of poets. After commenting that 'the greatness of a poet depends upon the two faculties, acuteness of feeling and command of it' Ruskin continues:

A poet is great, first in proportion to the strength of his passion, and then, that strength being granted, in proportion to his government of it; there being, however, always a point beyond which it would be inhuman and monstrous if he pushed this government, and, therefore, a point at which all feverish and wild fancy becomes just and true. Thus the destruction of the kingdom of Assyria cannot be contemplated firmly by a prophet of Israel. The fact is too great, too wonderful. It overthrows him, dashes him into a confused element of dreams. All the world is, to his stunned thought, full of strange voices. 'Yea, the fir-trees rejoice at thee, and the cedars of Lebanon, saying, "Since thou art gone down to the grave, no feller is come up against us".' So, still more, the thought of the presence of the Deity cannot be borne without this great astonishment. 'The mountains and the hills shall break forth before you into singing, and all the trees of the field shall clap their hands.'[4]

Ruskin's account of the prophet of Israel is reminiscent of Mary Warnock's account of Coleridge's identification of the strong music of the soul with joy. 'Imagination then, which is characterized as "shaping", is essentially connected with joy'.[5] That joy, that astonishment necessarily expresses itself in accessible words, however heightened the expression may be.

It is well known that at Jeremiah 23.9-40 we have a series of prophecies organised under the heading 'Concerning the prophets'. Arranged with considerable rhetorical effect the four oracles (the fifth 33-40 added by a later hand) speak more and more effectively of the criteria for reliable prophecy. Among the several important points being made is the confrontation between the word and the dream. Here the prophet is giving to prophecy a more reasonable basis. Against those who repeat the magical incantation 'I have dreamed, I have dreamed' the prophet places those who have stood in the council of the Lord, 'to perceive and hear his word'. That, however, manifestly does not mean the elimination of the vision. It rather asserts that there is a moment at which 'all feverish and wild fancy becomes just and true', when the imagination shapes and controls what is being said; or perhaps we should say, when the imagination shapes and controls by what is being said. R. E. Brown's remark about prophets in the Didache and Johannine community might be applied to their predecessors the Old Testament prophets, from whom they are sometimes too sharply distinguished. 'I suggest that teaching by word or deed, not ecstasy, is the mark of the prophet in both *Didache* and among Johannine secessionists'.[6]

We do not have to go beyond Jeremiah himself to see how the simple image points beyond itself. Associated with his call Jeremiah is twice asked: 'What do you see?' The answer is first (1.11–12) 'a sprig of almond tree' (*shāḵed*), and the divine response or significance 'I am awake (*shoḵed*) over my word to accomplish it'. This is a straightforward instance of wordplay (cf. Amos 8.1–2). To recognise the effect we might need to remind ourselves of Shakespeare's play upon the word 'state' in the ninth and tenth lines of Sonnet 64:

> When I have seen such interchange of state,
> Or state itself confounded to decay,
> Ruin hath taught me thus to ruminate,
> That Time will come and take my love away.

In each case the play upon the word arrests the reader, and switches his attention to greater matters only to reinforce the implications of what is being said, in the case for the prophet (who now begins to learn what it means to have God's word put in his mouth), in the other case for the poet who fears to see that Time's fell hand may take his love away.

> This thought is as a death, which cannot choose
> But weep to have that which it fears to lose.

In Jeremiah's case the full force of the image of the sprig of almond tree is further reinforced by the second image to which it is tied by the repetition of the question 'What do you see?' 'A boiling pot with its mouth open and its steam being blown by the north wind.' The God who watches over his word in the prophet's mouth to perform it is also present in the threat from the north: Jeremiah's ministry is given the widest context, and that ministry is made the more awesome.

So we could go on multiplying examples of the prophets' 'power of engaging attention and alluring curiosity' (as—I think—Dr Johnson put it), because their attention has been engaged, their curiosity allured by an image, a vision in search of words to express it. One is tempted to suggest that prophetic inspiration must have been very like those 'auditory hallucinations' which Nadezhda Mandelstam describes as 'something in the nature of an occupational disease' for a poet.

As many poets have said—Akhmatova (in 'Poem Without a Hero') and M. among them—a poem begins with a musical phrase ringing insistently in the ears; at first inchoate, it later takes on a precise form, though still without words. I sometimes saw M. trying to get rid of this kind of 'hum', to brush it off and escape from it. He would toss his head as though it could be shaken out like a drop of water that gets into your ear while bathing. But it was always louder than any noise, radio or conversation in the same room.

Akhamatova told me that when 'Poem Without a Hero' came to her, she was ready to try anything just to get rid of it, even rushing out to do her washing. But nothing helped. At some point words formed behind the musical phrase and then the lips began to move.[7]

Beside this we might put Jeremiah's 'If I say "I will not mention him, or speak any more in his name", there is in my heart as it were a burning fire shut up in my bones, and I am weary with holding in, and I cannot' (20.9). Lindblom suggested that a combination of 'purely psychical and ordinary moral elements' are at work here contributing to what he calls 'the higher prophetic consciousness'.[8] We should perhaps add to this our understanding of some of the known processes of literary composition.

It has often been noted that, in Walther Zimmerli's words, 'prophets know a "word" that creates reality, indeed in itself anticipates reality. For the prophet, the "word" is not only the expression of a thought or idea: it is an event'.[9] Again, to quote Lindblom on the inaugural vision of Jeremiah in which the prophet heard Yahweh saying, See I put my words in your mouth; this day I give you commission over the nations and kingdoms to root up and to pull down, to build and to plant (1.9 f): 'Here it is said that Jeremiah's message, whether of judgment or of salvation, would be not only a statement about doom or salvation, but also a power which really created ruin or prosperity for the nations'.[10] Such observations which are perhaps commonplace among Old Testament scholars bring their studies close to those of some twentieth-century literary critics who wish to assert that meaning is not something which predates language. Meaning depends upon language. To quote one such critic:

> The hallmark of the 'linguistic revolution' of the twentieth century, from Saussure and Wittgenstein to contemporary literary theory, is the recognition that meaning is not simply something 'expressed' or 'reflected' in language: it is actually *produced* by it. It is not as though we have meanings, or experiences, which we then proceed to cloak with words; we can only have the meanings and experiences in the first place because we have a language to have them in. What this suggests, moreover, is that our exper-

ience as individuals is social to its roots; for there can be no such thing as a private language, and to imagine a language is to imagine a whole form of social life.[11]

This, of course, explains why the prophets knew the agony of belonging with their people; and it explains why their words excited fear or hope among their contemporaries. Their writings were not *belles lettres*: they effected something by writing.

II

What are these prophetic writings with which we must engage? That too is a problematic matter; but the problems raised bring biblical criticism within reach of one of the interests of contemporary literary critics.

One of the great gains of recent decades has been the picture now available to us all and not simply to Old Testament specialists of the growth and development of the prophetic books. We have for a long time accepted the tripartite division of Isaiah: Isaiah of Jerusalem, deutero-Isaiah and trito-Isaiah. And we were prepared to concede that scholars could properly perceive the interpolation of apocalyptic fragments into the first thirty-nine chapters. Perhaps our perception of this was rather too much in modern European editorial terms. What has come to the non-specialist with all the excitement of a fresh discovery is the way in which, for instance, a little book like Amos is the product of many hands over many decades, indeed centuries.

We only know what we do know of Amos 'because he appeared as the messenger of Yahweh in Samaria and Bethel (and perhaps also here and there in other Israelite localities) during a period of at least a few weeks but scarcely longer than several months'.[12] From that brief beginning there unfolds a verbal and literary tradition, in which we are able (according to the analysis of Hans Walter Wolff) to distinguish 'three eighth-century strata, all of which for the most part derive from Amos himself and his contemporary disciples. Three additional strata can be recognized as later interpretations by their distinctive language and different intentions. They derive from the following centuries'.[13] So here we have, within one relatively brief document, writing and re-writing, a verbal and literary tradition which begins with Amos in the eighth century and passing through the hands—or rather the ears and lips—of his disciples is taken up in the seventh century with the destruction of Bethel by Josiah in view, fastening on catchwords such as 'Bethel' and 'altar' which may be reinterpreted in polemical style; the whole was then elaborated in the sixth century by a Deuteronomistic editor who betrays a more 'comprehensive historical interest and a special concern for the phenomenon of prophecy'; finally in the post-exilic period we have Amos' word of judgment supplemented by words of salvation and hope: 'the postexilic theology adds, briefly but distinctly, that Yahweh's sentence of death is not his last word'. This final disturbance of the older text and message is no recent discovery. We may recall Wellhausen on the conclusion:

> Roses and lavender instead of blood and iron ... Amos means what he says ... After he has just surpassed all his earlier threats, he cannot suddenly blunt their sharpness, he cannot let milk and honey flow from the cup of Yahweh's wrath at the end ... It is a later Jew who has appended this coda, and removed the genuine conclusion, because this sounded too harshly in his ears.[14]

What is new, and is the great achievement of the twentieth century, is to see this whole development as an aspect of the social history of Israel. 'You cannot just "write the truth"; you have to write it *for* and *to* somebody, somebody who can do something with it', wrote Brecht. In Amos, but not only in Amos, in all the writing prophets, we see this process of re-writing or re-interpretation at work.

For long this process was regarded as 'corruption', perhaps because biblical scholars had cut their teeth to some degree on textual criticism which for long had assumed that the older text was 'purer'. Now we are not so sure in either case. There are voices which suggest (quite rightly) that the processes of redaction must be taken with a new seriousness and (more doubtfully) that what in the end we must deal with is the canonical form of the text.[15] Life is more complicated: there is no 'end' just as there is no definitive starting-point. What is clear, however, is that without the critical process we shall not hear the text in any of its forms. To take but one example, without the aid of historical and literary analysis we shall not be able to discern the subtle development, inter-relation and gathering rhetorical force of the five visions of Amos: 7.1–3; 4–6; 7–9; 8.1–3; 9.1–4. We need to be able to re-write Amos in order to hear him.

Such an undertaking, which has been going on for some time, may commend itself as congenial to some recent literary critics. The books of the Old Testament which bear the names of prophets all bear the mark of being re-written, some of them many times. They have fulfilled the conditions laid down by Jacques Derrida:

> To write is to produce a mark that will constitute a sort of machine which is productive in turn, and which my future disappearance will not, in principle, hinder in its functioning, offering things and itself to be read and re-written ... For a writing to be writing it must continue to 'act' and to be readable even when what is called the author of the writing no longer answers for what he has written, for what he seems to have signed.[16]

Such language may seem exaggerated when applied to many of the literary texts which we are accustomed to think of as fixed. It is, however, literally true of the texts which we have under the names of the prophets in the Old Testament. Moreover these texts continue to be interpreted and re-interpreted in such different ways by Qumran and Philonic and Mediaeval Judaism, by New Testament writers, by the Church Fathers, in the Reformation and by post-critical scholarship that while Terry Eagleton's use of the words 're-written' and 're-writing' in the quotation which follows may seem exaggerated in relation to Homer and Shakespeare, it is more than a plausible metaphor for what has happened to the prophets.

'Our' Homer (he writes) is not identical with the Homer of the Middle Ages, nor 'our' Shakespeare with that of his contemporaries; it is rather that different historical periods have constructed a 'different' Homer and Shakespeare for their purposes, and found in these texts elements to value or devalue, though not necessarily the same ones. All literary works, in other words, are 're-written', if only unconsciously, by the societies which read them; indeed there is no reading of a work which is not also a 're-writing'. No work, and no current evaluation of it, can simply be extended to new groups of people without being changed, perhaps almost unrecognisably in the process; and this is one reason why what counts as literature is a notably unstable affair.[17]

The recognition of what some critics call the 'iterability' of the text may or may not be necessary or desirable for the reading of Homer or Shakespeare.[18] It is certainly necessary for the understanding and interpretation of the prophets. The very process by which the prophetic writings have reached us is one of iteration and reiteration, of interpretation and reinterpretation. Whether that is best called 're-writing' is a quibble compared to the facts.

These facts may perhaps best be understood if we make an effort to free our minds of modern Western ways of transmitting literature through publication, and that of course is what Old Testament scholars have tried to help us to do with their talk of the school of Amos, of Hosea's disciples, of the presentation of the prophet's teaching in the form of *memorabile* and so on. It may help us to enter imaginatively into understanding how this transmission could occur when we remember one of the most remarkable feats of preservation of a poetic tradition in our own century: the memorising of the poems of Osip Mandelstam and Anna Akhmatova during the Stalinist period in Soviet Russia, and then the recording of that period by Nadezhda Mandelstam in the two volumes *Hope Against Hope* and *Hope Abandoned*. Akhmatova called it a 'pre-Gutenberg epoch'. Among the many lessons to be learnt from that now recorded experience two stand out as relevant for our interest in the survival of the message of the prophets. The first is the way in which poetry precedes prose. The importance of this distinction and relationship is a commonplace of Old Testament scholarship. The precedence is more than chronological. Writing about Nadezhda Mandelstam's memorisation of her husband's poems, those of other authors, of 'certain ideas, ethical principles—everything that couldn't survive otherwise', Joseph Brodsky wrote:

> And gradually those things grew on her. If there is any substitute for love, it's memory. To memorise, then, is to restore intimacy. Gradually the lines of those poets became her mentality, became her identity. They supplied her not only with the plane of regard or angle of vision; more important they became her linguistic norm. So when she set out to write her books, she was bound to gauge—by that time already unwittingly, instinctively—her sentences against theirs. The clarity and remorselessness of her pages, while reflecting the character of her mind, are also inevitable stylistic consequences of the poetry that had shaped that mind. Both in their content and style, her books are but a postscript to the supreme version of language which poetry essentially is and which became her flesh through learning her husband's lines by heart.[19]

That story may cast some light upon the way in which the minority opinion of eighth-century prophets survived among their followers. But they did not simply survive; and this is the second lesson to be learnt. Again we may use Brodsky's words about Nadezhda Mandelstam:

> Her books were not so much memories and guides to the lives of two great poets, however superbly they performed these functions; these books elucidated the consciousness of the nation. Of the part of it at least that could get a copy.

In some such similar manner the teaching of the prophets became the conscience of the Jewish nation. The style and the content burnt themselves into the consciousness of the Jew, and subsequently of the Christian until it hurt—or healed.

III

Every literary critical approach to a piece of writing must take account of three things: author, text, reader. Usually one of these is made the point of entry to the discussion. We have already tried to suggest some ways in which imagination shapes the prophetic author. We have looked at some of the problems associated with those imaginatively highly charged texts which are the prophetic books. All this assumes that there is a reader, a reader who goes to the text with pre-suppositions, who assumes that there is more to the text than meets the eye, who would have his or her curiosity satisfied. In other words there is a reader who brings his or her questions to the text, comes with quickened imagination.

In literary criticism there is now a consderable literature on Reception Theory.[20] In New Testament studies Rudolf Bultmann focused upon the reader in his demythologising programme, although it is not clear that the problems associated with the existence of a Vorverständnis have been systematically applied to the study of the Old Testament. Nevertheless the expectations with which readers have approached the prophets could hardly vary more widely. There are those who have hoped to find there predictions about the end of the world, Armageddon (although not mentioned in the prophets!). At the other end where extremes meet are those who only expect to find in the prophets support for their indictment of contemporary society. To be treated more seriously, no doubt, are recent productions which avowedly use disciplines developed elsewhere to gain from the text significance hitherto undisclosed or inadequately emphasised. In his commentary on Micah in the Hermeneia series,[21] Delbert R. Hillers parts company with the redaction-critical or developmental analysis put forward in analysis of this as of other prophetic writings by Hans Walter Wolff. Adopting some of the analytical insights of contemporary social scientists Hillers used an understanding of 'revitalisation' or 'millennial' movements at other periods of history to investigate the book of Micah. He seeks to show that elements characteristic of such movements are apparent in the situations to which the book of Micah is addressed. After describing what he conceives to be some of the weaknesses of Wolff's approach he describes his own, using a term now widely current in literary criticism: he writes 'out of preference for the promise that may lie in a synchronic approach, to reading the book as arising for the most part out of one situation'.[22] Presumably Wolff's approach is diachronic.

As this essay was being written there appeared two volumes which provide further contrasting approaches,[23] and no doubt there are many others with which we are unacquainted and many to come. They belong to a proper debate, to a proper liberating of 'the text from any possible enclosing context', and belong in any consideration of how the imagination discerns that the text has yet more truth to yield, and seeks to disclose it. Such studies all await the judgement of their peers not simply today but tomorrow and the day after.

We may conclude this small excursion into strange lands with a different kind of consideration. If anything is clear about the prophetic books of the Old Testament it is that they are word events. As we have already observed the prophets spoke words which effected events. Supremely this was the character of the Word of God (Isaiah 55.11), but it is the character of all words—for better or for worse—to effect something, to trivialise life or enhance it. It is not surprising therefore that the prophetic word was sometimes accompanied by a sign ('*oth-semeion*), a physical act or event which is no mere illustration but a demonstration of the reality which may yet be accomplished in its fulness. So in many generations the passing on of the biblical message has not been in the mind alone, a communication of an inner experience or the sharing of a psychological effect. It has frequently been accompanied by an imaginative work, a painting, a sculpture, a musical cantata or other composition which brings the reality into the presence of the observer or hearer, and brings him or her into touch with the reality of which it speaks. What Eastern Christians perceive about ikons is true of all representational works of art which take the biblical story as their theme. They too trivialise or enhance it, but they do not leave it alone.

Some biblical passages and events lend themselves more than others to such treatment. Supremely among Old Testament figures, Moses and the stories surrounding him give rise to such treatment; and in the New Testament the nativity and the passion have constantly been interpreted and re-interpreted in imaginative ways other than by words alone. Not so the prophets. Jeremiah is represented a little because his story could be presented as a prefiguring of the passion. On the whole individual prophets, or their message, appear little in the iconography of the Church—little that is compared to the great quantity of artistic representation of other biblical themes. The reason is not far to seek: the prophets are word events. Apart from the word the prophet is nothing. Their support therefore, the sign which must accompany them down the ages of the Church, will be verbal.

In a volume in honour of a distinguished Scottish theologian it may therefore be appropriate to conclude with a plea that these writings with all their power to astonish and enlarge our faith and understanding be taken up (again, if necessary) from the pulpit. It has been said, sometimes in a deprecatory way, that the sermon was once as much a part of the cultural as of the religious life of Scotland. But that was no bad thing. From twelve thousand miles away it is impossible to know whether that is still the case. One can but hope. The prophets and their message will live again and again only if interpreted and re-interpreted: that is their character. And they must be accompanied by a sign, a verbal ikon. There are some indications that men and women of imagination might look this way again. Old Testament scholars have prepared the way: no generation before this has had such a clear picture of the form and content of the prophetic books. Literary critics can teach us how to open our minds and exercise our imagination in a fresh understanding of some of the greatest imaginative writings of mankind. Sometimes it appears that only the Church lacks an awareness of its true identity, its vocation.

In the last resort (wrote Miskotte), the church becomes a peculiar fellowship solely through this hearing of the Word; provided that the church clearly sees what has become perfectly clear, namely, that the authority and outgoing of the Word through prophecy (preaching) frees the Scripture from the self-estrangement which it suffered by having been treated as a book. Precisely when the book is removed from the mountain of tradition under which it is buried, from abstract speculation, from liturgical formalization, precisely when the book again becomes the independent, rude, verdant, symphonic thing that it is (not a catalogue of proof texts for dogmatics, not a daily calendar for pietists, and not a target for bourgeois critics and know-it-alls), precisely then does the power of the Word rise up from the rediscovered Book like a phoenix, the divine bird, the winged sun. 'This is why, along with the pelican in her piety and the roaring of the lion of Judah, the phoenix appears on the pediments of the cathedrals as a symbol of Christ' (Schmidt Degener). But it is even more a symbol of the constancy of the Scripture which had languished and died in its own nest.[24]

What then are the expectations with which we may approach the books of the prophets? They must, in Bennett's phrase, be free from 'any possible enclosing context'. That includes freedom from the way in which they happen to be used by New Testament writers, who are only one generation of those who subsequently have used them. If, as James Barr has recently asserted, 'the New Testament never set out to be an interpretation of the Old and did not turn out to be one either', that 'the business of the New Testament is not primarily to tell what the Old really means, but to declare a new substance which for the Old was not yet there, although it was understood that it had prophesied its future coming',[25] then in a sense the Old Testament texts have been set free. The window at Chartres rightly shows Isaiah carrying Matthew on his back, but that is not the only function which either Isaiah or Matthew must perform. Certainly the texts of Old Testament prophecy need to be liberated from their current limited use.

In an eloquent passage[26] Wilhelm Dilthey admits that 'the possibility of experiencing religious states in one's own life is narrowly limited for me as for most of my contemporaries'. 'But,' he adds, 'when I read through the letters and writings of Luther, the reports of his contemporaries, the records of religious disputes and councils, and those of his dealings with officials, I experience a religious process, in which life and death are at issue, of such eruptive power and energy as is beyond the possibility of direct experience for a man of our time.' Then he adds 'But I can re-live it.' Such is the presupposition with which we may approach the prophets, if we exercise imagination. They speak of a living reality of God, a reality which is limited for most of our contemporaries; but the word of judgement and salvation, of denial to many of our ways of thought and life and yet of promise and hope is there in all its eruptive power and energy. Who would not wish to hear it, and to re-live it?

> We, too, make noises when we laugh or weep;
> Words are for those with promises to keep[27]

NOTES

1. *Imagination* (London, 1976), p.108.
2. *The Summa Theologiae* of St Thomas Aquinas, Vol.45, ed. R. Potter OP (Blackfriars, London & New York, 1969) 2a 2ae Qq. 171-8. For comment see Paul Synave OP and Pierre Benoit OP *Prophecy and Inspiration* (Desclee Company, New York, 1961), and Ray L. Hart *Unfinished Man and the Imagination* (Herder and Herder, New York, 1968), pp.328-34.
3. *Modern Painters*, Vol.III, Pt.IV, chapter XII, 9.
4. *Op. cit.*, 14.
5. *Imagination*, p.78.
6. *The Community of the Beloved Disciple* (Geoffrey Chapman, London, 1979), p.140. In this Fr Brown is supporting Conzelmann contra Käsemann: Conzelmann 'Was von Anfang war' in *Neutestamentliche Studien für Rudolf Bultmann* (BZNW 21, Berlin, 1954), pp.194-201.
7. Nadezhda Mandelstam *Hope Against Hope* (Collins, London, 1971), p.70.
8. J. Lindblom, *Prophecy in Ancient Israel* (Basil Blackwell, Oxford, 1962), pp.195-6.
9. W. Zimmerli, *Old Testament Theology in Outline* (English translation, T. & T. Clark, Edinburgh, 1978), p.103.
10. Lindblom, *op. cit.*, pp.117-18.
11. Terry Eagleton, *Literary Theory, an Introduction* (Basil Blackwell, Oxford, 1983), p.60.
12. Hans Walter Wolff, *Joel and Amos* (English translation, Hermeneia, Fortress Press, Philadelphia, 1977), p.91.
13. *Op. cit.*, pp.106-13 on 'The Formation of the Book of Amos'.
14. *Die Kleinen Propheten* (1898), p.96 quoted by O. Eissfeldt, *The Old Testament: an Introduction* (Basil Blackwell, Oxford, 1966), p.401.
15. See the controversy between James Barr and Brevard S. Childs, and in particular Childs *Introduction to the Old Testament as Scripture* (SCM Press, London, 1979) and Barr *Holy Scripture: Canon, Authority, Criticism* (Clarendon Press, Oxford, 1983).
16. Jacques Derrida, *Of Grammatology* (Baltimore, 1977), pp.180-1, quoted by Tony Bennett 'Text and History' in *Re-reading English* ed. Peter Widdowson (New Accents, Methuen, London, 1982), p.223.
17. Terry Eagleton, *op. cit.*, p.12.
18. Tony Bennett, *op. cit.*, p.227, summarises Derrida: 'The "iterability" liberates the text from any possible enclosing context, be it the context of the originating moment of inscription favoured by interpretative criticism or the context of the semiotic code favoured by structuralism'.
19. *New York Review of Books* (date missing).
20. For an impression of the range of questions involved see Susan R. Suleiman and Inge Grosman (eds) *The Reader in the Text: Essays on Audience and Interpretation* (Princeton University Press, 1980).
21. Delbert R. Hillers, *A Commentary on the Book of the Prophet Micah* (Fortress Press, Philadelphia, 1984).
22. P.4.
23. Bertil Wirklander, *Prophecy as Literature: A Text-Linguistic and Rhetorical Approach to Isaiah 2-4*. Coniectanea Biblica Old Testament Series 22 (CWK Gleerup, Stockholm, 1984); and Norman K. Gottwald (ed.), *The Bible and Liberation* (Orbis Books, New York, 1983).

24. Kornelis H. Miskotte, *When the Gods are Silent* (English translation, Collins, London, 1967), p.331.
25. James Barr, *Holy Scripture: Canon, Authority, Criticism* (Clarendon Press, Oxford, 1983), p.70.
26. Wilhelm Dilthey, *The Construction of the Historical World in the Human Studies*, Vol.VII (See Dilthey: *Selected Writings* edited and introduced by H. P. Rickman, CUP, 1976), p.227.
27. W. H. Auden, 'Their Lonely Betters', *Collected Shorter Poems 1927-57* (Faber, London, 1966), p.280.

« 9 »

D. M. MACKINNON : THE EVANGELICAL IMAGINATION

This chapter provides some reflections on Professor Frank Kermode's treatment of the narratives of Christ's temptation in the wilderness.

Kermode has recently published a fascinating essay entitled: *Instances of Interpretation: Death and Survival*,[1] in which he has sought to illustrate the complexity of the work of interpretation, involved of necessity in the writer's activity, by discussing two episodes in the record of Jesus' ministry that are treated very differently by individual evangelists, namely the temptation in the wilderness, and the so-called triumphal entry into Jerusalem. The former is very differently treated by Mark from Matthew and Luke, and has no place in John's record, and there are very important differences between the narratives of Matthew and Luke. Again the so-called cleansing of the temple is separated by John from the triumphal entry, and set at the onset of Jesus' ministry, and Professor Kermode is closely attentive to the significant differences in the way Jesus' arrival in Jerusalem for the last week is treated by Matthew, Mark and Luke. The whole essay is successful in raising in the sharpest way the question of how the Gospels are to be received, how indeed they were conceived by the men who wrote them, what were the sources of their inspiration, that led them to treat the material before them as they did.

Professor Kermode is obviously fascinated by the elusive, laconic brevity of Mark's account of the temptation of Jesus, confined to two verses (I 12, 13), showing the one whom a voice from heaven has addressed as the 'beloved Son in whom I am well pleased' cast by the Spirit into the desert, there to be tempted for forty days by Satan among the wild beasts and to receive the ministry of angels. Again he is obviously impatient with the late Professor Vincent Taylor's treatment of Mark's account of the relation of the cursing of the fig tree to the cleansing of the temple as a typical Markan muddle, indicative of the primitiveness of the author's version: something is being said that is obviously important; but that something does not lie on the surface. Oddly enough Professor Kermode makes no reference to the strange statement in Mark's account that Jesus did not allow anyone to carry any article of furniture through the temple (Mark 11 16). No other version of the events includes reference to this interference with the conduct of temple affairs. It goes far beyond the question of angry protest at the behaviour of money-changers, sellers of *objets de piété* etc. To bar the carrying of *skeruē* through the temple *might* just suggest a challenge to the preparation in train for the coming Passover. But Kermode is certainly right to demand the closest reading of Mark's text.

Where the narrators of the temptation in the wilderness are concerned, again the reader is called to the closest scrutiny of the stories as Matthew and Luke tell them. Where Matthew in particular is concerned, Professor Kermode is indebted to the very important article that Dom Jacques Dupont OSB contributed to *New Testament Studies*[2] but it is impossible (as we shall see) not to regret his apparent neglect of the book: *Les Tentations de Jésus au Désert*,[3] in which Dom Dupont develops in full his understanding of this material. (Of this more later.) But where the material itself is concerned, Professor Kermode's close-packed essay is a powerful, even an unanswerable protest against those who would seek to transcend the human experience which the Gospels have sought to realise, and which the rich variety of their complementary traditions reveals as almost from the beginning a various, a diverse, even at a superficial level, a contradictory inheritance. We must not seek refuge from this inevitable subjectivity, splendidly creative as it has proved itself to be in quest of supposed, irrefutable fact.

Professor Kermode has brooded on the pages devoted by Père M. Steiner in his book on *La Tentation de Jésus dans l'interpretation patristique de Saint Justin à Origène*,[4] and seems ready to endorse Steiner's judgement, that Origen is the 'first great exegete' (p. 107). He is alert to the pervasiveness in the history of Christian exegesis of the controversy between Alexandrians and Antiochenes. He knows also that in the theological schools of Western Europe, the Antiochene tradition has long provided the norm of intellectual respectability. Steiner indeed is at pains to defend Origen (arguably the greatest of the Alexandrians in intellectual stature) against a biased judgment that would dismiss him as a lover of allegorical subtlety at the expense of a deep concern with what happened and was done. Rather his aim is to provide the instruments which will enable the student properly to assimilate what he is being told happened and was done. And here total context is important.

But although Kermode's sympathies are with the Alexandrian tradition, he is before all else a student of literature, and insists that we remember that each of our three versions of the Temptation story, and our four of the triumphal entry, makes its own 'synthesis of acts', to use Aristotle's expression. We must read, re-read, read again what is before us. The tools provided by typological exegesis, and by 'redaction-criticism' are alike indispensable. The latter (for all the ugliness of the name) embodies a standing protest against a view of the

Gospels which in the name of an entirely laudable concern with their factual basis, risks in the end reducing Matthew and Luke to scissors-and-paste compilations, turning aside from the theological density of Mark, and finding in the fourth Gospel something ultimately intractable. This though a closer scrutiny might have suggested that it is John among the four, who is most deeply, if almost unconsciously, concerned with the factual, with the *Logos sarx genomenos*.

If one applies the lesson that Origen taught, of the importance of context for an adequate understanding, one may extend it a good deal further than Professor Kermode has had space enough to do, to the Lukan temptation narrative which finds the climax of Christ's ordeal in the suggestion that he cast himself from the pinnacle of the temple.

The theme of the temple is profoundly significant in the structure of Luke's narration of Christ's ministry. His first recorded words are spoken there when, at the age of twelve, his parents take him to Jerusalem for Passover, and he delays behind to be sought by them anxiously and found in conversation with the doctors, who are greatly impressed by his precocious learning and wisdom. 'Did you not know,' he says in answer to his mother's reproach, 'that I must be involved in my Father's affairs?' And the temple is the inevitable site of that involvement (Lk. 2.41 ff.). After the expulsion of the traders, following the triumphal entry, Luke adds (19.47) that he was daily teaching in the temple; (certainly in Luke's version the duration of his ministry in Jerusalem could seem to extend beyond two or three days). But most significantly in the final climax of the crucifixion the themes of temptation and temple are again woven together in an unforgettable tapestry at once sombre and triumphant.

From the very moment the preparation for this climax is set in hand, the interpenetration of triumph and catastrophe is traceable in Luke's presentation. The journey to Jerusalem is introduced at 9.53, a verse which uses in respect of Jesus' resolve to go there the aorist active verb (estērixen), whose perfect passive (estēriktai) occurs significantly in the parable of Dives and Lazarus to mark the gulf between the place of torment and Abraham's bosom. If it is fashionable to characterise Luke's picture of this last journey as one of triumphal progress ending in exultant acclamation by the descent from the Mount of Olives, defended by Jesus from Pharisaic criticism (Lk. 19.40) by the claim that if human voices were silent, the very stones would cry out, the very next verse (19.41) corrects this picture. 'And when he drew near and saw the city, he wept over it, saying that "if you knew even in this day the things that pertain to your peace"' etc. The tone is one of utter weariness, of sadness in the face of a prophet's defeat. (The classical student may be moved to contrast the cry *Thalassa, Thalassa*, with which Xenophon's *Anabasis* reaches its term.) And the same note is struck again with almost brutal harshness, in the rebuke with which (in Lk. 23.27–31) Jesus dismissed the emotional sympathy displayed toward him by the women on the *via dolorosa*.

When with Lk. 22, the Passion-narrative proper begins, the references to Satanic temptation come clear and strong. It is Satan who has entered into Judas Iscariot; it is Satan who sifts Peter as wheat, even though he is foremost among those who are named by Jesus as those who have continued with him in his temptations; it is with a plea on his lips to his disciples to rise from sleep and pray that they do not enter into temptation that the detachment led by Judas come upon Jesus to arrest him. But inevitably it is in the crucifixion itself that temptation reaches its sharpest. From Lk. 23.35 to Lk. 23.43 the challenge to descend from the cross provides the setting of the whole scene, including the exchanges with the malefactors crucified with Jesus. 'Save thyself.' 'Save thyself and us.' The language is resonant with that of the earlier, lesser ordeal. 'If indeed you are the chosen one, the Christ of God.' It is the final invitation to Jesus to validate himself and his cause in a totally convincing way: or at least to try to do so and in failure, learn the scale of his error. But as on the earlier occasion, Jesus remains steadfast, refusing to put God to the test, daring to make the mysterious promise of Paradise to the malefactor, who, in penitence, has confessed him, and through his steadfastness, enabled himself to say at the last: Father, into thy hands I commend my spirit; words strongly resonant of his first reference at the age of twelve to his Father's affairs. But the last words are spoken on the cross; the veil of the temple has already been rent in twain. Whereas in Mark's version the death of Jesus precedes the rending of the temple-veil, which immediately follows it to be followed in turn by the centurion, who saw him breathe his last and heard his last great cry, confessing him as truly Son of God (Mark 15.37, 38). In Matthew (27.50ff) the order of these events is the same as that of Mark. The rending of the temple-veil is, however, there included in a list of portents, comprising also an earthquake, a rending of the rocks, and a resurrection of saints buried in the environs of Jerusalem who went into the holy city and appeared to many after Jesus' own resurrection. It is the experience of these portents that moves the centurion and others watching with him to great terror and confession of Jesus as Son of God. The apocalyptic embroidery changes the starkness of the Markan narrative with its sudden intrusive reference to the rending of the temple-veil coming between the statement that Jesus breathed his last with a great cry and the centurion's confession. But in Luke the order is significantly changed. The catastrophic sign of the approaching end of the Temple with all that it portended must take place before Jesus, who had begun his concern with his Father's affairs in that place, dies, commending to that same Father his spirit. For his fidelity is a greater thing than the cultus which the temple safeguarded, and this the centurion implied when he confessed Jesus not Son of God, but *dikaios*, a just, even more particularly an innocent, man.

Yet of course this is not the whole sense of the tale. In what I have written, I have, like Professor Kermode, continuously drawn on the resources provided by what is arguably the greatest contribution in English to the interpretation of Luke's treatment of Christ's temptation: namely John Milton's *Paradise Regained*.[5] The haunting, mysterious lines with which Milton concludes the dialogue between Christ and Satan (Book IV lines 560–1)

> To whom then Jesus: Also it is written
> Tempt not the Lord thy God, He said and stood

convey in their many-layered density, the heart of Luke's vision of Christ's victory. He *said and stood* (italics mine). He does not put to the test his understanding of his status and his mission by an act which would either validate his conviction and overwhelm to confession of his dignity those on whom suddenly he descended, or else by ending his life, in another way settle once and for all by the fatal end of his (to him presumptuous) experiment, the question that must continually engage him. It is the manner of his relation to his Father that is at issue. The way of the cross reaches its term when he says: 'Father, into thy hands I commend my spirit'. So nailed to his cross, he stands when challenged to save himself and to overwhelm all questioning by descent from the cross.

Yet of course such descent (if successfully consummated) would withdraw him from the society of the penitent malefactor, whose tentative plea to be remembered of Jesus when he enters into his Kingdom is answered by the promise that to-day he will be, with the partner of his present agony, in paradise. A Jesus who descended from the cross would be for ever withdrawn from close association with such men and women as this rogue. Similarly it is surely no accident that Luke, who finds Christ's climactic temptation in the desert to lie in the challenge to cast himself from the pinnacle of the temple, presents him remorselessly as the friend of tax-gatherers and harlots, includes in his teaching such parables as the tax-gatherer and the pharisee, the two brothers, the good samaritan, and in his life finds place for such episodes as the harlot's extravagant devotion in the house of Simon the Pharisee, and the gratitude of the Samaritan leper who, alone of the ten cleansed, returns to thank the healer. If a descent from the pinnacle of the temple gave Jesus a bloodless victory in the sense of winning him the awe-struck confession of his dignity by those to whom he came, the cost might well be entanglement with the spiritual élite, even with the Sadducaic priesthood or with the morally superior Pharisees in their less admirable aspects. The betrayal of his Father's mission, of his very Sonship of God, would at the same time, keep him of necessity aloof from the rag-tag and bob-tail of the society in which he moved. Yet again one must not simplify: there was in this open-ness conferred upon him by his fidelity, by his readiness to live in ambiguity, a tragic element. And this we have already glimpsed by reference to the tears shed over Jerusalem, and in the harshness of the words with which he seems to rebuff the women who lament on him as he treads the way to Calvary.

What has been done so far in this essay? Luke's treatment of Christ's temptation has been studied as a creative interpretation of a tradition which he seems to share with Matthew, but handles very differently. As Dupont well brings out, for Matthew the recapitulation of the experience of Israel in the desert is crucially significant. Luke by no means disdains this typology. Indeed in writing of Christ's transfiguration he says that he spoke with Moses and Elijah on Hermon of the *exodos* he would accomplish in Jerusalem. Yet the context that Luke's whole Gospel (and in particular his Passion-narrative) provides, distinguishes the sense of his temptation narrative from that of his fellow-evangelists.

What can one say in summary of this sense? And here admittedly we cannot detach our judgment from our memory of John Milton's reading of the narrative, which itself belongs to a particular setting at once cultural and biographical. (Kermode insists in much the same way that our recollection of the cleansing of the temple in the Synoptics is likely to be coloured and embellished by recall of detail peculiar to St John who locates the episode chronologically quite differently.) As Milton read the temptation story he was no doubt familiar with an exegesis which compared its argument with that of the book of Job, a book whose curious similarities with Aeschylus' *Prometheus Vinctus* has encouraged some commentators to suppose (almost certainly wrongly) that the author knew the tragedian's work. As we read the passage, we cannot, if we are literate, ignore the imprint in our imagination of Milton's rendering. And he was himself responding to what Luke had done with a tradition before him. We do well to heed the fact that we are dealing with great literature, where the imagination of a creative artist has transcended the limitation of bare factual record, in Luke's case an imagination liberated by freedom to indulge in acceptance of the miraculous as part of the furniture of the world in which he lived: (this though he is careful to differentiate Christ's acts of mercy, etc. from the merely thaumaturgical, more careful in his Gospel than in his supposed sequel, the Acts of the Apostles, where the discipline is much more relaxed, and the achievement considerably less).[6] But the question remains: are we dealing with, are we engaged with, that which is somehow factually referential?

Dupont insists emphatically that the tradition has its origin in Christ's own self-disclosure to his disciples, a self-disclosure that inevitably fastens on the secret of his relation to his Father. According to orthodoxy, this relation is the very ground of his being; yet all his ministry to its bitter end, shows this ground as something at once received, and yet precarious. Even in the Fourth Gospel it is something to be affirmed again and again in a prolonged exercise of 'infinite self-abnegation' (the phrase is Dean Inge's). The temptations touch most intimately on this relationship and this is implied even by the laconic Mark, who insists that the Spirit casts Jesus forth into the desert; the initiative is not his own; its spring is the love of the Father for the Son, and the Son's response.

It is by no means incredible that the relationship was presented by Jesus as something that he had to affirm at the very outset of his mission against every sort of subtly suggested misconstruction, that he had to wrestle himself in his humanity into the counterpart of that total receptivity which was the very substance of his being. Only (to revert to Luke's narrative) in the setting of that relationship (that total preoccupation with his Father's affairs and self-submission to his Father's verdict) is the openness to all and sundry, to outcast and disreputable, possible without lapse into antinomian sentimentality. The two elements in Jesus' relationship to God, and to men and women are complementary, and their complementarity is the final hard-won expression of his fidelity. What engages us has its hard factual basis.

Further there are serious students who protest that the ultimate concern of Jesus' temptations in the wilderness is far removed from the very ordinary temptations seemingly envisaged by the writer to the Hebrews when he spoke of Jesus as tempted in all ways as we are: 'yet without sin'. The engagement in the desert seems to suggest issues which by the very density of their presentation are made to lie outside the experience of human kind. Yet the victory (to use traditional language) of Jesus in the wilderness leaves him exposed to the particularities of his experience in ministry. If the angels indeed had then charge of him to keep him, as he fell, they would have done so because their rôle was to keep him in *all* his ways. Should he thus have rendered himself invulnerable, cocooned against the daily testing of his fidelity? The way appointed him by his Father was one of continual exposure; it was (to use traditional language) the way of incarnation. It is a manifest weakness of much traditional Christology that it has evacuated the mystery of God's self-incarnation of so much that must take time, that must be endowed with the most pervasive forms of human experience, its successiveness, its fragmentariness, above all its ineluctable choices, fraught equally inevitably with tragic consequence. It is a paradox that in a narrative, in which in the form in which we have received it, the mythological, the typological, even the contrived framework seem to take charge, we have in fact a standing protest against failure to take seriously the sheer concreteness of God's self-incarnating.

We need the tools of literary study, above all the discipline of close reading, to enable us to reach through the apparent flight from fact to fantasy, back towards the coldly factual basis. I say coldly factual; I am, of course, referring to the unique, unrepeatable presence of the transcendent in and to the world around us. To capture even the outskirts of that drawing near demands every resource of imagination that we possess. We have to enter into the experience of the Evangelists as best we can, and find beyond and conditioning their diverse presentations, what men were able to grasp of the self-interpretation[7] by deed as well as word, of the central figure of the Gospels. If there were to be a sub-title of this essay, it might be a twentieth-century footnote to Milton's *Paradise Regained*. And because it belongs to the twentieth century it cannot finally neglect historical questions, and especially that which with revived interest by Jewish as well as Christian scholars, has pre-occupied much recent attention, namely the question why Jesus was rejected, how he was put on trial, on whose initiative, by what sort of court was he condemned, etc. The poignancy of such issues in the age of the Holocaust is beyond question. For Christians have a very good measure of responsibility for preparing the way for the unspeakable enormities of the death-camps by the kind of sentiments expressed for instance by the greatly respected Anglican hymn-writer and scholar, Dr William Bright, in the nineteenth-century hymn:

Though the blood betrayed and spilt
On a race incurred a doom

And it is claimed that the sanction for such judgement can be extracted from the New Testament, from Acts and John as well as from Matthew. So the quest for the historical Jesus is complemented very properly to-day by that for the historical Pilate.

A sequel to the treatment of Christ's temptation in the desert in this essay might well be provided by one engaging with the passion-story and especially the passion-story of John, which would begin by recognising that it is dominated by an essentially tragic dialogue, the confrontation of Christ and Pilate. The setting is surprisingly naturalistic. Apart from the prostration of the band of temple-police come to arrest Jesus at the self-identification of his *ego eimi*, there is no miraculous embroidery of any kind. Although the reference at the onset to 'lanterns, torches, and weapons' reminds the reader that the arrest takes place in the dark, into which Judas passed from the supper, it is surprising that a Gospel, whose symbolism so stresses the contrast between light and dark, has no mention of 'darkness over the face of the land' at the hour of the crucifixon. Malchus is more precisely identified; but his injury goes unhealed. One could continue the theme for a long time.

But at the centre lies the reality of judgement, of Christ before Pilate, of the prisoner who is the Son of Man by whom this world is judged, and found wanting—the worlds of government, of piety, of speculation. The dialogue is devastatingly ironic. Certainly for John the initiative is taken by the Jewish ecclesiastical authorities who see (not without reason) a threat to the continued existence of Temple and cultus in the activities (however well-intentioned) of the Nazarene. The symbiosis of Jewish church and occupying power was precarious at the best of times, and its stability was menaced by any sort of agitation, especially with a prefect of Judea as brutal and even unbalanced as Pilate. For although the passion-narrative sometimes suggest a weak man, the fuller portrait (in John as well as Luke) is of someone rather different. Whether or not the evidence of Philo's *Legatio ad Gaium* establishes that he was 'a creature of Sejanus' (and there is substantial doubt on this point by Roman historians), Pilate in his situation and with his record is better seen as a man vulnerable to pressure discreetly exercised rather than as a weakling. He must avoid unnecessary brutality; yet at the same time he must never appear as other than Caesar's friend. If he seems to compensate for previous cruelty and folly by connivance in the continued activity of a strange, always disturbing prophet (whom some regarded as a king), he may find himself in very deep waters. So he collaborates with the priestly initiative and condemns Jesus to the cross. But Pilate's anger is still strong in him; and there is fury, contempt most certainly for himself as well as for the Jews, in the famous: 'What I have written, I have written'.

The presentation John offers of what to him is the judgement of this world is a masterpiece of tragic irony. It is a narrative that invites historical evaluation by reason of its immanent psychological credibility. We cannot accept it as it stands, as an historical record; but the tragic theological and historical dimensions of these pages so interpenetrate that the two forms of criticism (the literary and the historical) must both be enlisted to aid the the distinctively religious perception, which finds the truth of what human beings ultimately are, not simply revealed but brought into being by the fact that Jesus leaves the place of judgement, carrying his cross himself. There is no mention of the Cyrenian: only of the condemned man going forth to die, and by his death, finishing the work given by his Father and establishing forgiveness and mercy as the *telos* of the whole affair.

'It is expedient that one man die for the people that the whole nation perish not'—'If we let him alone, the Romans will come and will destroy our place and nation'. Caiaphas speaking as high priest is regarded by John as prophesying; but the obvious sense of his words lie in the expression of a sage, ecclesiastical *raison d'état*. I say: sage, not cynical; for indeed the Romans came, and temple and nation were alike destroyed. As long as the temple stood, as long as Jews flocked to Jerusalem for Passover, as long as the cultus was maintained, so long the Jewish nation survived as an identifiable entity. One could call this policy collaborationist as indeed it appeared to extremists. But it reckoned with the realities of power; also, remembering the past, there was hope that the Jewish people would not only survive, but as Yahweh's chosen, outlive their Roman oppressor. There was every sort of danger in disorder, and Jesus with his reputation as a healer, together with his very disturbing teaching, might not advocate, but could easily occasion, a dangerous sterile *émeute*. So if the Roman authorities were already taking notice of him, and that was more than likely, would it not be wise to go along with them, even to prod them into action? Caiaphas is surely, at least as much as Creon in Sophocles' *Antigone*, presented as a tragic figure. If Jesus implies that Judas' guilt is greater than Pilate's, that does not obliterate his tragedy any more than it exonerates the prefect. As Dostoevsky suggests in the 'grand inquisitor', in *The Brothers Karamazov*, Caiaphas' dilemma is that of ecclesiastics across the centuries. One recalls the situation of responsible Church leaders vis-à-vis *résistants* during the earlier years of the Nazi occupation of western Europe in the forties. They were compelled to acquiesce in abomination, or at least supposed themselves so for a time, that 'the whole nation perish not'. But for them as for the Jewish authorities, in John's passion-narrative, the road they chose too often led to the place of apostasy where they too cried (however hard they might seek to disguise its significance from themselves) that they had 'no King but Caesar', no source of order but the occupying power. John's insight into such responsible ecclesiastical mentality is devastating.

It is a paradox that the one thing a 'Church leader' cannot very often do is to lead. He sees his task more as one of preservation. Not always, I agree, but often enough to make the Johannine Caiaphas intelligible not as providing a shallow excuse for anti-semitism but for understanding the ultimate tragedy of Jesus of Nazareth.

And that tragedy is implicit in the Lukan temptation story. In one sense (as I have suggested) his victory set Jesus free; but in other ways it bound him fast. For if he had nowhere to lay his head, the Son of Man was, by that rootlessness, torn apart from very much in his society that was not despicable, but even sometimes wise and faithful. Was there no other way? We return to the reality of choice and behind that choice, to a mystery of divine self-emptying that we have hardly yet begun to fathom. But we render remote our chances of even approaching the furthest outskirts of the mystery, the shallowest waters of its impenetrable ocean, if we disguise from ourselves by apologetic dexterity, the fact that the victory by which the world was overcome and its prince cast out was profoundly tragic. 'A victory' said a gushing woman to the Duke of Wellington 'must be the most exhilarating thing in the world'. 'A victory' the Duke replied, 'is the most tragic thing in the world, only excepting a defeat'.

NOTES
1. *Essays on Fiction* (1983). Routledge & Kegan Paul, pp. 185-200.
2. *N.T.S.*, Volume 3 (1956-7).
3. Desclée de Brouwer (1968).
4. Paris: Gabalda (1962); see especially pp. 107ff.
5. I owe very much to Professor Barbara Lewalski's treatment of this poem in her book: *Milton's Brief Epic* (Providence: Brown University Press, 1966).
6. Cf. the excellent comments on the Acts of the Apostles by Fr. Noel Dermot O'Donoghue ODC on pp. 41ff of his book: *The Holy Mountain* (Glazier, Delaware, 1983), where referring to the morally repulsive episode of Ananias and Sapphira, he mentions their pitiless and self-righteous slaying, endorsed if not occasioned by Peter, adding that Satan entered the mind of Ananias and Sapphira, in order to enter the mind of Peter. In telling the tale, Luke shows his mind 'contaminated', blithely disregarding that on this occasion, Satan indeed entered Peter to sift him as wheat, and distract him from any impulse to strengthen his brethren, as a man turned again. In spite of the wealth of critical study devoted to the book of Acts from F. J. Foakes-Jackson & Kirsopp Lake to Ernst Haenchen, we still want a work which (granted that Luke–Acts form a single work from a common hand) will explain why the latter volume is so markedly inferior to the former in theological and spiritual perception.
7. And indeed his Father's interpretation of him.

« 10 »

N. D. O'DONOGHUE : MYSTICAL IMAGINATION

I

It can be said that as perception has to do with percepts, and conception with concepts, so imagination has to do with images. So: I perceive this particular tree; I conceive the concept or idea of tree-in-general; I imagine the tree I wish to see grow in front of my door. Here, already, from this everyday observation, a strange fact emerges. It is this: my perception is bound and bounded by the individual tree; my conception is bound and bounded by the idea of tree; but my imagination is free, totally free, almost wildly free. I can form an image of a tree as tall as the sky, as wide as the earth, as varied as the rainbow. I can imagine a tree that grows out of a mountain crag, or on top of a steeple, or in the depth of the sea. So, as against his other ways of knowing, man's imagination is wild and free, so much so that it can be seen as totally irresponsible and fantastical, and therefore as synonymous with fancy or fantasy. It is no wonder that a grave and wise man like St Thomas Aquinas will have nothing to do with it; indeed Plato long before him had rejected the poets, the image-makers, the fantasy-weavers from his well-ordered community.[1]

But what if this wild and wilful energy can be harnessed to the chariot of knowledge? What if instead of cutting loose from the sober world of eye and ear, on the one hand, and from the abstract and motionless world of ideas, on the other, this energy should rather serve to give vibrancy, radiance and movement to the whole scene, so that the perceived tree glows with fire and the abstract tree becomes a heavenly Tree of Life? Is this the end of truth or rather its beginning? Has wisdom lost its wits or begun to live its true life?

As soon as we begin to enter deeply into the world of any of the great philosophers we find ourselves in what can be described as a vibrational field; unless we make some contact with this force we never really meet the philosopher, however much we may analyse and measure him, however lucidly we expound him, however trenchantly we criticise him and point out his fallacies and unproven assumptions. We have at best measured his intelligence; we have not met his imagination.

So, to read the *Phaedo* and to describe, dissect and destroy (partially or entirely) the argument or arguments is but to perform an autopsy. It is only as we are lifted and carried along by the sweep and power of the vision of everlasting man, and his divine destiny, that we can be said to encounter the man who speaks and the man through whom he speaks. One might object that Locke, or Kant, or Aristotle demands the same response, as they oppose *their* vision to that of Plato, but this kind of objection misses the point. I am not saying that the reader must finally agree with Plato (or Kant, or whoever), but that what is most directly encountered and assimilated in a great writer is not in the order of ideas and speculation but in another order, that of imagination. Nor do I think that Plato and Aquinas really rejected this energy. I shall return to this point later.

II

The mystical is seen by some as an extension of everyday perception, a kind of sixth sense, a psychic power of clairvoyance or clairaudience, a whole rather disconcerting world of experience that in recent times has provided the material for the (barely respectable) science of Parapsychology. It is seen by others as an extension of the conceptual, as a kind of exalted thinking that tends to go beyond the range of words, that goes beyond metaphysical discourse yet is somehow continuous with it. In this sense Plotinus was a mystic as Descartes was not, Spinoza was a mystic in a way that Kant was not.

It cannot be denied that either of these extensions of ordinary ways of knowing may be termed mystical, though most people would probably feel happier with the second way of using the term, seeing Plotinus as more properly a mystic than Paracelsus.

But mysticism may also be seen as concerned with the mystical as an extension of imagination, of that free and unbounded form of knowing that I have tried to describe in terms of a vibrational field, something common to the poet, the artist and the philsopher. In this understanding of mysticism Plotinus might still be seen as a mystic, not inasmuch as his conceptual thinking moves beyond the limits of ideas and of language, but inasmuch as a visionary excitement, encountered in all true or strong philosophical discourse, becomes ever more intense as the reader 'tunes in', until it is at once steady, all-consuming, and indicative of what William Wordsworth calls 'unknown modes of being'. Not only are we asked to look beyond concepts and language, but also to share in an experience of that which lies beyond the threshold. This extension of imagination may issue in visions and 'showings', as in the case of St Teresa of Avila or the Lady Julian, or in poetical and artistic visualisations as in the case of William Blake; or it may issue in powerful poetical symbols, as in St John of the Cross; or it may generate philosophical and theological insights as in the case of Meister Eckhart and Angelus Silesius. But it is in all cases the same spirited steed of imagination, harnessed indeed to personal vision and personal destiny (and, therefore, disciplined), yet for all that free and mettlesome, that carries the mystic forward and upward towards what traditional theology names the *fontes*, the 'fountains' or springs of eternal truth.[2]

It is with mysticism as understood in this third way that I shall be mainly concerned in what follows, that is to say with mysticism as personal and imaginative involvement with unknown modes of being. This latter phrase, as I have said, comes from Wordsworth, and I have no hesitation in choosing this Romantic poet-philosopher as a guide to the understanding of mystical imagination. This is not to raise the question as to whether Wordsworth was a mystic but only to agree with Mary Warnock that, when the philosophers have had their say, this poet has in fact the last philosophical word to say.[3] Clearly, to understand imagination in general is to be well on the way to understanding mysticism as the extension of imagination. Besides, in Wordsworth's case theory and practice go hand in hand, and the total integration of theory and practice is one of the marks of genuine mysticism. Just as the mystic lives what he describes and describes what he lives, so at the level of poetic imagination, Wordsworth explains what he is doing by doing what he explains.

We know, for example, that the sight of a bank of daffodils beside a lake fired Wordsworth's imagination, not immediately but in recollection, not merely through the memory of the scene but through the feeling or shaft of delight that the memory brought along with it, breaking in on lonely and vacant moods. *The Daffodils* expresses with marvellous simplicity and economy how this feeling arises as the memory of the scene flashes upon the 'inward eye', which is the eye of the imagination. The inward eye is no longer bound and bounded by the object as given in perception and memory, as the outward eye is bound and bounded. It is free to recreate the scene around the emotion as alive within the memory. It can discriminate, highlight, rearrange, omit, embellish, transform. This is creative *Poiesis*; this is Pegasus, the fiery steed whose 'bright and battering sandals' are simile and metaphor, whose wings are rhythm and rhyme. In *The Daffodils* clouds and stars, marching armies and dancing children provide a forward movement that is directed and borne upwards through metre and the delicate interweaving of sound and silence.[4]

Elsewhere Wordsworth shows how this transformative vision of the inward eye opens up its own inward horizons, not only 'unknown modes of being' but 'something far more deeply interfused', the sense of 'a motion and spirit' that meets man's nature at levels too deep for utterance, too deep even for tears. We are here at the threshold of the mystical understood as the extension of that 'shaping spirit of imagination' (Coleridge), which is the ground of all creativity. We must now try to see what lies beyond this threshold.

III

It seems to me that it is best to begin by taking a bold step across the threshold, and I have chosen the following remarkable passage from *Blake and Tradition* by Kathleen Raine as a way of doing this: 'Samuel Palmer recalls . . . (William) Blake's great love for St Teresa whom he delighted to quote to his disciples. In *Milton* he names her, together with Fénélon, Whitefield and Madam Guyon, among the "gentle souls who guide the great winepress of love". It was for her understanding of the soul's love of God that he admired and loved her; and Oothoon seems to use one of St Teresa's images; for she too understood that sin is extraneous to the soul, like a cloud over brightness. She writes of the soul's relation to the Divine Lover and Beloved: "it seemed to me that my soul was like some clear and pure looking-glass . . . and in the very centre thereof Christ our Lord was represented to me, just as I am wont to see him. It seems to me that I see him in all the parts and portions of my soul as in a looking-glass" (Song of Solomon 2:14). Blake has made the looking-glass water, perhaps for consistency with the Neoloplatonic imagery of water, the Narcissus myth of the mirroring pool and the rest, but the thought is St Teresa's'.[5]

On the basis of this passage it is possible to distinguish three levels of similarity between the Catholic mystic (in the tradition of St Gregory the Great and Osuna) and the dissenting Christian mystic (in the tradition of Boehme and Swedenborg). There is, first and most deeply, the level of the love of God, and to this I shall return presently. There is, secondly, the level of metaphor and symbol, which is the basic dynamism of imagination. Thirdly, there is the level of vision and visualisation, and the question of the reality-status of mystical 'revelations'.

Kathleen Raine, in the paragraph I have transcribed, is mainly concerned with the second level. There is clearly much that could be said about the similarities and dissimilarities between Blake and St Teresa at this level, and there well may be other discoveries to be made in the matter of the influence of St Teresa on Blake—as far as I know only Kathleen Raine has noticed this influence. But I mention it here only to leave it aside, for I am more directly concerned with the other levels.

The question of the reality-value of the visions and 'revelations' of mystical writers such as St Teresa and William Blake—if the devotees of the one and the other will allow at least a common problem here—is usually posed in terms of a naive 'out there' epistemology. But when we make due allowances for the relativity of all human knowledge and agree that subject and object are entirely relative terms, even if we were to go the whole way with Bishop Berkeley and agree that the being of that which is perceived consists in its *being* perceived, we are still faced with the difficulty that only Blake sees Blake's visionary world, only St Teresa sees St Teresa's visionary world. Perhaps one could add that only St John (or whoever) saw the Woman Clothed with the Sun, the Four Horsemen, and the rest. Indeed it is strange that for all the hundreds of Christian fundamentalists, ranging from Isaac Newton to the latest mindless television evangelist, who have confidently *interpreted* the Book of Revelation, not one has claimed to have a direct vision of St John's world. There would seem to be as many private worlds as there are visionaries. There is no common world of mystical imagination as there is of perception and conceptual thought. It is as if, to borrow Wittgenstein's image, each mystical author played her/his own language game, played it indeed with amazing skill and consistency and obedience to the rules, but played nevertheless a game that nobody else can really play. In our own day, or near it, Rudolf Steiner has played this game with astonishing virtuosity and consistency, and has moreover claimed that the game can be taught (though, of course he does not use the Wittgenstein image), yet it is quite clear that none of his many followers have managed to master it.

It can be maintained that a certain degree of individual freedom and idiosyncrasy is not only to be allowed but even to be regarded as necessary in the order of imagination, and especially in the order of mystical imagination. At this point, however it is necessary to bring up again, and very firmly, the distinction between the mystical as an extension of perception and the mystical as an extension of imagination. Is St Teresa in her vision of Hell proposing to open up for us a terrifying actual world continuous in some way with the everyday world, and therefore supremely to be feared? Or is she giving us an imaginative account of the reality of evil? Are Blake's engravings supposed to represent an actual world, however deep and hidden, or do they rather illustrate Blake's insights about human destiny? Is Steiner's (or, for that matter, Edgar Cayce's) Atlantis no more than a footnote to Plato, or is it presented to us as actual in the way that the earth of the dinosaurs (whose bones are in our museums) is presented to us as actual, and therefore continuous with our present and past human experience and history? It is only when we are dealing with the mystical as an extension of perception that these questions arise. At that level they are important questions, and I shall return to them again. But they are not questions directly bearing on mystical imagination, and they must be put aside while we look at the question or questions which do bear directly on mystical imagination: the questions, distinguishable but closely related, of responsibility and commitment.

Imagination is free, mystical imagination is free in the highest degree. But, here as elsewhere, freedom is inseparable from responsibility. It is said that J. R. Tolkien was unhappy with his friend

C. S. Lewis' imaginative writings because, as Tolkien saw it, Lewis failed in creative responsibility in merely sketching his world of imagination, in not *realising* it fully by living in it in all its detail, as in fact Tolkien lived in the world of *The Lord of the Rings*.[6] There is question here (if one may accept Tolkien's point, purely as an example) of artistic rather than moral responsibility, though it may be argued that the one should not be dissociated from the other. The question becomes in any case a more serious one for the author who asks the reader for total commitment to the world he/she claims to discover at the horizons of spiritual experience. Artistic responsibility here becomes the moral responsibility of total commitment. This is fully exemplified in St Teresa, as it is fully exemplified in every mystical writer worthy of the name.

Now this commitment is not primarily and principally seen as obedience to a moral imperative. Indeed it is not seen at all in moral terms; insofar as it is, the mystic is no longer a mystic, though he/she may be a reliable spiritual guide. For the mystic as such the commitment is, first and last, finalised and energised by an experience of the source of all man's words and works, an experience of the source of man's being and of all goodness. All truth and beauty as well. It is from this experience that all mystical imagination flows. I call it 'the source-experience', and it is with the understanding of this that the present study is mainly concerned.

IV

A well-known passage from St Augustine's *Confessions* will show us the way at this point. It will be found in the tenth chapter of Book Seven, where this fifth century philosopher-bishop is describing his first (definitive?) conversion from Manicheism to Christianity by way of Neoplatonism. This came by way of a 'light above the mind' (*supra oculum animae meae, supra mentem meam, lucem incommutabilem*), 'above' not in any spatial sense, nor yet in any sense continuous with the physical, but 'above' as revealing another region of reality, a region of such dazzling presence and power that in the light of it evil disappears into shadows and unreality.

We are here in the world of the transconceptual mystical, the second of our three categories named above. But the passage ends with a statement that seems to take the whole experience into another dimension, a statement that comes quite unexpectedly in the context of an account of an intellectual change by way of a light above the *mind*. The statement is: love knows this light (*caritas novit eam*). In a later passage (Book 10, ch. 17) this light is invoked as 'Beauty ever ancient and ever new', and we are in the world of imagination. The call of love has transformed mystical knowledge into mystical imagination. The margin has been released, so that a systematic and binding conceptual discovery passes over into the celebration of a Presence at once free and uniquely precious (with the total responsibility which this implies for the recipient). It is, at another level, the landscape that opens up for Wordsworth to the vision of the 'inward eye'. It is memory that conjures up this world of light and love, a world that glows with its own special radiance named by Wordsworth himself as 'the light that never was on sea or land, the consecration and the poet's dream'. This is not the memory of the mind, but the memory of the heart: 'my heart remembers how', said Robert Louis Stevenson, as far away in the South Seas he remembers a windy day on the Scottish uplands.[7] This light of the heart remembering glows all through the ten autobiographical books of St Augustine's *Confessions*, and culminates in the celebrated eulogy of memory in the tenth book. Here we have the greatest theologian of the West at home in his own heart, in the house of creative imagination, and not, as in some of his later writings, toiling along the desert paths of controversy.

There is a remarkable resemblance in style, vocabulary and content between the passage from St Augustine with which we have been concerned and the account which St Teresa gives of the vision of the Holy Trinity which is for her the culmination of the life of mystical prayer. It will be found in the first chapter of the Seventh Mansions of *The Interior Castle*. She tells us that, though this vision of the Trinity is in her terminology an 'intellectual' vision, yet it comes by way of the heart: 'the spirit becomes enkindled (*con una inflamación*) by way of a cloud of surpassing brightness'. This illuminating experience is, as with St Augustine, dramatic and definitive, establishing its recipient in a new way of being and doing. Yet while the effect on mind and heart is similar, the doctrinal articulation of the experience differs: for Augustine it is the Exodus experience of the God Who Is; for Teresa it is the Christian experience of the Trinity-in-Unity. In both cases there is a kind of inner Divine speech in which the doctrine is stated and impressed on the heart (Augustine) or soul (Teresa). In both cases—and this is important—the inner Divine speech is subsequent to the core experience, which thus stands by itself independently of the doctrinal formulation. Indeed we have here a situation which is the exact converse of the process so aptly described by Flannery O'Connor: 'to me a dogma is only a gateway to contemplation'.[8]

What I have been trying to do in this section is to isolate and focus the source-experience from which, I contend, all authentic mystical imagination flows. Or, perhaps it would be more accurate to say: whose depth and authenticity (in terms of responsibility, commitment and self-giving) is the measure of the value of mystical imagination. This experience is at once entirely simple and richly complex. In the section that follows I shall venture to try to describe some aspects of this mysterious phenomenon.

V

By the source-experience I mean primarily experience *of* the source. There may be question of a single, once-and-for-all experience, or of a series of experiences usually culminating in a single crowning experience such as that which St Teresa describes in the passage from *The Interior Castle* quoted in our last section. This experience of the source becomes itself a source, the source from which the visions, symbols and insights of mystical imagination flow. Clearly it is only by an understanding of the source-experience that we can hope to understand the kind of discourse that flows from it.

There are, it seems to me, five main aspects of the source-experience, and I shall deal briefly with each of these in turn. Each of these aspects can be seen as fanning out into a much fuller discussion, and there are many other subordinate aspects of this rich and diverse phenomenal field. There have been many, mostly reductionist, studies of what is called the psychology of mysticism; very little has been done in the way of a descriptive phenomenology of mysticism which would try to relate the given diversity of claimed experience and expressed discourse to their source in the mind and heart—or, if the term is preferred, the subjectivity—of the mystic. It is to this kind of approach that the following analysis belongs.[9]

A) The source-experience is a heart-experience. The depth, quality and 'flow' of the experience is nowhere more powerfully and poignantly expressed than in the poems of St John of the Cross, especially in *On a Dark Night*, in which the 'soul' (that is to say, the whole personality as open to love) goes forth in darkness to seek the Beloved, because it is 'on fire with love', and is led onwards to the source by the fire in the heart, and not by any material or intellectual light. So, too, the *Cloud of Unknowing* speaks of the 'drawing of that love and the voice of that calling', a phrase taken over by T. S. Eliot to describe the resolution of man's ceaseless exploration, in his great mystical poem, the *Four Quartets*.[10] Both St John and the author of the *Cloud* (as well as Eliot) are speaking of an experience still on the way to fulfilment, whereas both St Augustine and St Teresa are speaking of a fulfilled and fulfilling experience. Yet, explicit in St Augustine and implicit in St Teresa, is the sense of further horizons, of a journey always beginning. Precisely because it is incarnational and other-regarding (*actively* salvific by way of the following of Christ) Christian mysticism is always *en route*, and is always profoundly untrue to itself whenever it claims perfection or realisation. The concept of a perfect or realised 'master' is alien to the Christian tradition and is, I suspect, a deformation or degeneration of what is best in the mystical traditions of the East.

To say that the source-experience is a heart-experience is not by any means to exclude the intellect. Rather is it to centre the experience along the axis of *erōs–agapé* while keeping the way open to the regions of sense-perception and philosophical-theological exploration. I would wish to argue that St Paul's eulogy of *agapé* in 1 Corinthians 13 is the fruit of a deep source-experience or experiences, yet it clearly includes the everyday practical and issues in a strong theological position.

B) It is clear that St Teresa's vision of the Holy Trinity and the experiences from which it flows is seen by the visionary herself as something *given*. It is not an active experience, a repeatable achievement; rather is it passive, or better, receptive. The 'turn' from activity to passivity is central to the tradition within which Teresa was formed, and this 'turn' is carefully described in the Fourth Mansions. In the first three mansions the disciple seeks God laboriously as a gardener might draw water from a well to irrigate his garden; in the Fourth Mansions the rain begins to fall and all is life and growth. God takes over; the Source Itself begins to flow in, and is experienced as abundance of light and fire—abundance of water too, but we must be careful here, for the metaphor has now become a descriptive term at the transphysical level. The metaphor of the gardener and the ways of irrigation comes from the *Life*, the book that Blake loved.[11] In the poems of St John of the Cross this experience of passive or receptive contemplation expressed itself in a whole shower of images; here the *Spiritual Canticle* is unique in the literature of Christian spirituality. We are here at the very centre of the world of mystical imagination, a world totally misapprehended by the people of 'clear and distinct ideas' and of a merely propositional theology. Nevertheless the border between imagination and the world of theological systematics is not closed from the side of imagination, and we find St John working out a dogmatics of mysticism by way of a commentary on some of his poems, though he makes it clear (in the commentary on the First Stanza of the *Spiritual Canticle*, for example) that the poetry must be given its own kind of hearing. The mystical cannot be translated into a systematic theology without remainder: the failure to appreciate this has led to very great confusion, and much strife and cruelty in the course of Christian history. The category of the 'heretical' usually emerges with the death of the mystical.

The poetry of St John of the Cross is more personal and less cosmic than that of William Blake, yet for all that, the imagination-world of these two great mystical poets has much in common, not least a total purity of life and vision, in the light of which all sham and pretentiousness fall away into dust and ashes. John remained, however uneasily, within the dogmatic system of the church of his time and place, while Blake rejected all the dogmatic and ecclesial systems of *his* time and place. Because of this, Blake did not feel any responsibility to translate his 'imaginations' into doctrinal form as John did. In both cases, however, the primary experience of the source came in full and glorious freedom as a gift perfect in itself. Perhaps all true poetry is thus receptive, a listening rather than a speaking, something that happens when the spirit is 'tuned in' to what Hopkins calls 'that fine delight that fathers thought'. Perhaps the mystic is the poet who has given herself/ himself completely, 'Purity of heart', says Kierkegaard, 'is to will one thing'.[12]

C) And so we come to the question of *continuity*. Is there continuity between poetic imagination (and, in general, artistic imagination) and mystical imagination? To put the question more concretely: is there continuity between the kind of inspiration that created Wordsworth's *Daffodils* and that which created St John's *On a Dark Night*? It seems to me that this continuity becomes clear when we relate each poem to the source-experience whence it flows. The experience is unique, entirely personal and unrepeatable, but the source is one and the same. At the centre of each poem is a moment of illumination, Wordsworth's 'flash' that strikes the inward eye in a time of relaxation and tranquillity, John's 'fire burning in the heart' that comes to recognition and expression only when his 'house is now at rest'. It is clear that Wordsworth's whole philosophy of imagination is a recognition that these flashes that are 'felt along the heart' are messengers from the source, sometimes coming as poignant intimations (in 'thoughts that lie too deep for tears'), sometimes as insights into 'the life of things'.

All this is for Wordsworth givenness, grace, as much as it is for St John or St Teresa. The main principle of differentiation is nearness to the source, and perhaps the best criterion for judging this is its effect on the whole of life: the givingness that responds to the givenness. Some Christians find a grace-filled givingness as well as a responsive givenness in the testimony of a St Teresa that they do not find in a Wordsworth or a William Blake. Some Catholic authors—Jacques Maritain, for example—will regard serious comparison between mystical writers within the fold and those outside the fold as out of the question.[13] I do not belong to this latter camp, but I do not want to confront this viewpoint directly here. Enough if it can be agreed that there is continuity or gradation within the range of a scale no matter how high or wide, an analogy not so much of being as of the *experience* of being. This, *pace* Maritain, is good Thomism.

D) In *The Lost Leader* the youthful Robert Browning accuses the ageing Wordsworth of betraying their common imaginative vision as poets of the free spirit. According to Browning, he and his companions of the younger generation saw Wordsworth as their leader, and 'lived in his mild and magnificent eye'. They felt betrayed because this leader had allied himself with the 'establishment' (the traditional enemy of imagination) by accepting a state sinecure. One does not have to accept the accusation as justified in order to admit that *The Lost Leader* poses acutely the difficulty of remaining true to the world of imagination in face of the various 'wordly' powers that would compromise its purity. St Teresa once posed the question why so few 'learned men' (that is, learned in theology, including spiritual theology, and seen by Teresa as better guides to follow than merely holy men) became mystics. She found the answer in their inability to let go of *honra*, human respect, the cold eyes of the world of common discourse.[14] Their concern for their image closed them off effectively from that flowing of light and fire that is at the source of the mystical: the mystical imagination was shackled by the image of themselves reflected back from the eyes of others. Receiving thus 'glory from men' they could not open their inner vision to the radiance of the source, the true 'glory of God'.

So it is that the source-experience demands of its nature total commitment. Indeed it was the emergence of this quality that led us on to see the source-experience as the key to the understanding of mystical imagination. Now this total commitment involves asceticism, especially the asceticism of detachment, and this at all levels. As long as there is at any level attachment to something other than the source, then full attachment to the source is impossible, impossible by a kind of mathematical impossibility. The first book of the *Ascent of Mount Carmel* of St John of the Cross is a shatteringly powerful statement of this principle. At a certain point indeed the mystical is as it were liberated, and runs freely ahead of the ascetical, yet the ascetical must always run along behind, and must not be left behind. Otherwise mysticism becomes gradually self-involved and self-indulgent.

This commitment to the source is not, however, some kind of impersonal ascetical deal. It is entirely personal, or super-personal. In terms first enunciated by Gabriel Marcel and later developed by Martin Buber and Emmanuel Levinas, it is an *I–Thou* relationship, in Buber's phrase, to the 'Thou of my existence'.[15] It is personal especially in that it questions the mystic in her/his 'ownmost individual selfhood, asking how far he/she seeks to draw the other(s) within the compass of the ego, and how far he/she is willing to be pierced and broken open so as to allow the ego to be surrendered and lost. This is the place of 'unselving' which the self can only *allow*; it is accomplished not by way of an intensification of the ascetical but by way of what St John calls the Dark Night of the Soul, an inflowing of the light that can come only as the lesser illuminations are totally extinguished.[16]

It is here especially that the ethical (*which is the essential basis of all true mysticism*) is taken beyond its proper limits and beyond its own built-in principles of balance and measure. This 'going beyond' the ethical is not a negation or a change of direction; rather is it a continuation of the ethical in its own inner direction and dynamism, after the manner of Aristotle's conception of the relation of 'heroic virtue' to ordinary virtue. It must not be confused with Kierkegaard's 'teleological suspension of the ethical' which is a denial of human dignity in the light of an overpowering divine righteousness. Rather is it the emergence of the latent 'obediential' possibilities of 'manwomanhood' created in the divine image and likeness.

Once a certain continuity with the ordinary and the everyday ethical is affirmed, at least in the mode of transcendence, it can be said that the mystical imagination goes its own way, making judgements that seem to commonsense paradoxical and unreasonable, as in the case of the 'hard sayings' of Jesus. Time and again this imagination has run wild—as witness the Fraticelli, the 'Children's Crusade', the early Quakers and Shakers, the wilder reaches of Revivalism—and the people of balance and good sense have tried to bring it to heel. Yet it can be asked whether these wilder expressions of mystical enthusiasm have really been called forth by total openness to the source, by a source-experience that has freed itself from possessiveness and narrow dogmatism. The source is the fountain of all creation and creativity and cannot be captured by some prefabricated notion or made to serve a religious cliché. To put it another way: there is no such thing as a mystic who is a bore; there are only bores who pretend to be mystics. Or, to put it more gently: as soon as a mystic becomes boring he/she is failing in imagination, and therefore failing in the relationship to the source. Nevertheless the last word here must be acceptance of the freedom and 'wildness' of mystical imagination, even when it challenges the orthodox and the everyday.

E) 'God is Love' says St John the Evangelist, enunciating the principle on which all mysticism rests. Now love is communication, pure and total manifestation of the lover to the beloved, and of the beloved to the lover. There is here, at the heart of the mystical, a hall of mirrors which only St John of the Cross has attempted to express. It is a hall of *living* mirrors, as John recognises. For each mirror and each mirroring has its own statement to make, its own communicative identity, utterly unique, infinitely personal.[17]

So it is that the source-experience is at every level an experience of mutual communication. This communication is sufficient to itself, yet since it is essentially communication, it is led by its very nature and inner life to further communication. The contemplation of the sunset, or the sea, or of a field of flowers is complete in itself, yet it seeks to overflow into further communication. This is the dynamism of all artistic and all mystical expression. Those who enter into the experience of the source must express this experience, must find ways of 'singing the praises of the Lord'. The urge to communicate may be channelled by Liturgy, or by the various charisms ('tongues', prophecy and the rest), or by the heart-to-heart discourse of 'soul-friendship', or by the bearing of witness, even the witness of suffering and death. So we have St Teresa in an exalted mood saying 'I die because I cannot die'; the urge to total witness becomes almost too strong for her to bear.[18] This, for Teresa or anybody else, can only be a mood and a special moment, but it expresses something that is at the very heart of mystical imagination.

This passion for communication expresses itself variously: through words, through deeds, through artefacts; through the journeys of St Paul; through the literary labours of St Jerome: through the sermons of St Ambrose and St Augustine; through Anselm's quest for understanding; through the bold speculations of Scotus Eriugena; through the great mind-edifices of Aquinas and Bonaventure; through the verses of Dante and Milton. Even when it is the conceptual intellect that shapes the work, it is the imagination, all afire with the Divine vision and as free as the wind, that sets the syllogisms moving. Not only faith seeking understanding, but love seeking ways of communication. So it is that the man who wrote the *Summa Theologiae*, that great logical tapestry that has dominated the speculations of the medieval schools, is the man who wrote the *Pange Lingua*: it is the one central experience of the God Who is Love that seeks communication in the one and in the other.

Communication generates light, indeed *is* light (as well as warmth). But in a world which, as a heart-world, is largely closed to the call and presence of the source, the light shines in the midst of darkness. In this situation the mystic is always a witness to the light, and the more this witnessing enters into the deeps of the world, the more it encounters contradiction, persecution, rejection, betrayal and death. 'I die daily,' says St Paul.[19] Of its very nature the light is communicative, as the source whence it comes is pure communication. Jesus by his very name of Saviour came to communicate with darkness, to flow into the darkness. This communication was of necessity the kiss of death for him, as it is for every mystic who descends from the Thabor of the source-experience into the valley of human darkness. The Christian affirmation is that Jesus was and is the source itself, who therefore not only survives the kiss of death but absorbs its power and indeed 'swallows down death'.[20] In his own place and according to his own measure the Christian disciple follows his Master into the darkness, but takes the new life along with him.

These then are the five positive aspects of the source-experience: it is a heart-experience (primarily and centrally); it is essentially gift, sought after but not achievable or even knowable, a grace received from the source itself; it is an encounter with the same source as that which every poet and artist knows in her/his own mode and measure; it demands total commitment, the total and unrelenting immolation of the self; it is communicative with an energy of communication that reaches the deepest heart of spiritual darkness. It is itself the source from which all mystical imagination flows.

But our analysis of the source-experience would be incomplete, one-sided even, if it did not take a straight and steady look at a matter that has been lurking in the shadows: the experience of the anti-source. It is a paradox attested to by all the great Christian mystics—and by many others as well—that any kind of deep, continuous contact with God involves as a kind of counterbalance contact with the adversary variously named Satan, Lucifer, Beelzebub, the Enemy, the Accuser, the Anti-Christ, the Evil or Wicked One (named *Ponēros* in the New Testament). St Teresa gives a vivid and terrifying description of her 'descent into Hell'; St John of the Cross talks in a chilling phrase of the naked contact of the human spirit with the Spirit of Annihilation (in the course of the experience of the Dark Night of Spirit).[21] The New Testament speaks again and again not only of the *Ponēros*, or Evil One, but of an utterly sifting and searching (and potentially annihilating) experience called *peirasmos* (the test or trial). The Lord's Prayer in both the Lucan and Matthean versions has an invocation concerned directly with the *peirasmos*; Jesus coming out of his ordeal in Gethsemane commands the disciples to pray this invocation, for it seems the time of the *Ponēros* has come.[22] It is impossible to read the New Testament as story or drama without giving a central place to this adversary, who is always present or near at hand, and is sometimes seen as immensely powerful. It is significant that the great imaginative restatements of the Bible, such as those of Dante and Milton, give a central place to the powers of darkness.

Now it can be said that the anti-source is eternally in opposition to the source, and it can be said that the religious imagination is powerfully activated by the sense of this opposition. Christian dogmatics, however, rejects this kind of final dualism, and tends rather to a subordinate dualism, which affirms an eternal opposition but sees the anti-source as created by the source, which it wilfully and sinfully opposes. This attitude provides great imaginative possiblities, and evangelical preachers tend to make the most of it: it fits in beautifully with the black-and-white rhetoric of this style of preaching. But it is only indirectly that this kind of theology stimulates the mystical imagination. Where the mystic finds a theological setting for his anti-source experience is in the doctrine which St Augustine took over from Plotinus, and which St Thomas and the medievals took over from St Augustine.[23] According to this doctrine the Evil disappears into non-being or nothingness, so that what opens up before the imagination is an immense void of unfulfilled being, or rather of the annihilation of all being, a void that would draw the human spirit into its depths in a kind of living death. Karl Barth, quite unphilosophically and untheologically called this void *Das Nichtige*, and the mystic in each of us can only be grateful for the word. It is imaginatively right.

It is St John of the Cross, among Christian mystics, who has most fully and powerfully explored the experience of the anti-source, which he calls the Dark Night of Spirit. He claims that he is doing no more than restating what is already there in Scripture, especially in Isaiah, Job, Jeremiah, Jonas and the Psalms.[24] For those who can follow him, John opens up a whole new dimension in Old Testament interpretation. He is curiously reticent about the New Testament, though the experience of the powers of darkness and their function as testing and sifting is clearly present in and behind the text. In any case the New Testament is for John the fulfilment of what the Old Testament expresses. As in the accounts of the passion, so generally, the Old Testament provides the script which is acted out in the events set down in the New Testament.

For John the Dark Night of Spirit comes only to those who have travelled far along the mystical path. Others are not strong enough to bear it. In the terms I have been using this is to say that there is a balance or equipoise between the source-experience and the anti-source experience. Moreover the Dark Night of Spirit brings a final purification to the human spirit by which it becomes more fully attuned to the purity of the source. Until the anti-source is experienced in itself (or in its anti-self) it can be said to be lurking within the source itself. To put it pictorially: for those who seek the face of God the one place that Satan can hide is in the face of God; so, too, the Bible is Satan's textbook, as is clear in the account of the temptation of Jesus. Indeed it may be said that every theological portrait of Christ runs the risk of allowing Satan to enter within the portrait. Thus we have the Christ of the fundamentalist preacher who crushes all the pathos and suffering brokenness of humanity. Or the Imperial Christ of the great empires of the past and the present, the Christ who sits at the right hand of Emperor or Prime Minister or President. More subtly, there is the Deity of the dominating spiritual leader, the Christ of the successful minister or 'defender of the faith'. It is perhaps only the direct and totally annihilating experience of the darkness that (for those who can take it) finally purifies the image of the source of all the lurking shadows and ambiguities. As St John of the Cross understands it, this is an experience far on the other side of the 'turn'; it is totally given, a grace that comes from above.

It is through this experience that the light shines fully into the depths of the darkness. We know that one of our greatest modern mystics, St Thérèse of Lisieux, felt that she was called to dwell in this darkness in her own time and place, and she spent the last eighteen months of her life in what she calls *le nuit de néant*, 'the night of nothingness'. She was, she tells us 'sitting at the table of the unbelievers', choosing to share that darkness to which they would awaken at death, in order that they might share the Christ-light that she carried within her, unfelt, unrealised, in total despairing darkness.[25] Here the mystic is the ultimate missioner. Here the mystical imagination touches its nether limits, as it touches its highest limits in the 'blessed vision of peace', the New Jerusalem coming down from Heaven.

VI

One consequence of the foregoing analysis is that all questions as to the value and validity of the vision-worlds of mystical writers depend finally on the depth and integrity of the source-experience. The visions are as authentic as their source.

As long as we stay within the world of mystical imagination, and all the freedom and variety which comes from a love that reaches towards infinite horizons, this position may be acceptable. But it is necessary to look again at the question of objectivity as it arises from the standpoint of mystical *perception*, or if the term may be used in low-key fashion, from the standpoint of the paranormal. Do the visions of mystics such as St Teresa and William Blake provide a source of real knowledge? Briefly, I would want to argue that philosophically speaking (and in contradiction to Descartes, or at least Cartesianism) there is the *possibility* of levels of reality beyond the doors of ordinary perception yet by no means of the order of pure spirit or *res cogitans*, and that from the point of view of *evidence* there is a massive weight of well-sifted material to push this possibility in the direction of *probability*. The question as to whether a *particular* witness to visionary worlds (regions other than the Cartesian dyad) is to be accepted or rejected is a question of the evidence as it is presented. There is, however, something to be said for some such approach as that of Richard Swinburne who has enunciated, and managed to defend, what he calls the *Principle of Credulity*, according to which normally truthful and reliable people should be believed in these matters until they are discredited; in other words, the onus of proof is on the prosecution.[26] It must be added, however, that we are still without any really helpful epistemology of the paranormal; nobody, as far as I know, has looked carefully at the question of the individual (as against the common) contribution to the human experience: if my experience of the deep-sounding sea is largely the creation of my (common) human powers of seeing and hearing, and is yet understood to be an experience of reality, why should not St Teresa's vision of Hell, albeit largely the creation of her individual human powers (and so very different from Swedenborg's vision of Hell), provide its own kind of access to reality? This kind of question is as yet not only not answered but not even fully asked. Here I must leave it, only remarking that no genuine mystic will have anything to do with what may be termed cheap knowledge, that is to say knowledge that does not have its ground of sowing and growth within the receiver. All mystical knowledge is an invitation to self-knowledge, not a substitute for it.

I have said little about the mystical as an extension of conceptual thinking, though I have put forward the notion that mystical imagination is always operative in the communicative *eros* of the great philosophers and theologians. Obviously the speculative élan of thinkers such as Plato and Hegel opens up towards a source-experience with a consequent 'poetic' enrichment of sober discourse; indeed it is in these enrichments that Plato and Hegel are most quoted and remembered. But there is, to borrow a phrase from an Irish poet, another 'hole in reason's ceiling' through which a ray of imagination shines in on the speculations of even the least imaginative philosophers.[27] This appears in its pure state in Kant's doctrine of the Categorical Imperative, which is, like the Agent Intellect of the medieval Aristotelians, a shaft of heavenly light breaking through the closed skies of systematic speculation. Wordsworth responds to this light in his Kantian *Ode to Duty*; George Eliot centres her whole world of imagination around it, as does Iris Murdoch in our own day (though she tries to enrich it with Platonism). Indeed it can be argued that Kant's Imperative cries out for imaginative expression and leads but an attenuated existence in the sober company of philosophical speculation.[28]

Where Kant speaks of the Moral Imperative, St Thomas Aquinas, in the Aristotelian tradition, speaks of Natural Law seen as 'the impression of the divine light' on the human mind. On the basis of this conception the medieval schoolmen were able to work out a formidable system of moral rules and prohibitions, a system that is still with us in all its enabling and confining power; it is the basis, for example, of the celebrated Papal Encyclical, *Humanae Vitae*. Within this system one small but precious principle allows room for imagination, allows an escape from the *Dieu Fabricateur* of Sartre's accusation. This principle came from Aristotle himself, and was named by him *epikeia*, usually translated as 'equity' or 'good sense'. It moderated and tempered the application of general laws to particular human situations. It was indeed enunciated very clearly by Jesus himself (citing the Pharisees against themselves) as: 'The Sabbath was made for man, not man for the Sabbath.'[29] Somehow, somewhere Western Christendom lost hold of this principle, if it had ever quite accepted it. Perhaps our future depends in no small measure on the discovery, or rediscovery, of this principle. It affirms respect and reverence for that unique individual manhood and womanhood, for that 'human form divine' which Blake discovered at the centre of his mystical vision, as in her own way and in her own idiom did St Teresa. For Teresa each individual soul is a noble castle of many mansions, where dwells that most undefinable and disconcerting of guests, the living God. Neither our churches nor our theologies have ever found enough 'space' for this overflowing presence. Perhaps it is the special work of man's mystical imagination to expand this space until it includes the furthest reaches of the world's darkness as well as ever new ways of access to the inaccessible light.

Who can guess the way ahead, or put limits to the strangeness of that journey?

NOTES

1. *Summa Theologiae* I. q 1.a.9. obj. 1. *Republic*, Book 10.
2. At its deepest the mystical is an extension of the *moral* order, but here I am concerned directly with its cognitive aspects.
3. Mary Warnock, *Imagination*, Los Angeles, University of California Press, 1978 (1976), p.195 (London: Faber, 1980). My understanding of Wordsworth is not the same as that provided by Dr Warnock, but it does not, I think, contradict it. I would, however, want to take Coleridge's influence on Wordsworth more positively than does Dr Warnock, though I would agree that Wordsworth is more consistent and illuminating, perhaps more truly original as well. It may be noted that this book begins with Hume and does not draw on more ancient sources.
4. *The Daffodils* will be found in any collection or selection of Wordsworth's poems. The following lines are especially relevant:

    I gazed and gazed, but little thought
    What wealth to me the show had brought.
    For oft when on my couch I lie
    In vacant or in pensive mood,
    They flash upon that inward eye
    Which is the bliss of solitude.

    Wordsworth saw these two lines as expressing the highest insight of true poetry. See Hunter Davies, *William Wordsworth*, pp.188 and 246 (Hamlyn, 1981).

    The Pegasus descriptive is taken from Hopkins' *Felix Randal*. The other Wordsworth references are as follows: 'Unknown modes of being' from *The Prelude*, Book I; 'Something far more deeply interfused' from *Tintern Abbey;* 'Thoughts that do sometimes lie too deep for tears' from the *Ode on the Intimations of Immortality from Recollections of Early Childhood*.
5. Kathleen Raine, *Blake and Tradition*. Princeton University Press, 1968, Vol.I, p.178. See the same author's *Blake* (Thames and Hudson, 1970), p.26. The quotation from St Teresa is not to be found in the (commentary on) *The Song Of Solomon* as Dr Raine places it, but in the *Life*, ch.40.
6. See *The Inklings* by H. Carpenter, Unwin Paperbacks, 1981 (1978), p.223 (IV.1).
7. Wordsworth, *On a Picture of Peel Castle in a Storm*; R. L. Stevenson, *Blows the Wind Today*.
8. Flannery O'Connor, *The Habit of Being*, New York, Vintage Books, 1979, p.92. See note 12.
9. Edmund Husserl's philsosophy as set down for instance in the *Paris Lectures* (The Hague, 1967), may be seen as an effort at relating the manifold of experience to its source in the *cogito*, the thinking subject. Husserl refuses to go with Descartes along the road of *cogito ergo sum*, but rather takes as his motto *ego cogito cogitata*, that is to say, he steps into the centre of the subject rather than out towards being, God etc. as *objects* of thought. But, as Sartre points out, the subject is encountering *something*. This Sartre sees as massive and threatening, and calls it the *It-Itself* (*Being and Nothingness*, Intro-

duction, par.6). This (though Sartre refuses to admit it) is simply a restatement of Kant's *thing-in-itself* (hidden, and in that sense mystical). Both are frozen entities which only the 'fire in the heart' can melt. The core of a mystical phenomenology is the description of the source through its reflection in the human subjectivity. Apart from the mystical, philosophy ossifies into either a scholastic realism of closed concepts (what Heidegger terms onto-theology) or a subjectivism faced with a dead 'thing-in-itself', or with an *in-itself* totally alien to the subject.

10. T. S. Eliot, *Four Quartets*: Little Gidding 5, in *The Complete Poems and Plays*, Faber and Faber, London, 1969.
11. 'The *Life* of St Teresa was among his favourite books' Kathleen Raine, *William Blake*, Thames and Hudson, 1970, p.26.
12. This is the whole burden of the minor work *Purity of Heart*. (Collins, 1961).
13. See Mary L. O'Hara, CSJ, *Gateways to Contemplation*; Mystical knowledge in *The Degrees of Knowledge* in *Selected Papers*, 1981: The American Maritain Association, St Louis. I am indebted to Dr O'Hara for the quotation from Flannery O'Connor given above. Maritain's dismissal of all non-Catholic mysticism is typically expressed in the following quotation from Dr O'Hara's article: 'It is a disastrous illusion to seek mystical experience outside of faith, to imagine a theological experience freed from theological faith' (*The Degrees of Knowledge*, English translation, Pelican, p.261).
14. *Ways of Perfection*, ch.12.
15. Martin Buber, *I and Thou* (translated by R. G. Smith) Edinburgh, 1937, p.76.
16. *Dark Night*, Book 2, ch.5.
17. *Spiritual Canticle*, Stanza 36 (35).
18. Poems I (Silverio numeration followed by translators).
19. I Cor. 15:31.
20. I have not been able to trace this phrase which I picked up as a student in Maynooth from the late Dr McGarry. Fr John Maitland-Moir has, however, found some similar phrases which he has been kind enough to share with me, e.g. in the Greek Liturgy of the Feast of the Exaltation of the Cross (Sept. 14th).
21. *Dark Night*, Book 2, chapter 23.
22. Luke, 22:46.
23. This does not mean that Satan is seen as a myth. He/she is real and personal, a deformed masterpiece. Here as elsewhere evil is *privatio boni debiti*. In this metaphysics there is an unstated possibility of the ultimate salvation of the evil, one which Christian theology has not been able to accept.
24. See, for example, the *Prologue* to the *Ascent of Mount Carmel*.
25. See O'Donoghue, *Heaven in Ordinarie*, Edinburgh, 1979, chapter 8.
26. *The Existence of God*, Oxford, 1979, pp.25ff. See S. J. Katz (ed.) *Mysticism and Philosophical Analysis*, especially the balanced approach of Peter Moore's contribution. (Sheldon Press, London, 1978).
27. The poet is Patrick Kavanagh who claims to 'have a feeling/that through the hole in reason's ceiling/we may come to knowledge/ without ever going to college.'
28. 'The agent, thin as a needle, appears in the quick flash of the choosing will,' Iris Murdoch, *The Sovereignty of Good*, London, 1973, p.53.

29. Mark 2:27. This is not to destroy the law (Matt. 5:17) whether revealed by God or written by nature in the heart of man and woman, but rather to apprehend it imaginatively as well as conceptually.

CONTRIBUTORS

JAMES P. MACKEY is Thomas Chalmers Professor of Theology in the University of Edinburgh, and author of *Life and Grace, The Problems of Religious Faith, Jesus the Man and the Myth* and *The Christian Experience of God as Trinity.*

GERARD WATSON is Professor of Ancient Classics (Greek) at St Patrick's College, Maynooth, and author of *The Stoic Theory of Knowledge, Plato's Unwritten Teaching* and *Phantasia in Classical Thought.*

JOHN DILLON is Regius Professor of Greek at Trinity College, Dublin, and author of *The Middle Platonists, A Classical Lexicon to James Joyce* (with Brendan O'Hehir) and *Proclus' Commentary on the Parmenides of Plato.*

THOMAS FINAN is Professor of Ancient Classics (Latin) at St Patrick's College, Maynooth. Author of various articles on the tragic dimension of ancient epic, the poetic imagination, the *Vita Nuova* and the Augustan Elegists, mystical experience in the *Confessions* of St Augustine.

PATRICK GRANT is Professor of English at the University of Victoria, British Columbia, and has written *The Transformation of Sin, Images and Ideas in Literature of the English Renaissance, Six Modern Authors and Problems of Belief, Literature of Mysticism in Western Tradition, A Dazzling Darkness: An Anthology of Western Mysticism* and *Literature and the Discovery of Method in the English Renaissance.*

JOHN MCINTYRE is Professor of Divinity at the University of Edinburgh and, among his other distinctions, is Chaplain to HM The Queen in Scotland. He is the author of *St Anselm and his Critics, The Christian Doctrine of History, On the Love of God* and *The Shape of Christology.*

A. D. NUTTALL is a Fellow of New College, Oxford, and author of *Two Concepts of Allegory, A Common Sky, Overheard by God, A New Mimesis* and *Pope's Essay on Man.*

MARY WARNOCK is Mistress of Girton College, Cambridge, and author of *Ethics since 1900, The Philosophy of J. P. Sartre, Imagination* and *Schools of Thought.*

J. DAVIS MCCAUGHEY was Master of Ormond College, the University of Melbourne, and is now Governor of the State of Victoria and author of *Christian Obedience in the University* and *Diversity and Unity in the New Testament Picture of Christ.*

D. M. MACKINNON was Norris-Hulse Professor of Divinity in the University of Cambridge, and is a life-fellow of Corpus Christi College. He has written *The Borderlands of Theology, The Problem of Metaphysics, Explorations in Theology* and *Creon and Antigone.*

N. D. O'DONOGHUE is a lecturer in Systematic Theology in the University of Edinburgh, and author of *Heaven in Ordinarie* and *The Holy Mountain.*

AUTHOR INDEX

Adams, Robert P.
  The Better Part of Valor. More, Erasmus, Colet, and Vives on Humanism, War, and Peace, 91nn8,12
Addison, Joseph, 144
Aeschylus
  Prometheus Vinctus, 180
Akhmatova, Anna, 165, 168
  'Poem Without a Hero', 165
Alexander of Aphrodisias
  De Anima, 55n3
Amos, 166-7
Anselm, 131-3, 134
Aquinas, Thomas, 48-53, 198, 199, 202
  Summa Theologiae, 49-53, 74, 135, 162, 186
Aristotle, 8, 32, 34-5, 71, 74, 153, 176, 187, 196, 202
  De Anima, 34, 35, 52, 55, 55n3, 56n8, 60n14
  De Memoria, 34, 55n2
  Metaphysics, 32n4
  On Divination in Sleep, 50-1
  Poetics, 129
Auden, W. H.
  'Their Lonely Betters', 173
Augustine, 22, 29, 42-3, 44-50, 52, 66n3, 162, 193, 199
  Confessions, 45, 68n7, 73, 79, 80, 191-2
  De Anima, 49
  De Civitate Dei, 44, 48
  De Genesi ad litteram, 44, 46-8, 49, 50, 51
  De Musica, 73
  De Trinitate, 46
  Genesis, commentary on, 53
  Letters, 45-6

Bacon, Francis, 86, 126, 129
Bailey, Benjamin, 125
Barbour, Ian
  Myths, Models, and Paradigms, 5-6
Barfield, Owen, 140
Barr, James, 167n15
  Holy Scripture: Canon, Authority, Criticism, 167n15, 172

Barth, Karl, 103, 110, 117, 199
Beatrice Portinari, 65, 66, 67-9, 70, 71, 73n13, 77, 82
Bennett, Tony, 172
  'Text and History', 168n18
Berkeley, George, Bishop, 130, 189
  Of the Principles of Human Knowledge, 130
Beyer, W. W.
  Keats and the Daemon King, 139
Birmelin, E.
  'Die kunsttheoretischen Gedanken in Philostrats Apollonios', 42n15
Black, Max, 6
Blair, Adam, 144
Blake, William, 4, 16, 127, 139, 187, 189-90, 194-5, 202
  Jerusalem, 139
  Milton, 189
  'Mock on, Mock on, Voltaire, Rousseau', 127
Blumenthal, Henry
  Plotinus' Psychology, 55n6, 56n9, 57, 62, 63n16
  'Plutarch's *De Anima* and Proclus', 57n12
Boethius, Anicius Manlius Severinus, 48, 68
  Consolation of Philosophy, 98
Brecht, Bertholt, 167
Bright, William, 182
Brodsky, Joseph, 169
Brown, Peter
  Augustine of Hippo, 49n23
Brown, R. E.
  The Community of the Beloved Disciple, 164
Browning, Robert
  The Lost Leader, 195-6
Brunner, Emil, 103
Buber, Martin, 196
  I and Thou, 196
Bultmann, Rudolf, 117, 169
Bundy, M. W.
  The Theory of Imagination in Classical and Mediaeval Thought, 33n5

AUTHOR INDEX

Burke, Edmund, 144
Burtchaell, James T., 7n12
Burton, Robert
  Anatomy of Melancholy, 137
Busnelli, G.
  Il Convivio, 74n14

Caiaphas, 183-4
Calcidius, 41-2, 46
Carpenter, H.
  The Inklings, 191n6
Catullus, Valerius, 72
Cavalcanti, Guido, 66
Cayce, Edgar, 190
Chenu, M. D.
  Is Theology a Science?, 4
Childs, Brevard S., 167n15
  Introduction to the Old Testament as Scripture, 167n15
Chrétien de Troyes
  Lancelot, 135
Cicero, Marcus Tullius
  De Natura Deorum, 39
  Orator, 37-8, 40, 61n15
Cloud of Unknowing, The, 193
Coleridge, Samuel Taylor, 18, 71, 75, 126, 129-30, 134, 135, 139, 143-4, 146, 150, 153, 161, 163, 188, 188n3
  'Dejection, an Ode', 140, 146-7, 149
  notebooks, 143-4, 149
  Statesman's Manual, 143
Collingwood, R. G., 111
Conzelmann, Hans
  'Was von Anfang war', 164n6
Copleston, F.
  Thomas Aquinas, 49n23
Cornford, F. M.
  Plato's Theory of Knowledge, 30n2
Coulson, John, 15n30
Courcelle, Pierre
  Les Confessions de S. Augustin dans la tradition littéraire, 48n21
  La Consolation de Boèce dans la tradition littéraire, 48n21
Crossan, John Dominic, 7n12
Cullman, Oscar
  Christ and Time, 111
Curtis, W. A.
  Jesus the Teacher, 117

Dante Alighieri, 15-16, 48, 53, 65-82, 199
  Convivio, 68, 70, 73, 74, 77n21, 80n31
  Divina Commedia, 52, 66, 67, 68-9, 70, 72n11, 74, 76, 77, 79, 80
  Eclogues, 68
  Letter to Con Grande, 80
  Vita Nuova, 66, 67-8, 69, 70, 71-2, 73n12, 74-82

Dante da Maiano, 66n4
Davies, Hunter
  William Wordsworth, 188n4
Davis McCaughey, J., 21
Derrida, Jacques, 168n18
  Of Grammatology, 167
Descartes, René, 3, 126, 187, 193n9, 201
  Discourse on Method, 134
  Meditations, 134
Dillon, John, 15, 42
  The Middle Platonists, 39n12
Dilthey, Wilhelm
  The Construction of the Historical World in the Human Studies, 172
Dio Chrysostom, 38, 39, 40
Diogenes Laertius
  Lives of the Philosophers, 36
Dodd, C. H., 118
  The Parables of the Kingdom, 114
Dodds, Eric R.
  Proclus. The Elements of Theology, 43n16
Donne, John, 135
  'The Canonization', 136
Dostoevsky, Fyodor Mikhailovich
  The Brothers Karamazov, 184
Dupont, Jacques, 176, 180-1
  Les Tentations de Jésus au Désert, 176
Durkheim, Émile, 12

Eagleton, Terry
  Literary Theory, an Introduction, 165-6, 168
Eckhart, Meister, 187
Eliot, George, 202
Eliot, T. S.
  Four Quartets, 193
Engels, Friedrich, 4n3
  On Religion, 4n3
Erasmus, Desiderius, 16-17, 89-92, 97
  Letters, 91n12, 92nn13,14
  Paraclesis, 91n9
  Praise of Folly, 86, 89-92, 93, 96
Eusebius of Caesarea
  Praeparatio Evangelica, 35

Fénélon, François de la Salignac de la Mothe, 189
Feuerbach, Ludwig Andreas, 12
Fichte, Johann Gottlieb, 10
Ficino, Marsiglio, 86
Finan, Thomas, 15-16
Foakes, R. A.
  The Romantic Assertion, 139
Foakes-Jackson, F. J., 180n6
Ford, Newell F.
  The Prefigurative Imagination of John Keats, 139
Freud, Sigmund, 12

Galileo Galilei, 3
  Il Saggiatore, 127
Gilkey, Langdon
  Maker of Heaven and Earth, 4n2
Gilson, E.
  Dante et la philosophie, 82
Gottwald, Norman K.
  The Bible and Liberation, 170n23
Grant, Patrick, 5, 16
Greene, Graham, 1
Grégoire, Franz, 11-12, 15, 19
  Aux Sources de la Pensée de Marx, Hegel, Feuerbach, 12
  Études Hégéliennes, 12n16, 14nn25,26, 15, 19
Gregory the Great
  Moralia, 79
Grosman, Inge (with Susan R. Suleiman)
  The Reader in the Text: Essays on Audience and Interpretation, 169n20
Guthrie, W. K. C.
  A History of Greek Philosophy, 29n1, 31n3
Guyon, Jeanne Marie Bouvières de la Mothe, 189

Haenchen, Ernst, 180n6
Haydon, Benjamin Robert, 125
Hegel, G. W. F., 7, 10, 11-15, 16, 19, 202
  Lectures on the Philosophy of Religion, 13, 15
  The Philosophy of Art, 13, 14
  Science of Logic, 11, 13-14, 19
Heidegger, Martin, 117
Heraclitus, 29, 30
Hillers, Delbert R.
  A Commentary on the Book of the Prophet Micah, 170
Hobbes, Thomas, 86
Homer, 39, 40, 71-2, 168
  Iliad, 71
  Odyssey, 71-2, 81n33
Homeric Hymns, 80n30, 81
Hopkins, Gerard Manley, 195
  'Felix Randal', 188n4
Hughes, Ted, 4
  Writers, Critics and Children, 4-5
Hume, David, 7, 8, 9, 22, 111, 113, 132, 133, 134
  A Treatise of Human Nature, 128, 129-30, 134
Husserl, Edmund
  Paris Lectures, 193n9

Iamblichus, 48n20
  De Mysteriis, 62
Inge, W. R., Dean, 181
'Isaiah(s)', 166
Israel, 180

Jack, Ian
  Keats and the Mirror of Art, 125n2
Jamieson, Storm
  Journey from the North, 152
Jeremiah, 163-4, 165
Job, 180
John (author of *Revelation*), 190
John the Evangelist, 175, 177, 180, 182-4, 197
John of the Cross, Saint, 187, 193, 194-5, 197, 199-200
  Ascent of Mount Carmel, 196
  On a Dark Night, 193, 195, 199
  Spiritual Canticle, 79, 194, 197
Johnson, Samuel, 65, 129, 164
Joyce, James, 72n12
  Portrait of the Artist as a Young Man, 72n12
Julian of Norwich, 187

Kant, Immanuel, 7, 8-9, 10, 18, 57, 67, 102-22, 143, 144-6, 187, 193n9, 202
  Critique of Judgment, 8, 107-8, 118-20, 121, 144-5
  Critique of Practical Reason, 102-3, 111-12
  Critique of Pure Reason, 57, 102, 106-7, 111, 119, 121
  Fundamental Principles of a Metaphysic of Morals, 103
  Religion Within the Bounds of Reason, 103
Kavanagh, Patrick, 202n27
  God in Woman, 82
Keats, John, 17, 125-6, 128-9, 130-1, 132-5, 136-40
  'La Belle Dame Sans Merci', 137
  The Eve of St Agnes, 134, 135, 136-40
  'Ode on a Grecian Urn', 139, 140
Kemp Smith, N
  A Commentary to Kant's Critique of Pure Reason, 104
Kempis, Thomas à
  The Imitation of Christ, 65
Kermode, Frank, 175-7, 179, 180
  'Instances of Interpretation: Death and Survival', 175
Kierkegaard, Søren, 112, 120, 196-7
  Purity of Heart, 195
Kirk, G. S. (with J. E. Raven)
  The Presocratic Philosophers, 29n1, 31n3
Kleist, H. von
  Plotinische Studien, 55n4
Kolakowski, L.
  Marxism and Beyond, 17n31

AUTHOR INDEX

Kristeller, Paul Oskar, 86
  Introduction to *The Renaissance Philosophy of Man*, 86n1
  Renaissance Thought. The Classic, Scholastic, and Humanist Strains, 86n1
  'Thomas More as a Renaissance Humanist', 86n1
Kroner, Richard
  The Religious Function of the Imagination, 102
Kuhn, Thomas, 6
  The Structure of Scientific Revolution, 5

Lake, Kirsopp, 180n6
Lang, W.
  Das Traumbuch des Synesius von Cyrene, 44
Lenkeith, Nancy, 88n5
Lesky, Albin
  History of Greek Literature, 36n8, 39n11
Levinas, Emmanuel, 196
Lewalski, Barbara
  Milton's Brief Epic, 179n5
Lewis, C. S., 153-5, 191
  Essays Presented to Charles Williams, 153-4
  A Preface to Paradise Lost, 35
  Surprised by Joy, 148-9, 154
Lindblom, J.
  Prophecy in Ancient Israel, 165
Lindsay, A. D.
  Kant, 105
Locke, John, 86, 126, 187
  Essay concerning Human Understanding, 127
Longinus
  On the Sublime, 33-4, 38, 40, 74
Luke (evangelist), 175, 176, 177-80, 181, 184
  Acts, 180, 182
Luther, Martin, 92, 96, 98-9, 172

MacDonald, George, 109, 111, 116-17
  A Dish of Orts, 102, 116
  Introduction to the Philosophy of History, 117
McFague, Sallie, 114
MacIntyre, Alasdair
  'Visions', 49
McIntyre, John, 18
Mack, Maynard
  'The World of Hamlet', 98
MacKinnon, D. M., 21
Maitland-Moir, John, 198n20
Mandelstam, Nadezhda, 168-9
  Hope Abandoned, 168
  Hope Against Hope, 164-5, 168

Mandelstam, Osip, 168
Marcel, Gabriel, 196
Mark (evangelist), 175-6, 177, 178, 181
Maritain, Jacques, 195
  The Degrees of Knowledge, 195n13
Marx, Karl, 10, 12, 23
  On Religion, 4n3
Mascall, E. L.
  The Openness of Being, 110
  Words and Images, 110
Matthew (evangelist), 175, 176, 177, 178, 180, 182
Maximus of Tyre, 39-40
Micah, 170
Michelangelo, 61
Milton, John, 21, 148, 180, 199
  'Methought I saw my late-espoused saint', 137
  Paradise Lost, 134-5, 136, 137
  Paradise Regained, 179, 182
Miskotte, Kornelis H.
  When the Gods are Silent, 171-2
More, Thomas, 92-3
  History of King Richard the Third, 92
Moses, 80
Muir, Willa
  Belonging, 147
Murdoch, Iris, 202
  The Sovereignty of Good, 202n28

Nabokov, Vladimir
  Lolita, 137
Nebridius, 45-6
Newman, John Henry, Cardinal
  Grammar of Assent, 15n30
Newton, Isaac, 190
Nineham, Dennis
  Explorations in Theology, 156
Norena, Carlos
  Juan Luis Vives, 87n3
Nuttall, A. D., 17-18
  A New Mimesis. Shakespeare and the Representation of Reality, 99n19

O'Connor, Flannery
  The Habit of Being, 192
O'Donoghue, Noel Dermot, 19, 20
  Heaven in Ordinarie, 200n25
  The Holy Mountain, 180n6
O'Hara, Mary, 195n13
  Gateways to Contemplation, 195n13
Origen, 176, 177
Ovid
  Metamorphoses, 80n29

Pafford, Michael
  Inglorious Wordsworths, 147
  The Unattended Moment, 147

Paracelsus, Theophrastus Bombast von Hohenheim, 187
Parmenides, 29-30
Paul VI, Pope
  Humanae Vitae, 202
Paul, Saint, 52, 77, 78, 80, 116, 194, 198
Perrin, Norman, 7n12
Phidias, 39, 61
Philo of Alexandria, 39
  De Legatione ad Gaium, 183
  De Opificio Mundi, 40
Philoponus (Pseudo), 62
Philostratus, 38, 39, 40, 41, 42
  Life of Apollonius of Tyana, 36-7, 55n3, 61n15
Pico della Mirandola, Giovanni, 86-8, 92, 96, 97, 99
  Oration on the Dignity of Man, 86-7, 89n7, 91
Pilate, Pontius, 182, 183
Plato, 9, 12, 29, 30, 31-4, 35, 37, 38, 39-43, 44, 72-3, 74, 202
  Cratylus, 33
  Phaedo, 186-7
  Phaedrus, 72, 73, 81
  Philebus, 33, 55n1
  Republic, 31, 33, 138-9, 186
  Sophist, 31-2, 41, 55
  Symposium, 61, 73, 81n32
  Theaetetus, 30, 32, 41
  Timaeus, 30, 32-3, 37, 39-40, 41, 43, 47, 53, 55n1, 56n7
Pliny the Elder
  Naturalis Historia, 46
Plotinus, 42, 45, 55-63, 187, 199
  Enneads, 45n18, 55-62, 63, 79n25, 139n21
  On the Intellectual Beauty, 61-2
  Problems of the Soul, 55-61, 63
Plutarch, 57n12, 62, 63, 81
  Eroticos/Amatorius, 81-2
Polanyi, Michael, 5
Pope, Alexander
  Eloisa to Abelard, 136
Porphyry, 42-4, 48n20, 53, 55, 62
  De Abstinentia, 44
  De Antro Nympharum, 43
  In Timaeus, 43
  Life of Plotinus, 42
  Sententiae, 43
Portinari, Beatrice, *see* Beatrice Portinari
Posidonius the Stoic, 42n15
Proclus, 48n20, 57n12, 63
  Euclid Commentary, 63
Proust, Marcel, 152
  Remembrance of Things Past, 149-50
Pseudo-Philoponus, 62

Quintilian, 38-9, 40
  Institutio Oratoria, 39

Raine, Kathleen
  Blake and Tradition, 189
  William Blake, 189n5, 194n11
Ramsey, Ian
  Religious Language, 115
Randall, John Herman, Jr (with P. O. Kristeller)
  Introduction to *The Renaissance Philosophy of Man*, 86n1
Raven, J. E. (with G. S. Kirk)
  The Presocratic Philosophers, 29n1, 31n3
Richardson, Samuel
  Clarissa, 137
Ritschl, Albrecht, 117
Robertis, Domenico de
  Il libro della 'Vita Nuova', 76
Rose, H. J., 36n8
Rousseau, Jean-Jacques, 152
Ruskin, John
  Modern Painters, 162-3
Russell, Bertrand, 4n3
  'A Free Man's Worship', 4n3

Sappho, 72, 78, 80-2
Sartre, Jean-Paul, 22, 152, 202
  Being and Nothingness, 193n9
  The Psychology of the Imagination, 142
Schaper, Eva
  Studies in Kant's Aesthetics, 108, 120
Schelling, F. W. J. von, 7, 10
Schleiermacher, F. E. D., 117, 120
Schoeck, R. J.
  'The Place of Erasmus Today', 91n8
Schonberger, O.
  Philostratos Die Bilder, 36n8
Seneca the Elder, 40
  Controversiae, 40
Seneca the Younger, 40
Sextus Empiricus
  Adversus Mathematicos, 35, 38
Shakespeare, William, 92-9, 168
  Cymbeline, 136-7
  Hamlet, 16, 86, 92, 93-9
  King Lear, 92
  Measure for Measure, 77n21
  Richard the Third, 92
  Romeo and Juliet, 135, 136
  Sonnet 64, 164
  The Tempest, 139
Shelley, Percy Bysshe
  Defence of Poetry, 130
Silesius, Angelus, 187
Simplicius, 35n7
Singleton, C. S.
  An Essay on the Vita Nuova, 76, 78

AUTHOR INDEX

Solmsen, F.
  Kleine Schriften, 36n8
Spinoza, Benedictus de, 187
Steiner, M.
  La Tentation de Jésus dans l'interprétation patristique de Saint Justin à Origène, 176
Steiner, Rudolf, 190
Stephanus, 62
Stevens, Wallace, 4, 21-2
  'Angel Surrounded by Paysans', 2-3
  Letters, 2-3, 4n7, 23
Stevenson, Robert Louis
  Blows the Wind Today, 192
Stillinger, Jack
  'The Hoodwinking of Madeline', 136-7
Strauss, D. F., 3, 14-15
Suleiman, Susan R.
  The Reader in the Text: Essays on Audience and Interpretation, 169n20
Swedenborg, Emanuel, 201
Swinburne, Richard
  The Existence of God, 201
Synesius
  On Dreams, 44, 48, 53
Syrianus, 48n20

Tacitus
  Annals, 46
Taylor, A. E., 30n2
Taylor, Vincent, 175
Teresa of Avila, Saint, 79n25, 187, 189-90, 191, 194, 195, 196, 197-8, 199, 201, 202
  The Interior Castle, 192, 193, 194
  Life, 194
Theiler, W.
  Die Vorbereitung des Neuplatonismus, 42n15
Thérèse of Lisieux, Saint, 200
Thomas à Kempis
  The Imitation of Christ, 65
Thomas Aquinas, Saint, see Aquinas, Thomas
Tobriner, Marian Leona
  Vives' Introduction to Wisdom. A Renaissance Textbook, 92n15
Tolkein, J. R. R., 190-1
  The Lord of the Rings, 191

Van Til, Cornelius
  The New Modernism, 103
Vandelli, G. (with G. Busnelli)
  Il Convivio, 74n14
Virgil
  Aeneid, 72n11
Vives, Juan Luis, 87-90, 92, 96
  Against the Pseudodialecticians, 86, 88-90, 92
  A Fable About Man, 87-8, 89n7, 91, 97
  Satellitum animae, 92

Walsh, W. H., 116
  Kant's Criticism of Metaphysics, 105, 107, 109, 111, 121
Ward, Aileen
  'Christian Day, 1818', 137n19
Warnock, Mary, 18, 22, 140
  Imagination, 3, 7-8, 9, 12, 105, 122, 161, 163, 188
Warren, E. W.
  'Imagination in Plotinus', 55n4
Wasserman, E. R.
  The Finer Tone, 139
Watson, Gerard, 15, 22
  Phantasia in Classical Thought, 32n4, 35n7
Wellhausen, Julius
  Die Kleinen Propheten, 167
Whitefield, George, 189
Wiles, Maurice
  'Myth in Theology', 3n1
Williams, Charles, 77n21
  The Figure of Beatrice, 73, 75n15
  Foregiveness in Shakespeare, 77n21
Wirklander, Bertil
  Prophecy as Literature: A Text-Linguistic and Rhetorical Approach to Isaiah 2-4, 170n23
Wittgenstein, Ludwig, 190
Wolff, Hans Walter, 170
  Joel and Amos, 166
Woodcock, Katherine, 137
Wordsworth, William, 18, 22, 73, 77n21, 146, 147-8, 150, 155, 187, 188, 195
  The Daffodils, 188, 195
  Ode on the Intimations of Immortality from Recollections of Early Childhood, 188
  Ode to Duty, 202
  On a Picture of Peel Castle in a Storm, 192
  The Prelude, 146, 150, 188
  Tintern Abbey, 188

Xenophanes, 29, 30-1
Xenophon
  Anabasis, 177

Yeats, William Butler, 12

Zimmerli, Walther
  Old Testament Theology in Outline, 165

SUBJECT INDEX

absolutes, 11, 12-14, 117
action, 21, 22, 23, 99
Adam, 134-5, 137
aesthetic judgment, 107-8, 119-21, 144-5
allegory, 143, 153; *see also* symbols
analogy, 6; *see also* symbols
angel(s), 2-3, 51, 96-7, 181
animals, 34, 35, 142, 151-2
anti-semitism, 182, 184
anti-source, 199-200
appearances, 30, 31, 32
art, 9, 12-15, 19, 36-41, 61-2, 145; and perception, 129; and reality, 140; and religion, 151, 154-6, 171; and responsibility, 190-1
artist(s), 1-2, 9, 12, 14, 17, 22, 40-2, 125, 133; the soul as, 32; whether unusual, 146, 147-8, 150, 155
ascension, 78
asceticism, 196
astrology, 50
autobiography, 146, 147, 152-3
autonomy, 87-8, 96-9
awe, 73-5, 77, 81, 144, 146, 147

beauty, 126, 127, 131, 133, 139, 140, 144-5, 191
Being, 29-30
Bible, the, 20-1, 47, 50, 102, 161, 166-8, 169-72; exegesis, 176-7, 180, 190, 200; *see also* Gospels
blasphemy, 82, 135
body: and soul *see under* soul!; resurrection, 46, 49

childhood, 11, 142, 150
Christ *see* Jesus
Christendom, 91, 92
Christianity, 42, 102, 112, 116, 118, 120, 148, 151, 171-2, 193, 202; and history, 153, 154-6; and the state, 184, 200; divisions in, 194, 195, 197; fundamentalist, 155-6, 190, 199, 200; Protestant, 135
'colligatory concepts', 116-18
commitment, 6, 22, 116, 190-2, 196

common sense, 88-9, 97
communication, 197-8, 202
conversion, 68, 70, 77, 148, 191
creation, the, 40, 82, 87, 119
creativity, 36-41, 42, 61-2, 87, 89, 119, 131, 149-50, 190-1
criticism, 55, 165-8, 169-70, 171, 186; Biblical, 165-8, 171, 176-7, 182; literary, 1, 21, 154, 161, 165, 166, 169-70, 171, 182

daimones, demons *see* spirits
devil *see* Satan
dialectic, 10, 11, 14
distractions, 56, 109-10
divination, 33, 50-1, 62
doxa see also appearances
dreams, 18, 23, 47, 48, 66, 134-5, 137, 138, 139, 143-4; and divination/prophecy, 50-2, 163-4; and truth, 125, 131; and visions, 43-4, 47, 49; power of, 21
dualism, 199

ecstasy, 52
education, 22, 30
Eleusinian Mysteries, 81
élites, 89, 91, 155
empiricism, 2, 17, 126-8, 130, 133, 138, 139; postponed, 139
'epiphanies' *see* joy
eros, 9, 72-3, 194, 202; *see also* love
eternity, 60, 98
Eve, 134-5, 137
evil, 190, 199, 201; *see also* Satan
exercises, spiritual, 56, 58-9
existentialism, 120

faith, 5, 18, 98, 103, 115-16, 119, 198
fear, 77, 78-9, 80, 81, 144, 153-4; *see also* trembling
femaleness of God, 82
folly, 90, 92, 95
foolishness, wise, 90, 92, 97
Forms, 33, 41, 139
Fortune, 98

214

SUBJECT INDEX

freedom, 17, 97-8, 142, 190, 201
free will, 87, 92, 96-9

genius, 125
God, 115, 118-19, 121, 122, 139, 172, 197, 198; and ideas of absolute, 11-12, 30, 110, 111; femaleness, 82; *imago*, 103; incarnation, 181; Kingdom of, 22-3, 114-15; knowing, 109, 110-12, 144, 145-6, 151, 156, 162, 192, 194, 196; oneness, 88; Plato on, 31, 40; playing at, 98; seeing, 44, 49-50, 51, 52, 79-80, 189, 192, 200; Word of, 170; Xenophanes on, 30-1
God-question, 1, 22-3, 102, 131-4
Gospels, 21, 153, 154-6, 175-84
grace, 98, 103

history, 151, 152-3, 154-6, 166, 167, 182, 190; Gospels and, 183
Holocaust, 182
hope, 150
Humanism, 86-99; defined, 86
humanity, nature of, 87-8, 96-9, 142, 151, 155, 156
hymns, 182, 198

ideals, 37, 145; *see also* Forms
images, 8, 36, 78, 106-7, 113, 131; distracting, 56, 109-10; dynamic, 58-9; *see also* symbols
imagination: and Christians, 42, 48, 102, 148, 155; and desire, 8; and divination, 62; and education, 22; and freedom, 17, 91-2, 190-1; and healing, 5; and knowledge of God, 109-12, 115, 122; and mysticism, 188, 194, 195, 197, 198; and perception/ordinary knowing, 3, 7-8, 18, 34, 55, 105-8, 113-14, 121-2, 139, 143; and reality, 17, 22, 36, 99, 128-31, 138-40; and reason, 19-20, 62, 65, 126, 142; and religion, 109-12, 115, 116-22, 150-1, 154-6; and truth *see under* truth; common to all, 155; creative, 36-41, 42, 45, 58-9, 61-2, 113, 131, 149-50, 190-1; dangers of, 45-6, 99, 109-10; definitions, 142; evangelists', 180; freedom of, 186, 190; 'higher' and 'lower', 56, 57, 59-61, 62-3; importance, 121-2, 152; leap of, 118; 'pathway to divine life', 15; power, 23, 147, 150; 'productive' and 'reproductive', 105, 113-14; reader', 153-4, 169-70; Romantics and, 127, 128-31, 138, 140, 146; starting-points, 73, 75; status, 15, 16, 29, 33, 55, 60-1, 63, 102, 155; synthesising, 115-18; truth-claims, 17, 18, 20, 21, 23, 140; use of word in Bible, 102
imago Dei, 103
incarnation, 181
individualism, 98, 202
ineffability, 80
inspiration, 163
intuition, 106

jealousy, 153
Jesus: as symbol, 154; doctrines about, 118, 181, 198, 200; life and work, 116, 117, 175-6, 177-84; teachings, 22-3, 114-15, 117, 177, 179, 180-1, 202
Jews, 169, 182, 183-4
jokes, 136
joy, 139, 147-50, 151, 155, 163, 192, 195; *see also* source-experience
judgement, 107-8, 182-3; aesthetic, 107-8, 119-21, 144-5

Kingdom of God, 22-3, 114-15
knowledge, 30, 103-8, 129-33, 189; and mysticism, 186-90, 201; *see also* perception *and under* God *and* imagination

language, 8, 35, 88-9, 91-2, 93-9, 134-5, 142-3; and reality, 96, 142, 145, 165-6, 170; and truth, 98; as performance, 95; evangelists', 177; wordplay, 164
life as a play, 90; *see also* masks
literary criticism, *see under* criticism
literary language, 89
literature, 129, 152-4, 161, 164-9; survival of, 168-9
logicians, 88-9, 90, 91
Logos, 29
love, 70, 71-3, 134, 135-6, 139, 146, 169; as absolute state, 11; characteristics, 70, 72, 77, 78, 79, 81-2, 143-4; courtly, 71, 135-6; Hegel's philosophy of, 19; Keats on, 125; mystical, 191-2, 193-4, 201; of God, 189, 197, 198; romantic, 72, 73, 135; sexual, 134, 135-6; types, 193-4; *see also eros*

Mammon, 23
man, *see* humanity
marriage, 90
Marxism, 17, 23
masks, 90, 95, 96, 99; language as, 98
meaning, 122; public, 99
meditation, 56, 58-9
memory, 55-6, 60, 87, 148-9, 152, 168-9, 192

mind, 11, 91, 142; and objects, *see* knowledge
moral choice, 6, 22, 191
moral life, 73, 196-7, 202
mysticism, 75-6, 78, 79-82, 187-90, 191-203; reality-status, 189, 190, 201
myth(s), 3, 20, 138; and Gospels, 154, 181

naming, 8; *see also* language
Nature, 11, 13, 73, 145
Nazis, 182, 184
negation/nothingness, 10-11, 14, 199-200
'negative capability', 125
Neoplatonism, 42-3, 46, 47-53, 62
nothingness, *see* negation

Ontological Proof, 131-4

parables, 7, 114-15, 177, 179
paradigms, 5
parapsychology, 187
people, *see* humanity
perception, 32, 34, 37-43, 104, 120, 127-31, 139, 189; and imagination, *see under* imagination; of beauty, 144-5; three classes, 49; *see also* knowledge
phantasia, 29, 30, 31, 33-48, 52-3, 55, 62-3; *see also* imagination
philosophers, 15, 19, 186-7
philosophy, 15, 68, 86, 102, 126, 134, 161, 188, 202; and religion, 13-14; of science, 5-6, 20
Platonism, 36, 37, 40-2, 52, 55, 72-3; Romantic, 138-9; *see also* Neoplatonism
play, life as a, 90; *see also* masks
pluralism, 104
poetry, 17, 39, 129, 146, 168, 195; *see also* art
poets, 162-3, 164-5; *see also* artists
pornography, 136
power, 91
powers (spirits), 22
proofs, 102, 109, 110, 131-4
prophecy, 47, 50-2, 66, 87, 161-6, 170, 171, 183
prophets, 161-9, 170, 171, 172
pseudodialecticians, *see* logicians
psychology, 20, 102, 130, 132-3, 142; of mysticism, 193; parapsychology, 187
public meaning, 99

qualities, primary and secondary, 126-8

rape, 136
rationalism, 17
realism, 129, 140

reality, 30, 118, 128-34, 138-40
reason, 9, 15, 16, 18, 92, 145; and emotions, 142; and imagination, 19-20, 62, 65, 126, 142
redaction-criticism, 176-7
Reformation, the, 89, 92, 93
religion, 112-13, 150-1, 155-6; and philosophy, 13-14; and science, 3-5, 6, 151; definitions, 14; universality, 121; *see also* Christianity
respectability, 195-6
responsibility, *see* commitment
reverence, *see* awe
romanticism, 127-9, 132, 134, 135, 136, 137-40, 146; and mysticism, 188
Russia, Soviet, 168

Satan, 137, 178, 199, 200
science, 3, 6, 9, 108, 126-8, 130, 145-6; and religion, 3-5, 6, 151; imagination's rôle in, 5, 6-7, 45; language, 89; Marxism and, 17; philosophy of, 5-6, 20
Scotland, 171
sense-perception, *see* perception
sermons, 171
signs, 170, 171
sleep, 43, 44
soul, 60; and body, 32-3, 43, 46-7, 51, 57-8; higher and lower, 55, 56, 57, 61; world, 60-1
source-experience, 20-1, 191-9, 200, 201, 202
speech, *see* language
spirit, 11-12, 13, 14; and body, 43-4, 46-7
spirits, 22, 43-4, 51
Stoicism, 35-6, 37, 38, 41, 42, 45
stories, 153-4, 156
stupore, 73-5, 77
sublimity, 144-5, 147
symbols, 7, 9, 20, 66-7, 71, 143-8, 151, 153; and religion, 1-2, 3, 4, 154, 156; in prophecy, 164

time, 60, 98, 151-2, 155; imagination and, 105
trembling, 70, 72, 77, 78-9
truth(s), 98-9, 126, 133, 139, 151, 167; imagination and, 2, 117, 18, 20, 31, 33, 93, 96, 98-9, 125, 126; limits of, 104; source of, 191
typology, 171, 176, 180, 181

USSR, 168
universal(s), 10, 11, 117, 155

vergogna, 73, 74
virtues, 73-5

SUBJECT INDEX

vision, *see* perception
visions, 33, 43, 47, 187, 189-203; *see also* dreams
vocabulary, *see* language

war, 16-17, 91, 92, 184
wheel of fortune, 98
wise foolishness, 90, 92, 97
woman, God as, 82
word events, 170